Penguin Education

The Economics of Imperialism
Michael Barratt Brown

Political Economy
Editor: K. J. W. Alexander

Penguin Modern Economics
General Editor: B. J. McCormick

Michael Barratt Brown

The Economics
of Imperialism

Penguin Books

Penguin Education, Penguin Books Ltd, Harmondsworth,
Middlesex, England
Penguin Books Inc, 7110 Ambassador Road,
Baltimore, Md 21207, USA
Penguin Books Australia Ltd,
Ringwood, Victoria, Australia
Penguin Books Canada Ltd,
41 Steelcase Road West, Markham, Ontario, Canada
Penguin Books (N.Z.) Ltd,
182–190 Wairau Road, Auckland 10, New Zealand

First published 1974
Reprinted 1976
Copyright © Michael Barratt Brown, 1974

Made and printed in Great Britain by
Cox & Wyman Ltd,
London, Reading and Fakenham
Set in Monotype Times

Penguin Modern Economics Texts

This volume is one in a series of unit texts designed to reduce the price of knowledge for students of economics in universities and colleges of higher education. The units may be used singly or in combination with other units to form attractive and unusual teaching programmes. The volumes will cover the major teaching areas but they will differ from conventional books in their attempt to chart and explore new directions in economic thinking. The traditional divisions of theory and applied, of positive and normative and of micro and macro will tend to be blurred as authors impose new and arresting ideas on the traditional corpus of economics. Some units will fall into conventional patterns of thought but many will transgress established beliefs.

Penguin Modern Economics Texts are published in units in order to achieve certain objectives. First, a large range of short texts at inexpensive prices gives the teacher flexibility in planning his course and recommending texts for it. Secondly, the pace at which important new work is published requires the project to be adaptable. Our plan allows a unit to be revised or a fresh unit to be added with maximum speed and minimal cost to the reader.

The international range of authorship will, it is hoped, bring out the richness and diversity in economic analysis and thinking.

B.J.McC.

Contents

List of Tables

Editorial Foreword

The study of past and present relationships between developed and developing countries is essential to an understanding of the modern world. Such relationships are in part economic and in part political. They are reflected in inter-governmental arrangements, in commercial ties and in financial flows, in the activities of multi-national companies and of supra-national agencies. The term imperialism is widely accepted to describe these relationships. The analysis of imperialism involves market and power considerations, requiring the approach of political economy rather than of economics.

Mr Barratt Brown has established a reputation for scholarship in this field of study which this book will further enhance. The key issues are clearly set out and the vast literature critically surveyed to suggest answers, or the difficulty of providing answers. Although a catholic range of writers and theories are covered the book concentrates on the Marxist analysis of imperialism. The Marxist focus is on the extent to which imperialism provides a necessary release for the otherwise explosive contradictions of closed capitalist economies. There is therefore treatment in depth of the characteristics of capitalist economies now and in the past. To the economic and political history of capitalism and colonization is added consideration of the changes brought about by the increasing importance of large multi-national companies. The decline of overt political imperialism is discussed and the concept of neo-colonialism critically examined. The established Marxist explanations are examined both from within Marxism and from the classical and Keynesian standpoint.

A most interesting and valuable aspect of the book is the extent to which it introduces the reader to the several and often sharply conflicting theories of imperialism which have Marxist roots. J. A. Schumpeter criticized the crude Marxist theory of imperialism as 'the formulation of popular superstitions', showing that 'nursery tales are no monopoly of bourgeois economics'. This book demonstrates that some Marxist scholars have left the nursery far behind. The study of the relationships between developed and developing economies is not the monopoly of Marxism, but cannot be conducted in ignorance of it. We have here an indispensable guide to what Marxists, and others, have to say about imperialism.

Key references are cited and a very full bibliography provided so that readers may follow up particular lines of thought and explore further the disputed issues referred to in the text.

K.J.W.A.

Preface

This book is based on a series of lectures given at the Centre for Advanced Studies of the University of Aligarh (India) in April 1972. I wish to take the opportunity of thanking my own University, the University of Sheffield, the British Council, the Indian University Grants Commission and the University of Aligarh for giving me the time and the opportunity to prepare and to present these lectures. The book is dedicated to my friends at the Aligarh Centre for Advanced Studies, who combine high academic standards with strong social and political commitment. It is aimed, with due modesty, to attempt that combination and, however far it falls short in achievement, should be read in that light.

I have been greatly assisted in writing this book by John Knapp. He has not only educated me over many years in the Keynesian approach to economic history, where his special contribution is acknowledged in the text; but he read through the whole of the first draft of this book and gave me both detailed criticisms and valuable suggestions for improvements. However, Mr Knapp has had no opportunity to comment in detail on subsequent drafts of the book, except that he has corrected my references to the views of Keynes and his successors where this was necessary. He should not be held in any way responsible for my views on other matters.

I have also to thank Stephen Bodington, who read the book in its final stages, for most helpful criticisms and suggestions. I have especially to thank Professor Kenneth Alexander for initiating the project of the book and for his encouragement and assistance throughout its preparation. There are many others to whose work I am indebted, particularly Robin Murray whose contributions are acknowledged in the text. Finally, it has to be said that without the patience and skill at interpreting my handwriting shown by Mrs Irene Gray, there would have been no book at all which anyone could have read.

1 Introduction: On Imperialism as a Concept in Political Economy

The concept of imperialism has only recently re-entered the social sciences as a respectable subject of economic study. There are two reasons for its eclipse. The first is recent, the second of longer standing. First, post-war decolonization and subsequent enthusiasm for international economic cooperation and assistance had relegated the concept to the historians and rendered its discussion as a current problem by social scientists either apparently irrelevant or actually subversive. Second, and lying behind this aversion of academic eyes from a painful memory, whose recollection became identified with Marxist economic analysis, there was the continuing devotion of social scientists to the whole body of liberal classical economic thought. Imperialism, and protectionism with it, were, according to this theoretical framework, like monopolies, unfortunate but temporary deviations from the true beliefs of Adam Smith.

Now the tide has turned. Ten years ago an attempt by this writer to call together a seminar of economists and historians, to consider problems of imperialism led to a meeting of just four people. A renewed attempt at Oxford in 1969 produced several gatherings of over a hundred social scientists and more than a score of papers, several of them subsequently collected together in one volume (Owen and Sutcliffe, 1972). For this, the first reason may be the emergence of a more radical population of students demanding a new response from their teachers; it certainly reflects widespread dissatisfaction with narrowly political explanations, in terms of 'defending the free world' or 'rescuing the achievements of communism' respectively, for what the United States has been doing in the Caribbean and South East Asia and the Soviet Union in Eastern Europe and on the Chinese border. The second and main reason must be the growing doubts about the efficacy of Adam Smith's invisible hand in reconciling public benefit and private gain, and maximizing utility for rich and poor alike. The irreplaceable resources of the earth are used up at an ever-accelerating rate and the ecological environment of man is put in jeopardy, while the gap between the wealth of some nations (comprising perhaps a third of the world's people) and the poverty of the other two-thirds has become wider and more glaring with each passing decade. Such untoward developments for liberal economic theory indicated that an earlier and neglected framework of Marxist analysis under the general heading of imperialism might be looked at again.

It would not be correct to suggest that only Marxists dissented from the optimistic views of the liberals. There has been a major holding action by those Keynesians who have sought to develop the critique of liberal theory first mounted by their master. Such a development was most perceptively foreshadowed by Knapp (1949). It has been maintained in the occasional writings of Harrod (for example, 1962, 1963a, 1963b, 1964) and Robinson (1966a, 1966b, 1970a, 1971a). Although these last two economists disagree sharply in practice (Robinson 1970b), they appear to share the view that, since a tendency to stagnation is endemic in the private enterprise capitalist system, state action has constantly to be taken to prevent this.[1] Governments in the past have been as deeply concerned to take such action as they are today; only their tools were more limited in the past, the main one being the control of imports and exports and of overseas economic activities. What

1. Readers should be warned that the references which follow throughout this book to Keynesian ideas relating to long-run historical developments must necessarily be impressionistic for two reasons: first, Keynes's *General Theory* was systematically concerned with the short run only. He was known to want to write about long-run problems in economic history in his later years, but did not live to fulfil that ambition; secondly, so far as Keynes's pupils and contemporary 'ultra-Keynesian' followers are concerned, they have always stressed the fragmentary, incomplete and preliminary character of what has so far emerged from their own work.

has distinguished these neo-Keynesians has been that they have remained critical of the assumptions of classical theories of resource allocation on a world scale during the period after 1945, when the success claimed for Keynesian demand management inside the developed capitalist countries temporarily obscured the failure to extend such Keynesian prescriptions to the international economy. Now, when Keynesian explanations for the post-war boom are under challenge,[2] and instead of confidence in the boom continuing there is uncertainty (Harrod, 1971, p. 83), and even talk of trade wars has begun again, there are good economic as well as political reasons for renewed interest in imperialism.

Imperialism is not a precise economic concept; it cannot be reduced to a set of general equilibrium models; but it has a long history as a framework for thought in political economy from the Mercantilists and Physiocrats through to Lenin and the neo-Marxists. The use of the word Imperialism, like Capitalism or Mercantilism, implies the need to combine political and economic analysis in explaining the unity of social phenomena. Those who limit their studies to pure economic theory believe they help us to understand the nature of international commerce, by analysing the causes and effects of the pattern of movements of goods and capital and thus estimating the 'gains' both generally and individually (and presumably the losses also) from such patterns (see Findlay, 1970, p. 134). Political theorists believe they can help us to understand the nature of inter-government relations by analysing the causes and effects of the pattern of power groups and thus estimating their relative strengths and their incorporation in political institutions (see Barry, 1965, p. 237). When economic and political theory are combined in political economy, it is not only economic and political motives and institutions which are considered together but the economic and political theories that the men and women involved in social activity held (or hold). For their actual estimates of benefits and losses, and of relative power positions, will have greatly influenced their behaviour. Theories, moreover, as Keynes was wont to insist (see

2. Above all from the Chicago School led by Friedman (1972).

Keynes, 1960, p. 383), continue to influence people's actions long after the events which gave rise to their formulation have passed away. And since theory helps to determine consciousness, false theory determines false consciousness. Theory is as much a tool of apologetics as of scientific inquiry.

In political economy, words which are used in a certain accepted sense in economics may have to bear a rather different meaning. Thus we may speak of models in political economy which are not the equilibrium models of economics but theories or hypotheses about political–economic relationships. The structure of categories in political economy which can be applied to interrelations in the real world will be different from the relationship of variables in equilibrium systems that are similarly applied in economics. There is even a difference in the use of the word 'economic'. This will have to bear a wider meaning as concerned with the production and distribution of wealth (goods and services for satisfying human needs) in different societies and at different times, rather than the narrower one of being subject to pricing in a market. Moreover, while economic activity may be said to be concerned with satisfying human wants, these are both large and varied. They include goods and services which satisfy our physical needs, but they also include money and power, which may itself be economic in form, i.e. concerned with production and distribution of goods and services, or achievable by economic means. Nor should we exclude the satisfactions from work itself. Furthermore we have to remember that there are group wants as well as individual wants to be satisfied.

Difficulties arise, however, when economic and political analysis is combined. The precision, indeed in economics the mathematical precision, of the statements that can be made disappears. The number of variables becomes unmanageable. The prediction of deterministic systems is ruled out. What then is the use of such general concepts where precise analysis and, therefore, accurate prediction within the limits assumed, are impossible? The answer is that useful insights can be obtained through the employment of a conceptual framework for the large continuities and changes in human activity, spread over a longer time or a wider area, than can be encompassed by either economics or political science alone. In the study of history, in the assessment of trends in our own times and in the future, we need some systematization of our collection of facts, and some criteria of the greater or lesser relevance of the facts collected. This implies the need to construct a general framework of thought – we may call it a model, from which specific hypotheses about causes and effects can be deduced and tested by their refutability. The alternative is to accept with Popper (1937) the view[3] that there are no generalizations to be made from history on which future actions can be usefully based, once we move from the narrow area, or short-term concerns, of economics and of what he describes as 'piecemeal social engineering'. Some historians may accept this view and spurn the 'speculations of the historicists' (Fieldhouse, 1967, p.194), but political economists are bound to reject it if they see their studies as contributing to man's greater knowledge and, therefore, more effective control over his conditions of life.

This is not to say that differences in ways of thinking about economic problems are identical with differences in the value judgements of those who adopt them. Nor are some economics (neo-classical) positive, or value free, while others (Marxist or Keynesian) are normative, or fail to distinguish between positive and normative elements.[4] What each social scientist selects to study, the factors to which he attaches importance, must follow what Joseph Schumpeter called 'the vision of things', which each brings to his analytical work (Schumpeter, 1955, pp. 41–2). Most economists, moreover, have had policy objectives in mind in setting about their work. None of this need mean, however, that value-loaded words and definitions are inevitable, or that the models and hypotheses that they offer for elucidating the working of the economic system at different times and places cannot be subjected to test. The tests may be concerned with the internal logic of the model, the correspondence with events as far as they are known which the model is

3. I have criticized this at rather greater length, see Barratt Brown (1970b, ch. 1).
4. For a full discussion of this problem see Hutchinson (1964, part 1).

supposed to represent, the insights provided for understanding other events and the energizing power of the model in generating action. Although this writer does not accept with Popper that history can give us no sure indications of future trends, he does accept his requirement that scientific statements must be made in a form that is open to the possibility of refutation (Popper, 1937, 1959).[5]

Imperialism as a concept of political economy may thus be regarded as a set of political and economic structures and relations which provide a framework of thought, or model, to help us in understanding what men have described as empires, from Persia and the Hans to the British Empire and the United States' 'grand design'. The model would have to be at a very high level of abstraction to embrace all these. Its explanatory power would therefore be limited to the most general propositions about human nature and human institutions (e.g. Lichtheim, 1971). In Marxist thought, imperialism is used as a technical term for a stage of capitalist development that spans the last hundred years (Kemp, 1967, pp. 1–7). In this book it is proposed to restrict consideration to roughly the last 400 years. The choice of period is determined partly by the extent of our knowledge, but mainly by the emergence in Europe in the sixteenth and seventeenth centuries of what we know as the nation state.

At all times the concept of imperialism has been used to encompass the outward drive of certain peoples (generally, since 1600, nation states) to build empires – both formal colonies and privileged positions in markets, protected sources of materials and extended opportunities for profitable employment of labour. The concept has thus been associated with an unequal economic relationship between states, not simply the inequality of large and small, rich and poor trading partners, but the inequality of political and economic dependence of the latter on the former. Of course, dependence is relative; no nation except China has perhaps at any time achieved or wished to achieve absolute independence, although some have been for a time totally dependent.

5. See Carr (1961, pp. 85–7 and p. 101) for a discussion of the latter.

This is a book which deals very largely with the institutional framework of economic activity, which most economists regard as a parameter rather than a variable. This distinction cannot be sustained in the larger range of analysis – both over time and space – with which political economy is concerned. What, then, is economic about imperialism? This is not only a question of the motives of individuals as critics of the economic interpretation of history generally suggest. Economic explanations may be concerned with results that no individual willed but yet can be related to causal forces.

In any politico-economic analysis we have to use categories – nation, state, ruling group, class, firm, plant – which inevitably embrace many separate individuals having widely varying aims and interests. In much of economics we are asked to assume that individuals pursue their own best economic interest in the different markets that make up an economy. In political economy we have to bring together the impersonal workings of markets and the personal decisions of powerful individuals and groups of men. This does not, however, mean that we are necessarily driven out into a sea of arbitrary decisions. There are economic and political structures to be identified within which decisions are made that may be partly related to the market, partly to the search for power in non-economic fields.

If imperialism is a model for elucidating the relations of nation states, does this necessarily involve the idea of one whole nation or people seeking to dominate another? Many writers on empire have spoken of a 'general impulse to dominate' and start from a review of warlike tribes and warrior nations leading on to a study of nation states,[6] where the balance of power among nations is identified as a cause of imperialist ambitions. This may be attributed to power-hungry politicians or to irrational group psychology, and particularly to the cultivation of nationalism which combines both attributes. Such a separation of political from economic factors runs through at least

6. To be found in such diverse writers as Schumpeter (1955, pp. 3–7 and 23); Robinson (1970a, pp. 34–5); Strachey (1959, pp. 217–18); Aron (1954, p. 59).

one whole school of theories of imperialism which set out to criticize the Marxist view of imperialism.[7]

For the Marxists the rise of the nation state and the growth of nationalism are inextricably associated with the rise of a capitalist class. Two alternative views will be noticed as a critique of the Marxist view that is followed in this book. One is the view of the Classical Liberal school, which associates imperialism with specifically pre-capitalist elements incorporated into capitalist society at its inception (Schumpeter, 1955); the other is the view of certain Keynesians who have developed an explanation of capitalist state activity in terms of a basically mercantilist motivation, one that is inherent not only in industrial capitalist societies but in earlier societies also.

Before the nation state there were city states and empires with a common money and laws, but only in the nation state have whole peoples come to believe, rightly or wrongly, that they had a common interest even overriding class interests, which the state could define and advance. This is regarded as an important assumption by economists – most explicitly in mercantilist thought, but implicitly also by Marxists and classical liberals.[8] It is worth emphasizing at the start that Marxist analysis is not simply a matter of looking for direct economic motives behind all individual actions or even looking for economic explanations for all social actions. This is an Aunt Sally of the anti-Marxists. In their original writings Marxists are above all concerned with political economy as the interconnection of economic and political structures in social formations: but they do give primacy to changing technology in understanding what determines these structures rather than to changing ideology or psychology. Social formations are a

7. These are examined from a Marxist view point in Kemp (1967, ch. 8), and are considered in chapter 2.
8. Hicks (1969) writes at length of kingdoms, city states and their colonies and of the Roman Empire and Han dynasty as guarantors of the security of traders and their money, but not at all of nation states and their empires, and indeed at one point rather wishes 'there were no nations' (p. 160); but in conclusion he speaks twice in italics of *the national interest* while emphasizing the failure of mercantilist regulation of the economy in the national interest.

complex totality for Marxists as for others, and economic or materialist interpretations are not to be applied mechanically but dialectically, that is, allowing for the feedback of human consciousness into the material world (Marx, 1904, p. 12).

If Marxist theory is not just a relation of economic motive and economic forces, nor is the classical liberal critique of this theory of imperialism, which we shall consider below mainly in the works of Joseph Schumpeter, just a matter of seeing political motives and political forces at work in societies. The Schumpeter thesis, so widely accepted by neo-classical economists, is that imperialism, like nationalism, is 'an atavism in the social structure'. That is to say that imperialism is a hangover, 'an element which stems from the living conditions, not of the present but of the past' – and, he adds, 'put in terms of the economic interpretation of history, from past rather than present relations of production'. 'A purely Capitalist world', Schumpeter maintains, 'can offer no fertile soil to imperialist impulses' (Schumpeter, 1955, p. 69). The Keynesians reject as myths both the inevitable conflicts of the Marxists' capitalism and the harmony of unregulated classical liberal capitalism. Capitalism for them was always managed and manageable. Imperialism was one way of managing it. There are other ways, depending on the interests of the ruling groups with power over the state and inter-state institutions.[9]

The differences between the three schools arise fundamentally from different ways of looking at economic activity. Marxists have tended to emphasize relations of men in the process of production, and particularly the property relations of owners and non-owners – in the case of capitalist economies the determining power of capital ownership – and to see imperialism in terms of the accumulation of capital and the exploitation of colonial and semi-colonial labour (see Lenin, 1933,

9. There is as yet no fully developed Keynesian work in this field but there are many indications of its lines of development in both the writings and activities of the master himself and subsequently in the works of Sir Roy Harrod and Professor Joan Robinson. I have no doubt that a developed work will be produced by J. A. Knapp in the course of time.

ch. 6). Classical liberal economists have emphasized the relations of exchange in the market, where goods for consumption are bought and sold (Hicks, 1969, ch. 3); trade may follow colonial settlement (p. 57) but imperialism is seen as a deviation from the ideal of free trade due rather to 'nationalist reaction ... arresting the liberal revolution' (Robbins, 1935; and see Schumpeter, 1955). The mercantilists have emphasized the role of the state in advancing the national, or at least the merchant's, wealth through management of a favourable balance of trade to encourage both home and foreign investment.

The critique of Marxism by the other two groups of economists will be studied also in their modern counterparts – the neo-Marxist, neo-classicist and the neo-Keynesian, or neo-mercantilist as one might call those who have taken up Keynes's rescue of mercantilist doctrine (Keynes, 1960, ch. 23). The neo-Marxists concentrate attention on the stage, as they call it, of monopoly capitalism, in which competition between capitalists survives but on a giant scale involving a world-wide struggle for monopolistic positions in relation to sources of raw material and markets. The neo-classical school continues to regard all restrictions on the free movement of goods, of capital and of labour, and all state intervention in the money market, including the foreign exchange market, as essentially nugatory and misconceived. The 'first mercantilism was a failure' they say (Hicks, 1969, p. 162) and look back longingly to the era of Free Trade and state their belief that 'if there were no nations ... the absorption of the whole human race into the ranks of the developed would be relatively simple' (p. 160).

The neo-Keynesians are not themselves mercantilists but use mercantilist type explanations of the behaviour of nation states. Some self-styled 'ultra-Keynesians'[10] follow Keynes in their emphasis on the importance of adequate knowledge in economic decisions, particularly knowledge which individuals in the market cannot have, but collectivities of individuals using the power of the state may attain (Keynes, 1932b, p. 318). They go further, however, to emphasize the dominant motives of personal and group (including national) power and prestige in the

10. The name is that given by Knapp (1973).

agents of economic activity, not just as an extraneous and irrational factor in economic activity but as lying at the very
centre of it (Knapp, 1973; Robinson, 1970a, pp. 39, 53, 59, 92).
This distinguishes their view of imperialism, therefore, from the
classical liberal view.

The essential link for the Keynesians between the human love
of power and prestige and the results in economic behaviour is
the desire for increased monetary wealth as the best route to
power and prestige. Given a chronic tendency for the inducement to invest to be weak, there is constant predisposition to
wars for foreign trade and colonialism. There is, thus, for the
Keynesians no exclusive causal connection between industrial
capitalism and imperialism. Imperialism may be found occurring both before and after the era that the Marxists designate as
capitalist.

While rejecting the liberal view, that imperialism was an
aberration from capitalism due to the hangover of the ambitions of a declining and underemployed feudal class, the neo-
mercantilists see the phenomena of Marxist imperialism as a
continuation of mercantilism by new ruling classes seeking to
use the state for the extension of their economic power in the
special circumstances of the nineteenth and early twentieth
centuries. Those liberal economists and economic historians
who have regarded the concept of imperialism largely as a
political and ideological one, like Fieldhouse (1967), for whom
trade literally follows the flag, have done so partly in reaction
to the more deterministic economic explanations of some
Marxists. The mercantilists saw trade and the flag moving
together as far as this could be arranged by nation-state governments. Modern states are seen in a mercantilist view as still
fighting for control over shares in total world economic
activity (Robinson, 1966b, p. 10).

What we shall do in this book is to select certain economic
problems of international relations to which the concept of
imperialism has been applied by political economists both in
the past, particularly in the past two centuries, and in the
present. These problems may be listed in summary form and in
the rough historical order in which they will be looked at:

1 What was the connection between the capitalist industrial revolution of the late eighteenth century in Britain (later in other countries) and so-called 'primitive accumulation' through treasure, tribute and slavery?

2 How was the world division of labour established and maintained between primary-producing underdeveloped states and industrialized developed states?

3 What were the pressures behind the opening up of empty or emptied lands by European settlers from the sixteenth to the middle of the nineteenth century?

4 What was the cause of European and United States competitive territorial expansion at the end of the nineteenth century?

5 Why was free trade replaced by protection and preference at the end of the nineteenth century in most industrialized countries, but apparently not in Britain?

6 What was the origin of the export of capital from Europe at the end of the nineteenth century and from all developed capitalist countries in our own times?

7 Does the present role of the large firm as the major accumulator of capital cut across the imperialism of nation states?

8 Are the terms of trade cause or effect of unequal economic relations between states?

9 Does the new relationship between metropolitan capitalist countries and their ex-colonies, which is described as neo-colonialism, differ enough from old colonialism to make possible some real economic development?

10 Is there a Soviet form of imperialism which is similar to capitalist imperialism?

11 What are the current prospects for inter-imperialist rivalry as the post-war hegemony of the US is challenged?

12 Finally, what possibilities are there of cooperation between groups in developed and underdeveloped countries which have an anti-imperialist orientation?

All these questions imply a basic question about the necessary connection between capitalism and imperialism in the Marxist framework of analysis. What we shall do in this book is to set out the traditional Marxist answers and subject them to criticism both from within the Marxist framework and also from classical liberal and Keynesian standpoints.

2 Classical and Keynesian Theories of Imperialism

In Schumpeter's words 'a purely capitalist world . . . can offer no fertile soil to imperialist impulses . . . its people are likely to be essentially of an unwarlike disposition . . . anti-imperialist tendencies will show themselves wherever capitalism penetrates the economy' (Schumpeter, 1955, p. 69). What sort of capitalist economy is it that the classical liberal writers were thinking about?

The classical view

The essence of the classical view of the economy is that it is a market economy. There are many markets, for goods and for factors, and many entrants to each market, none of them big enough to influence the price or rate of exchange by entering or holding back. Employers in a capitalist market system are essentially traders like their mercantile predecessors, distinguished only by having access to liquid funds,[1] to lay out as factors of production whose supply is given, in such a way as 'to minimize the cost of his product and to maximize his own return' (Robinson, 1962, p. 59). So it is that 'a man has almost constant occasion for the help of his brethren . . .' comments Adam Smith; although 'it is not from the benevolence of the butcher, the brewer or the baker that we expect our dinner, but from their regard to their own interest' (Smith, 1812, p. 27). With such a harmonious adjustment of self-interest, it is not to be thought of as surprising that the competitive system should engender pacific behaviour.

The classical vision of an economy where there is perfect competition reaches its apogee in the Theory of Free Trade. A

1. Hicks (1969, p. 144) describes these as circulating capital to be distinguished from fixed capital, a point which will be taken up later.

static condition is assumed without movements of capital or of labour *between* countries, but with complete factor adaptability to ensure full employment *inside* each country. Then movements of relative prices equalize the values of imports and exports, and the pursuit of individual profit leads each country (as it does each individual in the home market) to specialize in producing those goods and services in which it has the greatest comparative advantage. The result is 'an equilibrium position in which competition leads to the maximum *utility* in the world as a whole being produced from given resources' (Robinson, 1962, p. 62).[2]

Once more competition does not imply conflict. 'Under a system of tree trade', Schumpeter avers 'there would be conflicts in economic interest neither among different nations nor among the corresponding classes of different nations' (1955, p. 76). 'Any forcing of exports whether of commodities or of capital,' he adds in a footnote, 'would be senseless' (p. 174).

Free trade and competition are, moreover, in the view of the classical economists, the source of innovation and the causes of economic growth. Widening markets and the commercial opportunities arising from the establishment of free trade are the factors which revolutionized industry in Britain and will do so everywhere else. 'So long as trade is voluntary it must carry an all-round advantage,' writes Hicks, and 'the fact that force has been used in the establishment of a trading colony does not imply that the colony after its establishment, is an exception to the principle of all-round advantage' (Hicks, 1969, pp. 44 and 51). The metropolitan country and its colonies are connected in mercantile expansion, not by the establishment of any unequal relationship, but rather by the need of traders for 'reductions in risk' (1969, p. 489). Economic liberalization in the nineteenth century is seen as the cause of the sharp rise of living standards in Europe and the USA; failure to liberalize as the chief cause of continued stagnation in the rest of the world. Poor endowment of resources might, of course, be another.

2. The problems involved in the concept of *utility* are discussed by Robinson but need not concern us here.

Tariffs were lowered. Personal unfreedom was abolished. Enterprise was freed. Monopolies were dissolved. International division of labour was extended. And the consequential increase in wealth was spectacular (Robbins, 1935).

This increase was only brought to an end in the 1930s, on this view, by the re-emergence of sectional monopolist and restrictionist principles. 'Nationalist reaction must claim the main credit for arresting the liberal revolution' (Robbins, 1935).

Lying behind the free market, as the ultimate cause of economic growth, is a combination of population pressure and the development of science, stimulating both institutional changes in the market and the invention of financial institutions. Thus, labour surplus caused by rising population on the land moves into towns and ports to find new job opportunities which science has opened up for exploration and for industry, and which are encouraged by a low rate of interest on capital following the creation of new institutions of banking and insurance (Hicks, 1969, pp. 79, 94, 135–6, 144–5, 157; North and Thomas, 1970, p. 1). Such changes in population and in basic science are regarded as autonomous factors, which the economy responds to but does not influence. The application of science, the emergence of merchants, entrepreneurs and bankers, and the division of labour are by contrast supposed to result from the freeing of trade and competition. The widening of the market follows likewise, although the opening up of new markets through reduced transport costs is regarded as in part exogenous, in part the result of competition.

It would seem that the vision of a harmony of interests and of a continuous expansion of wealth through free trade could not survive the withdrawal of the assumption of perfect competition inside and between nations. Joan Robinson, whose summary of the classical argument we have just quoted, goes on to write:

It is obvious enough that any one group of sellers can normally do better for themselves collectively by agreeing to keep up prices than by competing individualistically. They do less business, but at a higher profit per unit. Similarly, any one nation within the conditions of the equilibrium model, may be better off with a smaller volume of trade at a higher price of exports in terms of imports than at the free trade position (1962, p. 64).

The incorporation into neo-classical economic thought of the possibility of imperfect competition did not, however, lead to any change in belief in the pacific and non-expansionary nature of the system. For Schumpeter this was: first, because restrictions on free trade only seemingly, but not really, advanced the interest of individual nations; secondly, because monopoly and monopolistic positions were, in his view, by their very nature, short-lived; thirdly, because 'export monopolism', so he believed, 'does not grow from the inherent laws of capitalist development. The character of capitalism leads to large-scale production, but with few exceptions large-scale production does *not* lead to the kind of unlimited concentration that would leave but one or only a few firms in each industry' (Schumpeter, 1955 edn, pp. 156–63). Writing twenty years later, Schumpeter argued that competition continued in the form rather of product improvement than of price cutting; he regretted the disappearance of the 'family motive' of the bourgeois investor and entrepreneur into the narrow bureaucracies of the modern corporation but still expected them to achieve the 'perennial gale of creative destruction' that ensured economic progress and at least 'another successful run' for capitalism (Schumpeter, 1943, p. 163).

Thus Schumpeter continued to believe that capitalism was not only 'democratic' and 'individualistic' but 'rationalistic and anti-heroic'.

The two go together of course. Success in industry and commerce requires a lot of stamina, yet industrial and commercial activity is essentially unheroic in the knight's sense ... and the ideology that glorifies the idea of fighting for fighting's sake understandably withers in the office among all the columns of figures (1943 edn, pp. 127–8).

Readers may judge how well this describes the soldier clerks of the East India Company or the internecine struggles of capitalist states. Schumpeter's essential point is the same as Hicks's – that among traders, whether merchants or industrial businessmen, the working of the market system requires mutual recognition of enlightened self-interest. Despite 'the conflicts ... born of an export-dependent monopoly capitalism', Schumpeter believed that 'deep down the normal sense of business and trade usually prevails. Even cartels cannot do without the custom of their foreign economic kin' (Schumpeter, 1955, p. 84).

Hicks writes in the same vein that legal institutions for settling disputes and for protecting property rights are needed by traders, but essentially they 'speak the same language'. However, he draws a contrasting picture:

Between merchants and non-merchants ... it is by no means easy to build up that understanding; and this is a major reason why on the boundaries of the mercantile economy (as we shall be calling them) there is so often friction – friction which attends the whole story of mercantile development from its beginnings even right up to the present day (Hicks, 1969, p. 35).[3]

Thus it is that in the classical liberal view the explanation for imperialism is to be found in the perpetuation into the mercantile economy of remnants of an earlier type of economy, both outside and inside its main centres. In Schumpeter's words, 'It is an atavism in the social structure' (1955, p. 65), and he goes on:

The bourgeoisie did not simply supplant the sovereign ... It merely wrested a portion of his power from him and for the rest submitted to him (1955, p. 93).

The militarism and nationalism of the absolute monarch thus survived into the era of capitalism not only in the institutions and personnel of the State but in the mental attitudes of the bourgeoisie themselves, and particularly towards peoples still not incorporated within their boundaries. It is from the financial interests of the monarchy that Schumpeter traces the origins of protective tariffs, of 'export monopolism', as he describes export-dependent monopoly-capitalist control over markets

3. It must be remembered that Hicks is using the words 'mercantile economy' to describe all market economies (see Hicks, 1969, pp. 161–2).

and raw material sources, and of the colonialism that emerged at the end of the nineteenth century. It was not, as the Marxists claimed, from the competitive system of capitalism, developing towards big enterprise (Schumpeter, 1955, p. 89).

The emphasis on royal revenue is taken up by Hicks in describing the earlier type of economy that survived into the era of the 'Mercantile Economy'. This is the survival of what he calls 'Command Economy' or 'Revenue Economy' in which 'a surplus of food and other necessaries is extracted from the cultivators and used to provide sustenance for public servants' (Hicks, 1969, pp. 23–4) whether the latter were royal retainers, classical bureaucracies or the households of feudal lords. It is elements of the command economy, and particularly the attempt to regulate trade in the national interest, that he sees as transforming the colonization of wider areas for the mercantile economy into something quite different (pp. 161–4).[4] This was colonialism, which involved 'the imposition of an alien rule', and was quite different from colonization, which was the widening of the market by peaceful trading. He makes it clear in a footnote that it is not the merchants who were mercantilist in seeking state regulation of trade but the rulers who 'become "mercantilist" when they begin to realize that the merchants could be used as an instrument for their primarily non-mercantile purposes' (p. 161).

This summary of the classical liberal view must be completed by reference to its explanation for the current underdevelopment of ex-colonial areas. The direct imposition of alien rule in colonies, it is said, so outraged national sentiment that it created an equal and opposite reaction in post-colonial nationalism and self-imposed autarchy; so that it is not only the Communist world but 'the underdeveloped world taken as a whole' that has 'carried their protectionism furthest' and

4. This regulation of trade in the national interest is, of course, as Hicks acknowledges, 'the so-called mercantilism of the seventeenth and eighteenth centuries', but he avoids using the word in the book because he wants to retain 'Mercantile Economy' to describe the whole history of the market 'not neglecting the relations with the State but keeping that, as it were, "outside"'.

'suffers most' from it, according to Hicks (1969, p. 163). Protectionism is an evil which Schumpeter expected to 'unleash storms of indignation among the exploited consumer at home and the threatened [colonial] producers abroad'. Yet, Schumpeter admits that there is a 'strong, undeniable economic interest' of these groups in 'countries that function in a monopolist role *vis-à-vis* their colonies' and thus 'submerge the real community of interest among nations' (1955, p. 84).

Hicks also concedes that 'strong as these political forces are . . . there is an economic reason' for protectionism in the underdeveloped world. This is that, while labour-saving improvements in machinery should, according to Ricardo (1912 edn) 'On machinery', lead to an increase in demand for labour out of increased accumulation from extra profits, this applies only to a single country where there is occupational mobility of labour.

In the international economy, even such as was created for a while by the dominance of Free Trade . . . the labour that is thrown out may be in one country, and the expansion of demand for labour, which is the effect of the accumulation of capital that results, may be in another (Hicks, 1969, p. 165).

Thus handloom weavers in India suffered long-lasting damage from textile machinery introduced in England; but Hicks still argues that, although this provides an understandable motive for protection, 'the high cost industries that are set up behind these shields do not engender the profit – to the national economy as a whole – which would serve as a basis for further growth' (1969, p. 165). Hicks is hopeful, however, that, although he believes that protectionism and hostility to international capital are obstacles to development, they may not be insuperable.

Forms of international investment less wounding to national pride can be and have been discovered. It is beginning to be recognized, on the other side, that to keep a socially unprofitable industry in permanent existence by protecting it is foolish (1969, p. 166).

On this view, government attempts to maintain full employment by influencing the balance of trade and thus the terms of trade are regarded as otiose. For one country to force the expansion of its exports only turns the terms of trade against it. For one country to restrict imports turns the terms of trade in its favour, but these imports are some other countries' exports, and in this way the whole level of international trade might be lowered through reciprocal action (Hicks, 1959, pp. 58–60). The argument that favourable terms of trade won for any country by restricting its exports would inevitably be bad for employment has considerable historical justification (Barratt Brown, 1970a, annexes to chapters 2 and 5); but the apparent corollary, that forced exports would only be self-defeating, is based on Say's Law and fails to take account of the possibility, or probability, that there may be underutilized resources, which, if brought into use, would raise the whole level of economic activity, both in the state taking such action and elsewhere. The classical free trade assumption that goods move between countries, but capital and labour do not, has been modified into a theory of dualism inside underdeveloped countries. Here the assumption is that goods move, but capital does not, and labour only moves from the subsistence agricultural sector to the developing industrial sector; and in this way economic development proceeds (Lewis, 1954). This assumption has been applied also to relations between countries where similar movements have taken place. In both cases the assumption has been criticized in logic and in fact (see Griffin, 1969, pp. 19–30).[5]

The classical liberal view is then, first, that the benefits of free trade will be shared between the parties (this we have already questioned) and, secondly, that the rate of economic growth depends upon the rate of saving, i.e. the availability of capital for investment in new machinery. Although Hicks quotes Ricardo 'On machinery', as recognizing the possibility that labour-saving inventions might reduce the demand for labour for a long period of time before the 'circulating component'[6] in capital accumulation was adequate to re-employ the redundant labour, he himself believes that a cheapening of

5. This is discussed further in chapter 10.
6. The distinction of a circulating component in capital is Hicks's own answer (1959, p. 144), as far as it goes, to the Keynesian criticism of neo-classical capital theory. See Robinson (1962, p. 60).

fixed capital would in time take up the slack even between countries. This was, however, in his view, subject to the proviso that groups of workers inside one country or in different countries do not establish privileged positions for themselves where they raise *their* wages 'well before the point was reached when the general surplus of labour was removed' (Hicks, 1959). Such trade union action, he believes, was the cause of the prolonged unemployment in the nineteenth century; otherwise, expansion would only have come to a stop in two special cases, namely where foreign trade was impeded or where there were adverse movements in the balance of payments, checking the rise of real wages (1969, p. 152).

Lying behind the neo-classical view is the assumption that Say's Law is inviolable:

It is plausible to argue . . . that from the long period point of view, discrepancies between saving and investment can be neglected, so that saving and investment are the same; and that, therefore, the rate of growth depends upon the rate of saving. If one adds the assumption (valid enough in many times and places and surely valid for industrial revolution England) that profits are the main source of saving, it becomes likely that there will be more saving the higher are profits. 'Inventions' will not be adopted unless they raise profits; higher profits mean more saving; a higher rate of saving means a higher rate of growth for the economy as a whole; and this at least on the average over a fairly long period, and on the average over labour as a whole should imply a more rapid growth in the demand for labour (Hicks, 1969, pp. 150–51).

The assumptions involved in the classical liberal view of imperialism, as we have taken it from Hicks, include the following (using 'capitalist economy' for his 'mercantile economy' throughout):

1 Competition in the international as in the national capitalist economy is typical, and the more perfect it is the better the utilization of resources will be; monopolistic positions are either short-lived by their nature or caused by non-economic influences of political power groupings.

2 Competition encourages innovation to reduce costs and

therefore economic growth. Say's Law operates in an industrial economy, as in any other commercial economy, so that the rate of growth depends upon the rate of saving, and, in both national and international economy, equilibrium is generally achieved at full employment of human and other resources.

3 The extension of the capitalist economy into non-capitalist areas has benefited the latter because in the capitalist economy costs are reduced by competition, enterprise is liberated and savings are generated for economic growth.

4 Competition between traders inside and between nations is essentially peaceful because all benefit from the individual pursuit of self interest within common rules and regulations.

5 The benefits of free trade are distributed between the nations in a roughly equitable manner.

6 The motivation towards economic activity of industrial capitalists need not be distinguished from that of merchant capitalists; all are traders despite the distinction of the holding of large proportions of fixed, or 'sunk', capital by industrial capitalists.

7 Where mercantilist policies of trade regulation are applied by rulers, the merchants and other traders are the instrument of these policies, and may be the beneficiaries, but are not the primary instigators.

8 Pre-capitalist institutions, ruling groups and attitudes carry over into the capitalist economy and continue to distort its free working over very long periods of time.

The Keynesian view

All these assumptions except 6, 8 and possibly 7 are challenged by Keynesians. Without exception all are challenged by Marxists. The main Keynesian challenge is to the assumption of perfect competition, 1, and of Say's Law, 2. These two affect their view of 3, 4 and 5 which are all concerned with the benefits of free trade and competition. We have already noted the Keynesian criticism of the assumption of perfect competition. The Keynesians' rejection of Say's Law, is, if anything, more complete. The freeing of trade need not necessarily encourage investment. Increases in competition do not necessarily increase demand, even if they involve cost-saving innovations. Employment might fall by more than it rose as a result of innovation and increased competition. Growth, in the Keynesian view, tends normally to be slow, distorted and subject to mercantilist restrictions.[7] It is not enough for the classical economists to fall back on population pressure or scientific discoveries as autonomous or exogenous factors, which free competition releases to give economic growth, and to make the widening market a partially exogenous factor. Demand in the market depends on the transmission of cost-saving innovations not only into lower priced products but into new employment of the savings. Otherwise, population pressure is unrelieved; the application of science to industry is checked. So Robinson (1971a, p. 89) writes of the neo-classical economists:

In their models it is explicitly assumed that there is and has always been correct foresight, or else 'capital' is malleable so that the past can be undone (without cost) and brought into equilibrium with the future; in short, they abolish time. But this is not enough to ensure full employment. They have also to assume that the wage bargain is made in terms of product; the real-wage rate finds the level at which the stock of 'capital' is squeezed up or spread out to employ the available labor force. Keynes took it for granted that in an industrial economy wage rates are set in terms of general purchasing power; and he brought the argument down from the cloudy realms of timeless equilibrium to here and now, with an irrevocable past facing an uncertain future. Money then comes into the argument as 'the link between the present and the future'.

Keynes's emphasis on the role of money and the desire for monetary wealth has given to the Keynesians a link between economic history and theory. The timeless and placeless equilibrium of classical theory could be replaced by a view of historical development. As Robinson has said (1962, pp. 78–9):

7. The fullest development of this view is again to be found in Knapp's writings, which he has kindly made available to me, and particularly in lectures (1956–7), a paper (1969) and his contribution to a course of lectures (1964–5).

... at least in connection with the accumulation of capital, we have learned to distinguish the desire to save from the inducement to invest and both from the supply price of a stock of waiting.[8]

Thus the tendency to hoarding, that is to saving without investing, Keynes's liquidity preference, has operated throughout the history of money-using societies (Keynes, 1960, pp. 242, 351). The result has been stagnation as the normal condition, with potential capacity to supply frustrated by lack of effective money demand. For 'money loving' leads *both* to inadequate purchasing power (underconsumption) and to inadequate inducements to invest.

Only special circumstances – Keynes humorously instanced the desire to build pyramids, medieval cathedrals and monasteries and mighty modern mansions – evoked the necessary incentive to invest 'out of savings [and so] increase not only employment but the real national dividend of useful goods and services' (Keynes, 1960, p. 220). More important instances are cited by Knapp (1956–7) – the demand for military supplies in time of war, the charting of new trade routes, the discovery of new sources of gold and silver, the opening up of new lands for settlement and development, the invention of new technology – where the preference for liquidity was overcome and dis-hoarding encouraged. The desire for personal power and prestige of ruling groups has led them in the past, as today, to procure armaments, protect merchant adventurers, retain bullion, assist colonization, extend markets and fields of development, encourage inventions. Keynes hoped that 'once we understand the influences upon which effective demand depends', 'it is not reasonable ... that a sensible community should be content to remain dependent on such fortuitous and often wasteful mitigations' (Keynes, 1960, p. 220). National defence remains a major incentive to invest, but other forms of public expenditure have grown since Keynes was writing.

While the Keynesians reject the assumptions of free competition and of Say's Law, they accept the classical economist's assumptions that there is no distinction to be drawn between

8. The reference is to Alfred Marshall's concept of profit as a reward to owners of capital for 'waiting' (see Robinson, 1962, pp. 60–61).

the motivations of industrial capitalists and those of earlier traders and that there is nothing inherent in industrial capitalism that leads to its necessary expansion. Exogenous factors – discoveries of gold and new lands, wars, inventions, national prestige – are required to explain the incentive to invest. The difference between the Keynesian and classical view is thus concerned with the way in which these factors work upon the economy. In the classical view they remain outside or should remain outside, since they distort the proper working of competitive markets to ensure the best and fullest use of resources. For the Keynesians they work right through the world economy both in generating monopoly positions and in encouraging investment which would otherwise flag for lack of incentive.

The logic of the Keynesian economic model based upon the love of money, including all forms of monetary wealth, which is universal between different classes of any population and different eras of the history of market economies, implies that this is not peculiar to the capitalist system. Stagnation and empire, as a way out from stagnation, become universal categories. Against this the Marxists would argue that capitalism, as a system of allocating resource according to the return to private capital, is not only the market economy *par excellence* but historically the system that effectively brought every part of every land in the world into one market economy. This was, as Marx saw it, the historic mission of capitalism. Robinson has herself, as a Keynesian, commented that:

... the exaltation of making money for its own sake to respectability, indeed to dominance, in society was the new feature of the capitalist system which distinguishes it from all former civilization. ... In the nineteenth century ... a society developed in which ambition and love of power could be satisfied by accumulating wealth, and this met with technical and historical conditions which enabled it to grow and flourish and stretch its tentacles over the world (1970a, p. 67).

These sentences appear shortly after the following:

To maintain 'law and order' so as to provide an environment for the creation and extraction of wealth, the capitalist-imperialist nations had to provide an administration in many lands and this required a number of wars of conquest but industrial technology had provided them with unchallengeable power, so that it did not cost them much (1970a, p. 65).

So it is the Keynesian's view that, while money making became the supreme motive in the capitalist system, this itself would have led only to stagnation if it had not been

that the capitalists had to present themselves as benefactors of society. They gave employment, they built up the wealth of the nation and carried Christian civilization to barbarous lands (1970a, p. 67).

This then for them is the source of imperialism. And why? Because, says Robinson, the capitalists wished to 'consider themselves gentlemen', to win for themselves that 'something inborn that could not be bought' that the landowning aristocracy had and they had not. In the last analysis, then, it is the personal motivation of the industrial capitalist – to dis-hoard and not to hoard – that matters. Expected profits allowing for risk and uncertainty must be greater than the relative rate of interest for investment to take place. This is the formal Keynesian model in which the marginal efficiency of capital is brought into relation with the rate of interest. But in explaining capitalist expansion Keynes himself said he relied more on the spontaneous optimism of 'animal spirits' of business men to maintain the rate of accumulation (Keynes, 1960, p. 161); and Robinson relies on their image of themselves as aspirants to the status of gentlemen.

The rejection by Keynesians of classical free trade theory has been greatly strengthened by recent criticism of neo-classical capital theory initiated by Pierro Sraffa and developed by the so-called neo-Ricardian school (Robinson, 1971b; and see Sraffa, 1960). This has important implications for any concept of imperialism as a form of international capitalist economic behaviour. Capital has a dual nature; it is both the property of capitalists, and as such can be said to have a supply price in the market (the price that is necessary to persuade the capitalists to 'abstain' or 'wait' or at least not to prefer liquidity); it is also capital equipment whose demand price depends on its utilization. This means not only that the price of capital depends on the profits obtained from production through using the equipment, but that the distribution of income between capitalists and workers in the last resort depends on the profits. This is a circular argument, however, and provides no determinant for profit ratios or profit shares, such as the concept of payment to capitalists for waiting or abstaining or overcoming liquidity preference seemed to carry with it. It also means that there is no determinant for the shares of different countries which exchange goods, in which there are different proportions of capital and labour because of different technical conditions of production.

This is of great importance for the international terms of trade, as well as for all other relative national prices, because the relative prices of any given combination of commodities cannot then reflect the marginal opportunity costs of each in terms of the rest, when the value of capital goods is not independent of the rate of profit. 'Capital is not malleable so that the past can be undone (without cost)' as we just quoted Robinson saying (1971a, p. 89; 1971c), and therefore it is impossible to change the forms of capital fixed in plant and machinery into different machinery at will according to changing demand. But this would be necessary if prices (and income distribution) were to be said to be determined independently of the rate of profit. Because only then could the technical relations between capital and labour – more of one substituted at the margin for more of another – be adjusted so as to give meaning to the idea of a reward to different factors according to their contribution to the best use of given resources. Only where technical relations are similar for all products – i.e. capital–labour ratios are identical – could prices in the market be independent of the rate of profit. For, at every rate of profit, prices would then be proportional to labour input. Where technical relations vary, there will be no single relationship between a certain capital–labour ratio and a certain wage rate or a certain profit rate.

If the prices of different commodities are not independent of profit rates, then both prices and the distribution of income will be the outcome in the long run of the bargaining power of trade unions and employers; and similarly in the terms of trade the profits and wages of producers in different countries will be the outcome of their respective bargaining power (Robinson, 1971c, pp. 36–7). The terms of trade cannot be said to be 'really nothing else but the old "law of demand and supply" which in these large matters seems to work pretty surely and infallibly' (Hicks, 1959, p. 60), as the neo-classical view has it.

Concerning the expansion of foreign trade, Keynes in his rehabilitation of the mercantilist doctrine recognized the role of state authorities in regulating the balance of trade, to make up for 'the insufficiency of the inducements to new investment', both at home and overseas, at a time when the authorities had no direct control over the domestic rate of interest or other means of encouraging home or foreign investment (Keynes, 1960, pp. 335–6). For the future Keynes looked forward to 'some coordinated act of intelligent judgement to manage saving and investment and their distribution between domestic and foreign uses' (1932b, p. 318). The state, however, in Keynes's view, should only 'do those things which at present are not done at all'. Keynes did not see these 'improvements in the technique of modern capitalism by the agency of collective action' as being incompatible with 'the essential characteristic of capitalism, namely the dependence upon an intense appeal to the money-making and money-loving instincts of individuals as the main motive force of the economic machine' (1932b, p. 319). This has become the basis of the neo-Keynesian view of the causes of economic development. It is the reverse of the Marxist view, which, as we shall see, regards the money-making motive as the product not the foundation of the capitalist system.

One important consequence for the Keynesians of their rejection of neo-classical theory, is that there is nothing necessarily peaceful to be expected in the relationship between capitalist states, no need therefore to look for some pre-capitalist explanation for wars and colonialism. The continuing instinctual elements in human nature are given emphasis over the changing social attributes. Distribution of income between persons and between nations is to be explained as the result not of economic competition only but of political and military power. The special geo-political conditions of the nineteenth century,[9] to which Keynesians ascribe Europe's rapid increase in wealth at that time, include both the opening up of new lands in the Western Hemisphere and Oceania, on the one hand, and on the other, the preponderant political and military power of Europe, and of Britain in particular, in relation to the peoples of every other land.

What this means for the Keynesian explanation of world economic and political relations is that a quite hard-headed view is taken of the use of political power for economic ends, and equally of economic power for political ends. In the nineteenth century, mercantilism was concealed or disguised; in effect it continued to run through the policies of states from the eighteenth century right up to our own times. The protection of home and colonial markets, colonization and colonial rule and the terms of trade are all to be regarded as expressions of a national policy of power, in which political, military and economic power reinforce each other (Knapp, 1973, p. 35). Political bargaining and the use of military-state power are seen by Keynesians as being often important expressions of national economic interest, where a neo-classical economist would deny the connection. Examples are rivalry in the search for access to markets and for control of low-cost supplies of producer goods not obtainable from domestic sources. Economic advantage, however, is sought, not for material gain so much as for the sake of domestic and foreign political ends. Knapp has suggested the lines along which Keynes's views might be developed. In a tabular summary of the ultra-Keynesian paradigm, he starts from the motivations of power and prestige, emphasizes the normalcy of restrictions and control of markets and the role of the state in the mechanism of growth of the market through time. He then describes 'the role of money (in the long run)' as 'immensely important, by way of linking desire for status with

9. Knapp can claim that he was the first to use Keynesian theory to explain the long boom of the nineteenth century as a period of quite special geo-political conditions, developed not by free trade but by a disguised form of mercantilism (see Durbin and Knapp, 1949).

stimulus to productive activity (technical progress and capital accumulation), by way of quest for wealth' and the 'role of the political process' as 'at the root of the matter ... [since growth] *interacts* with vicarious satisfaction of prestige-drives of the underprivileged to strengthen regional, national and ethnic cohesion and conflict, irrespectively of class loyalties' (Knapp, 1973, p. 36).

We may here make a preliminary statement of the Marxist view. This is not that the use of political and military-state power is *always* the expression of economic interest. It is that particular social formations based on particular economic and technological structures necessarily involve particular forms of economic expansion. Thus, Marxists see capital accumulation necessarily driving capitalist societies to assimilate and transform non-capitalist societies, just as land grabbing was necessary to a feudal society and slave raids to a slave society. Keynesians would see these only as different expressions of an unchanging human nature, while Marxists, recalling that there were, and are still existing, primitive societies not based on the domination of man by man, and showing no signs of aggressive behaviour, because cooperation is essential to survival, look forward to future societies at a higher level of technology, where such domination and aggression can be expected to end because once more cooperation is essential to survival. Such past and future societies are in fact recognized by Robinson (1970a), but this does not lead her to articulate in the Marxist fashion a view of the necessary correspondence between the structure of economic relations that human beings enter into at particular levels of technology and the superstructure of legal, political and military institutions that frames their consciousness.[10]

10. Lest this highly compressed statement of a complex set of ideas should be thought to imply a deterministic system, it is necessary to point out that Marx allowed for the influences on human consciousness both of the remnants of the superstructures of past social formations and of the glimmerings of those of future social formations which can be seen to be required when the existing structure of economic relations is no longer appropriate to a radically changing technology (Marx, 1904, preface).

3 Marxist Theories of Imperialism

Marx saw the social formation, capitalist society, as the latest of a number of historical social formations. Each could best be understood by studying their mode of production – the way in which men get their living, combining 'the productive forces', as he called them, or technology as we should say, and the relationships they enter into in getting their living, which he called 'the production relations' or economic structure. Upon this base was built the 'superstructure' of political and legal forms. Ideas, men's consciousness of their lives, were to be understood not as creating but as emerging from these structures – past as well as present and including those that formed nuclei for the future.[1]

Thus, imperialism, in the Marxist view, is to be seen both as a political form and as a set of ideas that emerge from a particular level of technology and from the economic structure that was appropriate to it. This structure in capitalist society, although it appears as a relationship between things – capital, land, labour and goods in the market – is in reality a relationship between people, between the few owners of capital and the many 'owners' of labour power who had been dispossessed of their property. The essence of this stage of technology was that machinery could be used continually to cheapen the costs of production, to economize in labour time and to increase output per man. Capital applied to the purchase of machinery, materials and labour power in order to produce goods for sale could be enormously expanded, beyond the wildest dreams of merchants whose profit came from the purchase and sale of goods which others had produced. In a competitive market,

1. This is a brief summary of the statement of Marx's 'vision' (1904, preface).

moreover, only those who continuously expanded their capital in order to further reduce their costs could hope to survive. The driving force of such a society was not the greed of the capitalist, although this was harnessed to it, nor the skills of the workers, although these too were harnessed to it, but the competitive struggle for capital accumulation.

This picture of an expanding economy fails at first sight to satisfy the Keynesians' requirement that there should be some reason to suppose that wealth accumulated will continue to be laid out on growing purchases of real equipment on an adequate scale, and will not be held in hoards of money or in paper titles to wealth instead, because of a weakness of fresh opportunities to invest in capital goods. The Marxist theory on the matter is different. *First*, the capitalist entrepreneur and his capital arise together with a new kind of technology out of a pre-capitalist exchange economy of handcraftsmen and other self-employed producers who are at a low level of productivity. The capitalist, in building up a stock of capital which he uses to increase his productivity in competition with handcrafts, does, in effect, by reducing costs create the possibility of extra purchasing power. Competition between capitalists to develop new cost-saving techniques, then, encourages them to go on investing. 'Modern industry,' Marx says, 'never looks upon and treats the existing form of a process as final. The technical base of that industry is, therefore, revolutionary, while all earlier modes of production were conservative' (Marx, 1946, ch. 15). At the same time, the new class that introduced modern industry 'cannot exist without constantly revolutionizing the instruments of production and with them the whole relations of society' (Marx and Engels, 1933).

Secondly, the check to investment arises when the process of accumulation comes up against limitations of realization in the market owing to the very source of the accumulation, that is the profit taken from the workers who have not only to create the profit but purchase the extra goods which new capital makes possible. Hence the periodic booms followed by slumps when labour is dismissed and re-engaged as capital is destroyed and restructured.

Thirdly, while the necessity to employ labour to make profits in order to sustain capital accumulation drives the capitalist on, the capitalization of profit becomes increasingly difficult with the larger and larger ratio of capital to labour, unless the cost of capital can be cheapened or the rate of exploitation of labour can be raised.

As one writer has put it, the contradiction in capitalism is for Marx 'between tendency and aim'. The aim of capitalists is to step up accumulation through higher productivity to increase their profit, but the tendency is not only for accumulation to restrict consumption, their own and their workers, but also for the technological changes involved to reduce the labour employed per unit of capital, and thus generally to lower the rate of profit.[2] In other words, although Marx rejected Say's Law, as Keynes did, he believed that most capitalists have no choice but to invest the same amount regardless of whether Say's Law is true or not (Marx, 1951, p. 358). Marx's insistence on the importance of the expropriation of the self-employed craftsmen by the capitalist (Marx, 1946, ch. 17) is not that the latter thus provided an expanded market – as the Keynesians point out, greater inequality of incomes would tend to reduce effective demand – but that the capitalist could then 'compel the working class to do more work than the narrow round of its own life-wants prescribes' (ch. 15).

Thus Marx saw the development of colonies as the most blatant example of the need of industrial capitalism for expropriated labourers. Where new lands were opened up, settlers could buy land cheap and become their own masters. 'In the colonies,' writes Marx, '. . . the capitalist regime everywhere comes into collision with the resistance of the producer who, as owner of his own conditions of labour, employs that labour to enrich himself, instead of the capitalist' (ch. 33). Marx quotes a Professor of Political Economy of Oxford, later of the Colonial Office, Herman Merivale, 'In ancient civilized coun-

2. The line of Marxist defence against the Keynesians adopted here follows in part from the essays on 'Karl Marx's economic method' and on 'The place of Keynes in the history of economic thought' in Meek (1967, p. 190); Glyn and Sutcliffe (1972, pp. 229–33).

tries the labourer, though free, is by a law of nature dependent on capitalists; in colonies this dependence must be created by artificial means'.

Owners of capital, who hoped in the colonies to establish plantations, mines, local industry, housing, transport, docks, etc., and work them for profit, had to destroy or enslave the local population and bring in from outside the African slaves, indentured Chinese labourers or English convicts to do the work. The only alternative was 'systematic colonization' where the government took over all the land and sold it dear so that an immigrant would have to work for a long time for wages before he could become an independent cultivator.

The resulting colonial societies made up of local capitalists with European ties, settler cultivators and slaves were to be found in North and South America, in Southern Africa and Australia. The subsequent tensions between settlers and slaves and between local and European capital have led some – critics of Marx (Gallagher and Robinson, 1963) and neo-Marxists (Emmanuel, 1972b) – to argue that the main pressure behind imperialism, both in the extension of empire and the intensity of exploitation, has been that of the colonial settler. Exploitation of wage labour in colonies as elsewhere was not primarily a matter for moral judgement, although Marx never overlooked that; it was a matter of economic relations. Profit is made and capital accumulated in only one way – out of the labour alienated from the human being who owns and sells it to the owner of capital, at a price that is less than the value of the net product. This is how surplus value is created. This is not a question of bargaining over slices of the cake.[3] The wage labourer does not know what is the value of his net product and has little freedom to take or to leave the price he is offered.

Imperialism is thus, for Marxists, an extension by industrial capitalists of that form of commodity production in which labour becomes itself a commodity. 'Capitalist production, therefore, under its aspect of continuous connected process, of a process of reproduction, produces not only commodities, not

3. For a succinct statement of this aspect of Marx's writing see Medio (1972, pp. 312–30).

only surplus value, but it also produces and reproduces the capitalist relations – on the one side capitalists and on the other side the wage labourer' (Marx, 1946, ch. 23). The driving force behind the extension of commodity production under capitalism is the competition of capitalists, even under conditions of oligopoly, and their need to find, not only new markets and raw material supplies, but new sources of accumulation from the profitable employment of labour – which is in effect the meaning of more euphemistic phrases about 'opening up investment opportunities'.

This is the point where Marx's analysis begins – in the process of the accumulation of wealth in a capitalist economy. Marx's famous phrase 'Accumulate, accumulate! That is Moses and the Prophets!' (Marx, 1946, ch. 24) is generally quoted as if Marx was writing about personal motivation. But Marx is clear that 'we shall see first how the capitalist, by means of capital, exercises his governing power over labour, then, however, we shall see the governing power of capital over the capitalist himself' (Marx, 1959, pp. 37–8). Robinson paraphrases this section of *Capital*: 'Capitalists invest because it is their nature to do so' (1962, p. 106). In the context in which she is writing, she seems to mean their nature as human beings. But Marx emphasizes that competition for the capitalist 'compels him to keep constantly extending his capital, in order to preserve it, but extend it he cannot, except by means of progressive accumulation' (1946, ch. 24, section 3, p. 603).

The driving force in Marx's model of the capitalist system is the competition for capital accumulation. Since 'expand or die' is the requirement of each individual capitalist, and since competition forces all capitalists to proceed likewise, this is reflected in the expansionary drive of capitalist nations. The origins of imperialism are to be found in the capitalist system itself; this is in sharp contrast to the classical liberal view which explains imperialism in terms of the subconscious atavism of a population inflamed by the nationalistic appeals of power-hungry politicians: it is equally in contrast to what one might expect a Keynesian view to emphasize in explaining the phenomena of imperialism, whether this was based on the personal motivations of the love of power and prestige or on national motivations of a mercantilist type that have overcome the chronic historical tendency for desired saving to exceed actual investment in all money economies.

The rate of accumulation in Marx's long-run economic model is the 'one independent variable' (Marx, 1946, ch. 25, p. 633). All others, the level of industrial employment and the unemployment rate, movements in wages and prices and the *pace* of technological change are dependent on it. The *possibilities* of technological change, arising from a wholly new form of technology, with continuously increasing opportunities for higher productivity, lie at the base of Marx's system. The rate of accumulation derives from a surplus for the capitalist, adequate, after allowing for his own consumption, to reproduce his capital (i.e. to provide for depreciation) *and* enable him to enlarge it. Surplus for Marx is a different concept from that of gross profit in modern economics, since it comprises the whole of the difference between costs of production and sales price, providing, therefore, for taxes, distribution costs and capitalists' consumption as well as for depreciation and net investment.

It is the part of the surplus that is reinvested that is necessary for the capitalist's survival.

The . . . law of capitalist accumulation says in fact only that *by its nature* accumulation excludes any decrease in the degree of exploitation, or any rise in the price of labour, such as could endanger seriously the steady reproduction of capital and its reproduction on a continuously expanding scale.[4]

By degree of exploitation, Marx means the ratio of surplus produced to wages paid in the case of each worker. Costs of production can be reduced in three main ways: (a) by reducing the cost of each worker, directly through lowering wages or indirectly through cheapening the commodities consumed by workers; (b) by reducing the cost of capital equipment through introduction of more efficient machines, through continuous operation and through cheaper or reduced inputs of raw

4. Marx (1946, ch. 25, p. 634) but the more felicitous translation of Steindl (1952, p. 231) has been used here.

materials and fuels; (c) by reducing the time taken by each worker to produce a given output through increased application of machinery to production.

It was Marx's view (appropriately in the Industrial Revolution and once again, perhaps, in the current Second Industrial Revolution) that this reduction in time was the most important, and led to the need of each competing capitalist to accumulate enough surplus for reinvestment in new machinery to raise his labour productivity. There might be other ways of increasing surplus by increased intensity of work and by employing slave labour, but the reduction of time taken in production was the essence of industrial capitalism and of the division of labour and economies of scale engendered by it (Marx, 1946, ch. 15, section 1). Only in this way could the capitalist hope for profitable investment and a steady rate of accumulation in competition with other capitalists.

This steady rate of accumulation would be likely to vary over the long period but it would be, so to say, a 'going rate', which competition between capitalists would make each of them try to adhere to.[5] Marx makes it clear that the rate of accumulation can exceed the rate of growth of population, (a) because new recruits to the industrial labour force can be found at the expense of agriculture and small proprietorships, and (b) because technological progress can release labour as productivity increases. In the short run, if rising real wages cut into the rate of accumulation, unemployment would bring them down again – how far would depend on trade union action. In the long run, Marx did *not* expect real wages to fall, but he did expect the share of wages in the value of the product to fall, because of his assumption that with the increasing application of machinery to production the organic composition of capital would rise. By this he meant the ratio of the value of capital invested to the wage bill (in his terminology, 'constant' compared with 'variable' capital).

5. This is not the same as the Keynesians' 'warranted' rate of growth of capital which is given not by the competition of capitalists but by the expectations of capitalists of profitable investment (see Robinson, 1971a, pp. 110–12).

Robinson has questioned whether this tells us anything more than that rates of profit will rise and fall with capital utilization, since Marx's organic composition depends on output per unit of capacity as well as capital per unit of capacity (Robinson, 1942, pp. 41–2). But, as Steindl has pointed out, Marx's formulation of the organic composition of capital inadequately expresses his meaning. It is the ratio of the value of capital invested to that of wages in the net product that he is actually talking about and Steindl is in no doubt that Marx has a logical argument why the share of capital in the net product must rise in time to permit the continuation of a given rate of accumulation (Steindl, 1952, pp. 234–5). On the same definition, it can readily be shown that the rate of profit must fall sooner or later as the ratio of capital invested to net output rises, but that individual capitalists may take offsetting action to avoid this, through higher productivity or a high rate of exploitation (Murray, 1973).

To maintain the rate of profit, which the competition of capitalists establishes at any time, each capitalist must find new opportunities for profitable employment of labour. But the more that all capitalists replace labour with machines, the more difficult this becomes. Using Marx's terminology: capital is laid out on capital goods and materials (c) and on labour (v) and must yield a surplus (s). As the cost of capital equipment and materials are increased per cost of labour (Marx's organic composition of capital or c/v), it will tend to become more difficult for capitalists as a whole to maintain the rate of surplus (s/v) that keeps up the rate of profit $\{s/(c+v)\}$ since this is the same as $(s/v)/\{(c/v)+(v/v)\}$. Or to put it in another way, if labour cost per unit of output $\{v/(c+v+s)\}$ is falling with rising productivity, and if capital equipment cost per unit of output $\{c/(c+v+s)\}$ is rising with new technology, i.e. the organic composition of capital (c/v) is rising, then the share of profits or surplus, $\{s/(c+v+s)\}$ will be hard to maintain because the rate of surplus (s/v) will tend to be smaller. Capitalists will try to increase the surplus or reduce the cost of labour (see Glyn and Sutcliffe, 1972; and Glyn, 1972).

The problem then for any capitalist is that the surplus

generated has all the time to be increased for him to stay in the competitive struggle; but the general conditions for such a process make it all the more unlikely that it will happen, since the rate of profit tends to fall with higher capital–labour ratios. Some capitalists will survive by establishing monopolistic positions, by cost-cutting innovations, by opening up new markets; but these are always subject to challenge from others. For capitalists as a whole from one country there are similarly possibilities of establishing monopoly positions in the world market, but once again these are always subject to challenge. Competition on a world scale forces capitalists everywhere to seek additional surplus in order to capitalize the profits they have already made.[6] Where capital–labour ratios are low, the surplus will be large per unit of labour, and this may be particularly advantageous for small capitalists and in circumstances where productivity cannot be increased; but the rate of profit per unit of capital will be determined on a world scale by the general conditions of production and productivity.

Although Marx undoubtedly envisaged a general crisis of capitalism as steadily deepening in severity as well as widening in the number of economies affected, he was concerned also with periodic crises, which were only overcome by destruction of capital, whether or not there was expansion into outlying fields. The path of capitalism is not a steady run down into stagnation unless 'a somewhat comprehensive socialization of investment will prove the only means of securing an approximation to full employment', as Keynes suggested (1960, p. 378), but a succession of crises of overproduction only rectified by destruction of capacity.

The enormous power inherent in the factory system of expanding by jumps, and the dependence of that system on the markets of the world, necessarily begets feverish production, followed by over-filling of markets whereupon contraction of the market brings crippling of production. The life of modern industry becomes a *series* of periods of moderate activity, prosperity, overproduction crises and stagnation (Marx, 1946, ch. 15) [Author's italics].

It was just in this context that Marx made his clearest enuncia-

6. This is the essence of Bukharin's thesis (1972).

tion of the reciprocal process of development and under-development, when a few lines earlier he wrote:

A new and international division of labour, a division suited to the requirements of the chief centres of modern industry springs up, and converts one part of the globe into a chiefly agricultural field of production, for supplying the other part which remains a chiefly industrial field.

The essence of the Marxist model is that capitalism contains by its very nature an expansionist force – the production of capital to produce more capital. As distinct from economic structures based on slavery, on land ownership or even on merchant capital, those based on the ownership of industrial capital must expand or die. Some capitalists may collude; how far collusion can be maintained even inside a nation state, let alone on a world scale, we shall study in later chapters. Industrial capitalism is concerned wholly with production of commodities, that is production for exchange in an imperfectly competitive market. Earlier economic structures involved mainly production for use. Before the middle of the eighteenth century, as Schumpeter himself emphasized, there had been only islands of capitalist economy embedded in an ocean of village and urban economy. Merchants were concerned with buying and selling, not with production. They might make profits or losses, but they could always give up and invest in land where older and simpler forms of economic power can be exercised, as many of them did, because their capital was in stocks and in ships and warehouses which could be disposed of. By contrast, the capital of the industrialist is tied up in labour and productive machinery, which has but a poor disposal value, as liquidators of bankrupt firms know very well.[7]

7. See Murray (1971b). It is interesting that Hicks sees as the outstanding characteristic of the industrial revolution the investment in fixed capital. 'Circulating capital,' he writes (1959, p. 144) 'is continually turned over; it is continually coming back for reinvestment. But fixed capital is sunk; it is embodied in a particular form from which it can only gradually, at the best, be released.' At the same time, he goes on (p. 155): casual labour becomes regular 'just because of the characteristic on which I have been insisting, its dependence upon the use of fixed capital'.

The destruction and restructuring of capital in periodic crises of overproduction are central elements in Marx's model. The reason why the Marxists remain unmoved by the Keynesian requirement that capital accumulated will be laid out on growing purchases of real equipment on an adequate scale for full employment of resources, is that they too recognize that frequently the scale will not be adequate. Capitalist economic growth is a process of booms *and* slumps. Individual capitalists are driven to keep up in the competition of capitalist accumulation, but from time to time they are all plunged into crises of overproduction just because Say's Law does not operate, although each of them individually assumes that he can sell what he invests to produce. Marx (1909), explores at length the role of money and credit in the process of capital reproduction and speaks of the 'superfluity of industrial capital' when a stoppage occurs in the phases of reproduction, 'but it is in a form in which it cannot perform its functions . . . commodity capital but it is unsaleable . . . fixed capital but it is unemployed. . . .' It is just here that Marx formulates the famous sentence of how he sees the course of capitalist crises in the overexpansion of productive capacity in relation to the consuming power of any population in which income is very unequally distributed:

The last cause of all real crises always remains the poverty and restricted consumption of the masses as compared to the tendency of capitalist production to develop the productive forces in such a way that only the absolute power of consumption of the entire society would be their limit (1909, ch. 30).

Robinson interprets these passages as an indication that Marx was trying to reach an underconsumption theory but failed to do so because he had still not abandoned 'orthodox theory that stands and falls with Say's Law' (1942, pp. 50–51). Steindl, as we have seen, has suggested an alternative interpretation on the assumption that Marx rejected Say's Law. This is that it is competitive overinvestment by capitalists that leads to excess capacity in relation to purchasing power and results in the failure, in Marx's language, to 'realize surplus value'. This 'fulfills the functions of an underconsumption theory,' as Steindl (1952, p. 245) puts it.

But Marx's model does not need its underconsumptionist mechanism. There remains the problem of capitalizing each new mass of surplus. Capitalists aim to produce surplus that they cannot capitalize – too much to be realized because of the poverty of their workers, but too little in the outcome to set all the workers to work on labour-saving machinery. Yet these are the tendencies of the system and counteracting tendencies are likely to be short-lived. If, however, a lower organic composition of capital yielding higher rates of profit can be retained by using cheap labour in colonies and semi-colonies,[8] as part of a type of dual world economy, where capital can move between the two sectors but labour does not move, then the rate of accumulation at the capitalist centres could be sustained. This will be possible even if the rate of surplus is lower in the colonial sector, so long as this rate can be isolated – by state guarantees, subsidies, etc. – from the going rate in the centres of accumulation. Extra surplus is then obtained without raising the organic composition of capital.

It is clear from the texts quoted above that Marx did not expect this to last for long before the colonies were developed within the capitalist framework. This is what has *not* happened, and we shall have to consider the implications of this fact for the rest of Marx's theory of colonialism. There would in Marx's view still be a realization problem for metropolitan capitalists at the centre because of the impoverishment of the colonial market; but the essence of the Marxist view of colonies and imperial expansion is that these function as a part of the contradictions of capitalism. Aims and tendencies are in conflict. This is not due to mistakes of foresight, as Keynes suggested (1960, pp. 367–8), but to inevitable contradictions in the

8. Laclau (1971) is one of the few modern Marxists to give what appears to me to be the correct interpretation of the central argument of Marx in this respect, but he does not see this retention of areas of low organic composition of capital as a type of dual economy, as is suggested here, because he is concerned with the neo-classical view of dualism, where labour moves but not capital, and rightly wishes to criticize this view.

system, which cannot be reconciled so long as the operation of the system depends on private capital accumulation.

Colonial exploitation was listed by Marx among several counteracting tendencies to his expectation of falling profit rates over time: an increase in the intensity of exploitation, depression of wages below the value of the necessaries of life, cheapening of capital goods, relative overpopulation making cheap labour available to new lines or new areas of production and, finally, foreign trade (Marx, 1909, ch. 14). This last worked in three ways. Foreign trade may cheapen the cost of materials and the necessaries of life, increase the surplus from a lower organic composition of capital; and expand the scale of production. Moreover, for a time at least (and it may be a long time), capitalists in an advanced country can gain a higher rate of profit by selling 'in competition with commodities produced in other countries with lesser facilities for production . . . in the same way that a manufacturer exploits a new invention before it has become general' (Marx, 1909, ch. 14, section 5). 'The favoured country receives more labour in exchange for less labour although this difference, this surplus, is pocketed by a certain class.' Finally, Marx adds that, 'capital invested in colonies, etc., may yield a higher rate of profit for the simple reason that the rate of profit is higher there on account of the backward development, and for the added reason that slaves, coolies, etc. permit a better exploitation of labour'.

Marx did not develop a theory of imperialism but all Marxist theories of imperialism have been built upon this one section concerning counteracting tendencies to the falling rate of profit, for Marx expected capitalists to attempt all these ways of escape, mutually self-contradictory as some of them may be. There is, in fact, little evidence in the last century that the ratio of capital invested to net output has risen or the share of wages and the rate of profit fallen (see Steindl, 1952, p. 236) except for fairly short periods (Glyn and Sutcliffe, 1972). The explanation could be that Marx's expected counteracting tendencies have been generally stronger than the underlying tendencies.

The Keynesians have criticized Marx for bringing his short-term analysis of the dependence of real wages on the degree of unemployment into his long-run analysis. The rate of profit depends, in Keynesian economics, not on low wages but rather on high wages because it requires a certain level of consumption to induce investment (or consumption by capitalists themselves). This is also understood in Marx's reproduction schemes in volume 2 of *Capital*, where surplus value must not only be 'produced' but 'realized' (1908, ch. 17), although it is not so clear in volume 1 of *Capital* where he is assuming that products are sold, i.e. the operation of Say's Law. But he explicitly removes this assumption in *Theories of Surplus Value* (1951, ch. 2, section 4c).

While in Keynesian short run theory the rise (or fall) of incomes (undifferentiated between capitalist and workers) provides just enough saving to finance induced investment, in Marx's long run theory the distribution of incomes between capitalist and workers (who don't save) yields the necessary saving to provide for (though not to guarantee) the given trend rate of accumulation. Steindl (1952, pp. 238–9) has shown that, at least in most parts of Marx's work, the check to accumulation is explained not in terms of 'underconsumption', i.e. an increase over time in the ratio of investment to consumption, which, as we have seen, did not happen, but in an increase in potential investment in relation to consumption, which shows itself in increased productive capacity. The essence of the matter is the capitalist's search to realize this potential. Marx's concept of 'overproduction' does not involve the overproduction of products but excess capacity to produce with each new technological advance, which reduces the opportunities for further profitable employment of labour. This is the result not of the competition of workers pulling down wages (as in volume 1 of *Capital*) but of the competition of capitalists, through increases in productivity, pulling down prices or, as oligopoly develops, reducing capacity utilization.

Competition cuts into the surplus, or in the case of oligopoly reduces capacity utilization, but each new expansion of production requires more capital per unit of output. A most important way in which this shows itself is in the disproportion between capital-goods production and consumer-goods production in a capitalist system. As capitalists are driven to lay out more and more surplus on new capital goods, the likelihood of demand for consumer-goods production continually needing new plant to take up all the extra potential capital-goods production is weakened. Empirical evidence shows that capital-goods industries have much wider amplitudes of output in the trade cycle and for long periods (Steindl, 1952, pp. 4–7) tend to operate below full capacity. So the need for finding new outlets for capital-goods production is an especial problem of capitalism. In one sense imperialism has consisted in retaining capital-goods industries in Britain and other advanced industrial countries and allowing only consumer-goods industries to develop elsewhere – an artificial world division of labour, caused in large part by the unbalance at home between capital-goods and consumer-goods production.

This is closely connected with Marx's picture of capitalists' competition leading to a process of concentration. It is, in fact, in the middle of his argument about the law of capitalist accumulation in volume 1 of *Capital*, which was quoted earlier, that he introduced the law of the 'centralization of capital':

The battle of competition is fought by cheapening of commodities. The cheapness of commodities depends, *ceterus paribus*, on the productiveness of labour and this again on the scale of production. Therefore, the larger capitals beat the smaller. . . . In a given branch of industry . . . in a given society the limit would not be reached until the moment when the entire social capital was united in the hands either of a single capitalist or of a single capitalist company (ch. 25, section 2 of the 4th German edn).

At one pole, then, Marx expected concentration of production and centralization of capital; at the other, more and more independent producers proletarianized, wider and wider enlargement of the capitalist world market, periodic reduction of the consuming power of society. As the distribution of income grows more unequal – in Marx's two-class model, between capitalists and wage earners – the conflict between expanded productive capacity and reduced consuming power leads to deeper and deeper crises; offset only by wider and wider extension of the area of capitalism.

This internal contradiction seeks to balance itself by an expansion of the outlying fields of production. But to the extent that the productive power develops, it finds itself at variance with the narrow basis on which the conditions of consumption rest (1909, ch. 15, section 1).

For the Marxists then, the imperialism of the last two hundred years is quite specific to capitalism and arises out of its essential operation which turns all individual motivation to its ends. In the era of oligopoly a Marxist critique[9] of the neo-classical assumptions may be summarized as follows. Competition is increasingly between large firms with certain monopolistic positions and is increasingly bitter as capital is more and more concentrated. Free trade hardens a quite artificial world division of labour which develops the centres of modern industry and underdevelops the rest of the world. Resources are widely underutilized in both developed and underdeveloped parts, as labour-saving capital investment outdistances in type and quantity the capacity for consumption and for new employment. Periodic crises are modified by state intervention in restructuring capital.

We must now consider how Marxists have developed Marx's work into a critique of Imperialism. Lenin in his essay on *Imperialism*, written in 1916, saw imperialism not only as arising out of capitalism but as an actual stage of development of capitalism – the 'highest stage', in his view, a so-called 'monopoly stage', which could be dated from the great depression, with increasing interconnections of industrial and bank capital (Lenin, 1933, pp. 43–5). At this stage competition between capitalists had led to monopolies (we should call them oligopolies) fighting it out the world over and using nation-state power to control markets and sources of raw materials, and especially markets for capital export. What Marx had seen as emerging out of the unplanned working of the capitalist system,

9. For a modern exegesis on the economics of time and agglomeration under capitalism see Murray (1972).

Lenin saw as the deliberate policy of new national capitalist groups rivalling those in Britain. The state finance of industry behind state-protected tariff walls in these capitalist economies had created a new combination of national financial and industrial interests, which Marxists described as finance capital, and which led Lenin to speak of 'the epoch of the development of monopoly capital into state monopoly capitalism' (Lenin, 1933, pp. 45–60).

Lenin's conception of 'finance capital' was based on Rudolf Hilferding's study of the role of German and United States banks in extending and controlling industrial capital. Hilferding entitled his study *Finance Capital – the latest phase of Capitalism*. He saw state protection of industry in the newly developing European and American capitalist nations moving from the establishment of monopoly positions at home to similar positions abroad. Of tariffs he wrote:

From being a means of defence against foreign conquest of domestic markets they become a means of conquering foreign markets, from a weapon of protection for the weak they become a weapon of aggression for the strong (Hilferding, 1923, pp. 384–9).

And of finance capital and the state:

Finance capital finally needs a state which is strong enough to carry out a policy of expansion and to gather in new colonies (p. 300).

The export of capital in Lenin's view of imperialism is explained by the decline of profitable uses for capital at home. Here Lenin comes very close to an underconsumptionist theory.

As long as capitalism remains capitalism, surplus capital will never be used for the purpose of raising the standard of living of the masses, for this would mean a decrease in profits for the capitalists; instead it will be used to increase profits by exporting the capital abroad, to backward countries. In these backward countries profits are usually high, for capital is scarce, the price of land is relatively low, wages are low, raw materials are cheap. The possibility for exporting capital is created by the entry of a number of backward countries into international capitalist intercourse, the main railway lines have either been built or are being built there, the elementary conditions for industrial development have been assured, etc. The necessity for exporting capital arises from the fact that in a few countries capitalism has become 'over-ripe' and, owing to the backward stage of agriculture and the impoverishment of the masses, capital lacks opportunities for 'profitable' investment (Lenin, 1933, ch. 4).

This statement of Lenin's assumes a surplus of capital – excess saving from profits – in conflict with correspondingly reduced purchasing power of the people at home. Without an expansion of purchasing power there can be no new profitable opportunities for investment, but capitalists cannot, from the nature of the competitive world in which they operate, raise the standard of living of the people. Workers are both producers and consumers. Lenin assumes with Marx that over time the proportion of capital to labour used in the process of production increases in relative values, so that the probability of maintaining the same rate of profit with the surplus created is reduced. There are counteracting tendencies as Marx indicated. But Lenin assumed that there were limited possibilities for these counteracting forces except for foreign trade and especially the cheapening of raw materials. He explained the 'feverish hunt for sources of raw materials throughout the world (as a cause of) the desperate struggle for the acquisition of colonies' (Lenin, 1933, ch. 6). Colonial rule makes possible both guaranteed sources of materials and also of monopolistic positions 'to make sure of orders, to strengthen the necessary "connection", etc.'.

If Lenin were right, it is hard to explain how, under capitalism, a long secular boom, albeit with ups and downs, spreading all over the world could have been sustained throughout the nineteenth century. This was the problem to which Luxemburg addressed herself (1951). For Luxemburg the export of capital is directly concerned with the export of goods. High profits from the export of capital after an initial enlargement of markets would tend to impoverish the market for the goods of the capital-exporting country. The ultimate justification of capital investment anywhere is the production of goods for consumption. Luxemburg's reworking of Marx's schemes of extended reproduction in volume 2 of *Capital*, seemed to show the inevitability of an overproduction of consumer goods (see Tarbuck, 1972, Appendix 1). It has often been suggested that this is simply a mistake because she assumed a stable level of productivity despite a rising organic composition of capital and she also assumed constant consumption by the capitalists. But Luxemburg's emphasis on another of Marx's suggestions concerning the importance of new outlets for consumer goods in non-capitalist areas of the world might still be of great importance at a certain period of time for the continuing profitability of capitalist investment. 'Imperialism', then, according to Luxemburg, 'is the political expression of the accumulation of capital in its competitive struggle for what remains still open of the non-capitalist environment' (Luxemburg, 1951, p. 446).

This suggestion is of special interest for us because it comes very near to the Keynesian view of the matter. Although Luxemburg did not take up other Keynesian-type suggestions of Marx on the importance of gold discoveries and the credit system for expanded reproduction, she did emphasize the important role of military expenditure (1951, p. 454). Her main argument is supported by Robinson, in an introductory essay to the English edition of Luxemburg's *Accumulation of Capital* when she writes:

Few would deny that the extension of capitalism into new territories was the mainspring of what an academic economist has called 'the vast secular boom' of the last two hundred years, and many academic economists account for the uneasy condition of capitalism in the twentieth century largely by the 'closing of the frontier' all over the world.[10]

It was not, however, an overproduction of goods that we saw as the central failing of the capitalist system in Marx's view. It was a tendency to overproduction of capital, to meet higher ratios of capital to labour, shown up in underused capacity resulting from an excess of competitive investment.

Hobson, from whom Lenin drew some of his arguments in his

10. Robinson (1951, p. 28). The reference is to a footnote of Hicks's (1939, p. 302).

essay on *Imperialism*, argued that excessive saving caused 'an accumulation of capital in excess of that which is required for use, and this excess will exist in the form of general over-production' (Hobson and Mummery, 1889, pp. iii–iv). Keynes comments that this is 'in fact a secondary evil which only occurs through mistakes of foresight, whereas the primary evil is a propensity to save in conditions of full employment more than the equivalent of the capital which is required . . . in response to the demand from actual and potential consumption' (Keynes, 1960, pp. 367–8). This is certainly the Keynesian view but it is not Marx's. It is not merely a mistake of foresight for two or more capitalists to be forced to try to outbid each other in labour-saving investment to capture each others' markets, and end up with excess capacity and with all capitalists reducing their employment of labour.

The essential difference between the Keynesian and the Marxist view is this: that where the Keynesians see mercantilist policies of nation-state governments, whether open and zealous or disguised and reluctant, to create 'vents' for potential supply through domestic investment and exports, in attempts to mitigate the inherent tendency to undue weakness of inducement to invest which has characterized private enterprise economies at all times,[11] the Marxists see in the capitalist mode of production the dynamic of competitive capital accumulation through investment in more productive, i.e. time saving, machinery. The emphasis placed by the Keynesians, and particularly by the 'ultra-Keynesians', in their critique of the neo-classical economists' reliance on the price system to ensure full utilization of resources (Knapp, 1973), leads them to concentrate attention on the problem for all entrepreneurs of holding down the price of labour without reducing the extent of the market (Robinson, 1970a). The emphasis placed by the Marxists, in their critique of the classical economists' reliance on the capitalists' surplus from increased productivity to ensure

11. Keynes (1960, pp. 347–8). Keynes's words here about the weakness of the inducement to invest rather than those quoted earlier about liquidity preference (pp. 247, 352) provide the jumping-off point for ultra-Keynesian theory.

continued accumulation, leads them to concentrate on the problem for all capitalists of realizing a surplus that is not too large for further capitalization, nor too small for the higher capital–labour ratios that increased labour productivity implies.

In the problem of the inducement to invest faced by the Keynesians, stagnation is relieved by special circumstances of new lands and new technology reducing absolute money costs and by state intervention to manage aggregate demand; in the problem of realization and capitalization faced by the Marxists, conflicts are resolved by periodic destruction and restructuring of capital, by unemployment and re-employment of labour, and by the steady concentration of capital in monopolistic firms and industries, which develop some parts of the world economy at the expense of other parts. Colonialism for the Keynesians has to do with nation-state measures to expand exports of goods, capital and labour and to increase the cost of unwanted imports. Imperialism for the Marxists has to do with capitalist firms seeking for surpluses and seeking to use their surpluses wherever they can by incorporating new areas of the world economy into their system of accumulation. What seems to the Keynesians as manageable at the margin by well-informed state intervention in a capitalist system seems to the Marxists as beyond the limits of state control over competitive capitalist accumulation.

This is not the same as the idea of Luxemburg, that foreign trade provides an extension in countries outside the capitalist system to a saturated market inside, which must ultimately reach its limit as the whole world is incorporated into the system. That would be quite alien to Marx's schemes. These do not depend upon a breakdown in the exchange of goods in relation to their production – which would comprise only the realization problem and would imply an underconsumptionist theory; they depend upon a breakdown in the formation of surplus value. As capital accumulates, surplus value is raised at a diminishing rate but more surplus is needed to set each new worker to work.

A question to be decided among Marxists today in a period of oligopoly is where a theory of imperialism based upon what Marx wrote would start from. Would it be from an excess of surplus value, owing to *reduced* competition between capitalists, and so direct attention to the search to find profitable uses for the surplus in armaments and the space race, and therefore on the struggle between capitalism and socialism? This is the view of some modern neo-Marxists who follow Luxemburg in this respect (see Baran and Sweezy, 1966). Or would it start rather from the continuing competitive struggle inside capitalism, within an oligopolistic framework today, of increasingly large corporations, to incorporate other producers and control their own markets and sources of raw materials, and carve up the world in the process? The struggle between capitalism and socialism would on this view be secondary.[12] This seems to be nearer to Marx's own view, as we saw it earlier (1951, pp. 413–14). On the first view, we should expect to see the polarizing force of capital accumulation in one place creating an equal and opposite effect of unemployment and impoverishment elsewhere. On the second, rival centres of accumulation could be expected to emerge, each searching for protected opportunities of development.

The manifest failure of capitalism to develop industrialization equally throughout the whole world, as Marx in some of his writings and even Lenin undoubtedly expected it would, has raised problems for Marxist analysis which have been the special concern of neo-Marxism. This is the problem indicated earlier of the driving force of capital accumulation pushing up against limits of capital realization, or in Keynesian language 'inadequate investment opportunities'. It was Luxemburg's work which made clear the view of a total world economy, 'assimilated to capitalism', in which Marx's categories should be studied (Lee, 1971). This was adopted by Bukharin despite his criticism of Luxemburg's underconsumptionism (Tarbuck, 1972); but Lenin's view of state monopoly capitalism, based on Hilferding, involved a narrower concept of capital export. The attempt today to explain development and underdevelopment as two sides of the same coin seems to modern Marxists to

12. This is the view of Mandel (1970a).

imply a view of 'a capitalist mode of production at a world level which requires imperialism to link up the different fragments' (Palloix, 1971, p. 31). This is in line with Lenin's total view of monopoly capitalism, but what this view lacks is an explanation of the priorities for metropolitan capitalism (see for example, Magdoff, 1972, pp. 157–8, 160). Which is the main aim among so many conflicting aims – to reduce material costs by an artificial division of labour or to expand sales by aiding economic development, to raise the rate of profit with cheaper machinery or to raise the rate of surplus with cheap labour, to win allies at home in protected labour-intensive industries or allies in a comprador bourgeoisie in underdeveloped countries competing with metropolitan products, to support governments that will behave as clients, but cannot develop their economies, or to encourage groups that can develop their economies but may become independent in the process? And amidst these conflicts, can capitalism develop lands that have been underdeveloped?

Marx, writing about the East India Company in 1853, saw England as fulfilling 'a double mission in India: one destructive, the other rejuvenating', He assumed that the 'means of irrigation and internal communication', 'the immediate and current wants of railway locomotion' could be the 'forerunners of modern industry'. He was cautious enough to add:

The Indians will not reap the fruits of the new elements of society scattered among them by the British bourgeoisie, till in Great Britain itself the now ruling classes shall have been supplanted by the industrial proletariat or till the Hindus themselves shall have grown strong enough to throw off the English Yoke altogether (Marx, 1950, p. 48).

But it is clear that he supposed that in the words of a later Marxist:

The general direction of the historical movement seems to have been the same for the backward echelons as for the forward contingents (Baran, 1957, p. 140).

Lenin in *Imperialism* clearly foresaw industrial growth in the colonies:

The export of capital influences and greatly accelerates the development of capitalism in those countries to which it is exported, while, therefore, the export of capital may tend to a certain extent to arrest development in the capital-exporting countries, it can only do so by expanding and deepening the further development of capitalism throughout the world (Lenin, 1933, p. 59).

A date can actually be given to the questioning by Marxists of this thesis. In September 1928, at the Sixth Congress of the Communist International, Kuusinen introduced 'theses on the revolutionary movement in colonial and semi-colonial countries' (Degras, 1960, pp. 526–48), which rejected the so-called 'decolonization' thesis. A major part of Marx's argument and much of Lenin's tone, if not of his analysis, were incorporated into the notion that capitalism, rather than developing all areas that it touches, can positively 'underdevelop'. This notion was taken up by Baran and later by Frank to explain the underdevelopment of some countries as a corollary, as the obverse, or even the cause, in fact, of the development of others. Frank sees a whole hierarchy of exploitation – a chain of metropolis–satellite relationships moving from the world metropolis, which is no one's satellite, *via* nations, capital cities, regional and local centres, large landowners and merchants, small peasants and tenants, right down to the landless labourer at the bottom. Thus surplus is extracted upwards and inwards as it is created, developing some areas at the expense of others (Frank, 1969a, p. 95).

Similarly, another present-day Marxist, Emmanuel, who also believes that the rich are rich because the poor are poor and vice versa, supposes that this is due to unequal exchange in international trade. More labour time is given for less. Marx is quoted, expanding what we saw earlier as the advantages of foreign trade:

And even if we consider Ricardo's theory ... three days of one country's labour may be exchanged for a single day of another country's. ... In this case the rich country exploits the poor one, even if the latter gains through the exchange ... (Marx, 1951, p. 93, quoted in Emmanuel, 1972a, p. 92).

This is quite out of keeping with Marx's general view, that

the productive process is prior to market relations as Bettelheim insists in criticizing Emmanuel. And the latter defends himself with what is, largely, a Keynesian-type argument, that it was consumption that determined investment, and not the reverse (Emmanuel, 1972a, appendices 1 and 2). Wages for Marx are the 'dependent variable', not as Emmanuel makes them, the independent variable. The rate of capital accumulation is the independent variable. Accumulation of capital and its concentration in one area polarizes the development of the productive forces. Where modern industry is first established, production acquires 'a capacity for sudden extension by leaps and bounds'. This is a cumulative process. Elsewhere the blocking of such development may result. But this is for Marx only one aspect of the general conflict throughout the capitalist world between the competitive expansion of productive capacity and the failure of employment opportunities, and of purchasing power among the exploited masses. The workers in rich and poor countries have a common exploiter; there is no sense in which the one can be said to exploit the other.

4 Foreign Treasure and Slaves

In the long history of empires the capture of booty and loot and the extraction of tribute have formed the chief justification, if not always the chief motivation. Ruling groups shared out some of the loot and the more there was to share the wider was their basis of support. There was, therefore, perhaps nothing new in the expansion of European empires in the sixteenth century. They were a natural response to the obstruction of overland trade with Asia and Africa by the Ottoman Empire. That in the process the wealth of the Americas was discovered and the superiority of European navigation established, did, however, create a new kind of empire – an overseas Empire – that generated a new kind of trade involving an exchange of manufactures for raw materials; a new kind of competition between European powers that hastened the formation of nation states; and a new class of traders that encouraged rapid technological advances. There can be no doubting the wealth that was brought back to Europe without recompense from Africa, Asia and the Americas in the sixteenth century. What the Marxist view implies is the association of this concentration of wealth with the establishment of European capitalism and its subsequent domination of the rest of the world.

The Marxist view of the rise of capitalism was that it depended, first, on a form of capital accumulation that involved the dispossession of many small owners from the land and their means of production, if necessary their total elimination and, secondly, on the emergence of a new kind of capitalist with a new kind of technology. What then was the importance of foreign treasure? Marx was insistent that the industrial capitalist class in Britain did not emerge out of the merchants and monopolists of the seventeenth century (Marx, 1909, ch. 20; Dobb, 1946, pp. 193–8) and he emphasized that colonial wealth did not lead to industrial capitalism in Spain or Holland (Marx, 1946, ch. 31). On the other hand, Marx saw the 'primitive accumulation of capital', as he called it, in the expropriation of the English peasantry; the 'genesis of the industrial capitalist' in the sea ports 'beyond the control of the old municipalities' and the 'chief momenta of primitive accumulation' in the 'discovery of gold and silver in America, the extirpation, enslavement and entombment in mines of the aboriginal population, the beginning of the conquest and looting of the East Indies, the turning of Africa into a warren for the commercial hunting of black skins'.

The wealth of the whole world ransacked, independent peasants destroyed and the loot brought back to England – these were necessary conditions for the birth of industrial capitalism but not sufficient conditions. The new class of industrial capitalist introducing a new kind of technology provided the missing condition, and the main field of his operations was trade and not plunder, the main source of his profit, wage labour not servile labour. That was not to say that he was above plunder or the employing of slaves, to replace an independent peasantry. Indeed, Marx regarded the use of slaves in colonies as typical of the need of industrial capitalism for expropriated labour.

With Marx's emphasis on trade, neo-classical theory is in profound agreement, but the inflow of bullion is regarded by the neo-classical school as positively damaging to trade along with other mercantilist policies; the use of slaves is seen as a 'relapse' in the evolution of the market economy due to the shortage of labour in new lands of settlement (Hicks, 1969, p. 137). The fall in the rate of interest at the end of the eighteenth century is said to result not from the inflow of gold but from the development of banking (1969, p. 45). It was just this point that Keynes challenged. The 'element of scientific truth in mercantilism' was for Keynes that a favourable foreign balance was the direct means to expand foreign investment and the indirect means to reduce the rate of interest and induce home investment, given a tendency to hoarding; or if not to hoarding, certainly to a weakness in the inducement to invest, and no other means available to governments. New discoveries of sources of precious metals, state spending on wars, and the opening up of new lands were the main special conditions suggested by Keynesians for overcoming the tendency to stagnation. The spread of the money economy in the sixteenth century from the wool trade as well as from the inflow of precious metals was on the Keynesian, as on the Marxist, view, an important cause of the dispossession of the peasantry (Robinson, 1970a, pp. 44, 55).

Merchant capital amassed from the conquest of India, 'the application of science to production and the permeation of money values into every aspect of life' together with the Protestant break with obscurantism created the conditions for the development of industry. 'The spark that fell upon all this tinder was the trade in cotton textiles' which led merchants to 'begin organizing production ... from putting out to household workers they developed factories and the employment of labour for wages' (Robinson, 1970a, pp. 61–2).

This is the Keynesian view and it can be seen that it differs from the Marxist view in one respect: foreign plunder expands the money economy, reduces the rate of interest and provides cotton as a suitable material for new forms of production by merchants, but the direct connection between foreign treasure and a new kind of capitalist – the industrialist – with a new kind of technology is not suggested. What sort of people were these early industrialists and what sort of technology are we talking about? Hobsbawm has made the point that the machines were really quite simple (1968, pp. 43–4), and so were the men – watchmakers, like the man whose invention Arkwright stole to make the water frame, millwrights like Thomas Brindley the canal builder, blacksmiths like Thomas Newcomen, inventor of the steam pump, instrument-makers like James Watt, who invented the steam engine, a colliery enginewright like George Stephenson, who designed and made the first locomotive. Abraham Darby, who discovered how to smelt with coal and

James Wilkinson who founded the Sheffield firm at first only leased their Shropshire furnaces. These were not just inventors; they became capitalists.

The 'old colonial' Empires, as they are called, of Spain and Portugal, of France and even of England and Holland in the sixteenth century, were manifestly not the work of industrial capitalists. Merchant capital was certainly involved but under the protective arm of absolute monarchs of still mainly feudal states. Royal monopolies gave high profits to those who had claims to extract precious metals or could capture existing trade routes and keep out foreign competition; but by the end of the sixteenth century there were too many 'outsiders' in the business and profits collapsed (Hobsbawm, 1954). The decline of the Spanish empire and later of the Dutch, and the rise of England to commercial predominance in the seventeenth century, alike support the view that 'old colonialism did not grow over into new colonialism; it collapsed and was replaced by it' (Hobsbawm, 1954, no. 5, p. 46). The United East India Company which received its charter from Parliament in 1708 really was a different company from the old East India Companies operating under royal charters of 1612 and 1661. The basis of the new system was precisely the development of Britain's manufacturing interest, not by the merchant monopolists but by the 'outsiders' who were indeed proto-industrial capitalists. That they were anti-monopolists is not to say that they were free traders. On the contrary their strength was built up behind Cromwell's navy and his Navigation Acts of 1650–51. The new colonies were to supply food and raw materials in exchange for English manufactures. The execution of Charles I marked the significance of these economic changes for political structures (Barratt Brown, 1970a, ch. 1).

That it was a major change justifying Marx's categorizing it as the beginning of a new era and a new mode of production can be seen from Cromwell's acts that followed at once after the King's execution. Christopher Hill has summarized these acts as 'the removal of the obstacles to the development of English capitalism' (1970, pp. 264–6). These included not only the suppression of the Levellers, but he instances the draining of the

Fens and the destruction of the historic commoners' rights, the conquest of Jamaica, the exploitation of Ireland, the restitution of the East India Company, the building of the navy, the Navigation Acts and all those acts that established the colonial trade. To understand the new colonialism of the proto-industrial capitalists, it is enough to see in Daniel Defoe's hero, Robinson Crusoe, 'a picture of the technical ability, the attention to financial detail, the inventive resourcefulness, the self-confidence, the assurance of command over native peoples to give us a surer picture of what was to be than all the wealth of the Whig merchants' (Barratt Brown, 1970a, p. 4).

It was, however, Crusoe's stock of guns, ammunition and tools from a superior technology that were crucial to his success, as Stephen Hymer (1971) has written in an essay on Robinson Crusoe and primitive accumulation. This is the story of the actual Crusoe, slaver, conqueror, early capitalist, the other side of the ideal trader, in whom so many economists have found the mythical origins of neo-classical theory. In this essay Hymer has shown how the story of Crusoe uncovers the secret of what Marx called 'primitive (or original) accumulation'. In this process money is in the first stage turned into commodities ('£40 in toys and trifles') to make into more money from an expedition to the Guinea coast ('gold worth £300'). Part of this is lost, but part turned into 'all sorts of tools, iron work and utensils necessary for my plantation'. With this cargo taken to South America, slave labour is employed, but slaves are scarce and more are sought from Africa and on the journey there Crusoe suffers his shipwreck. On his desert island the use of his tools is of value only for his own needs, until the place is populated. With the capture of Man Friday by force and his initiation into slavery, Crusoe has labour power to set to work to meet present needs and future growth. The beginnings of expanded reproduction are possible. More labour is captured and Crusoe's people are 'perfectly subjected' in his dominion.

Among so many prescient insights in Defoe's allegory there is one particular herald of the future form that capitalist imperialism was to take. This is the Spaniard whom Crusoe releases from his native captors, to whom Crusoe gives his pistol and sword, whereupon three natives are immediately butchered, and whom Crusoe then employs as his ambassador and finally leaves on the island as his overseer and agent to manage his colony of Spaniards, convicts and slaves, when a chance shipfall enables him to sail back to England. His plantation had prospered and on his return to civilization, he finds himself 'master all on a sudden of above £5000 Sterling in money and had an estate, as I might well call it in the Brazils, of above a thousand pounds a year'. The island he visits again much later and shares into parts among the Spaniards; and as Crusoe concludes, 'reserved to myself the property of the whole but gave them such parts respectively as they agreed on and having settled all things with them, and engaged them not to leave the place, I left them there'.

Written at the beginning of the eighteenth century, *Robinson Crusoe* provides the clearest picture we could have of the roots of capitalism in colonialism, not the merchant capitalism of the old colonialism in which goods were bought and sold at a profit, but the new colonialism in which slaves were set to work with the tools and weapons of a new technology as wider and wider areas of the world were incorporated into capitalist economic relations. Crusoe, as Hymer shows him, is a transitional figure, but 'the secret of his capital is revealed'; this is not based primarily upon the discovery of treasure, although this gives him his start, but 'is based on other people's labour and is obtained by force and illusion' (1971, p. 35).[1] Before him the story of European conquest can be read in Prescott's *Conquest of Mexico* and *Conquest of Peru*, after him in Orme's *History of the Military Transactions of the British Nation in Indostan*. These histories provide the most striking contrast between the plundering Conquistadores of feudal Spain and the clerks of the East India Company's factories in Madras. The flow of precious metals continued, but in the seventeenth century it was from the profits of traders (Knowles, 1928,

1. All the quotations are from Hymer (1971), except the last but one which comes from Defoe, *Robinson Crusoe* (p. 394), World Classics edn.

p. 72). Apart from slaves, which we shall consider in a moment, there was little direct booty or tribute to come again from the colonies until the middle of the eighteenth century when Clive's victory at Plessey returned 'such a prize in solid money'. By the time of Clive the stage was set for England's industrialization and the crucial role of India in that process.

If colonial possessions provided no more than a protected exchange of manufactures for raw materials, protected that is from rival nation states, we could accept Fieldhouse's dictum to substantiate the Schumpeter model: 'It is perfectly possible,' Fieldhouse writes, 'to construct a model for the economic development of modern Europe on the assumption that the Continent had no possibility of outside investment, without necessarily accepting as a consequence a stop to the process of investment or the accumulation of capital. Economic development would certainly have been very different and might have been slower; but it could still have taken place' (1967, p. 188). Fieldhouse had narrowed down the Marxist connection between capitalism and imperialism to the expansion of overseas investment in the last half of the nineteenth century, because he was examining Lenin's view of that period as an age of imperialism, and the 'highest stage of capitalism' (Lenin, 1933). But this is a variant, and, as we shall see later, one by no means consistently held by Lenin himself, of the general Marxist model of the inextricable connection of capitalism and imperialism. We may, therefore, take Fieldhouse's dictum to cover the whole period of capitalism and ask whether capitalism could have developed in Europe without colonial sources of capital accumulation; albeit somewhat more slowly and in a different manner. In his latest book Fieldhouse says that he has 'modified (his) earlier views on the role and importance of economic factors in the imperialist process'; but in so doing he limits himself to a definition of this process as one of territorial annexation (Fieldhouse, 1973, pp. 3–4).

The inflow to Europe of treasure in precious metals in the sixteenth century could not in itself assure capitalism's economic development. As Midas discovered, an accumulation of gold cannot be consumed. There are, however, three ways in which it might have encouraged development: (a) by permitting capital accumulation and thus giving purchasing power over labour and materials; (b) by raising prices and therefore profits in relation to wages; and (c) by providing a base for extended credit, both individual and national. It is enough for our argument only that governments should think that bullion import had these effects, so long as it led them to encourage exports, although what we have to show is a necessary connection with the emergence of capitalism in Europe.

Economic theories, as we have already quoted Keynes as suggesting, are generally applied to periods when they are no longer applicable. The mercantilist theory that a nation is strong in so far as it imports bullion took hold of England and France in the late seventeenth and eighteenth centuries but it was from sixteenth and early seventeenth-century experience that it arose.[2] It certainly had the most powerful effect on nation-state policies until Adam Smith began its demolition in 1776. The substance behind the theory came from what Heckscher (1969) termed a 'fear of goods' and a belief that bullion imports created employment, while imports of goods destroyed it.

Mercantilism was not only a theory of merchant capital but of early industrial capital. Merchants are equally interested in both exports and imports, although they want imports under their control in order to assure them of monopoly profits. The ordinary citizen has a love of goods, in Heckscher's terms, although he may also have a 'fear of goods' as an industrial worker. It is, however, the industrial capitalist, who cannot realize his capital until his goods are sold, who has a really strong 'fear of goods', and wants policy directed to encourage the export of goods as well as to protect him against imports. The strategic importance of agricultural self-sufficiency and of naval power (recognized even by Adam Smith) was woven into mercantilism but basically it was a protectionist

2. Thomas Mun, the first English Mercantilist writer, compiled his book on *England's Treasure from Foreign Trade* in the 1620s although it was not published until 1664.

view. It is not difficult to understand its origin in the stagnation of English cloth exports in the second half of the sixteenth century after their meteoric rise in the first half (Fisher, 1954, p. 153). Markets in Europe were glutted and English and other traders began to look overseas.

Mercantilist theory, however, not only saw imports of precious metals as preferable to imports of goods, but as positively beneficial to a state. Money was identified with capital in that it yielded an income in the same way as land, but it also increased circulation as a means of exchange. An increase in the quantity of money, if not hoarded, would lower the rate of interest and yet not lower prices and profits. This was most explicitly argued by John Locke (see Heckscher, 1969). That this was believed, not only by his patrons, the Shaftesbury family with their wide political and colonial interests, but by seventeenth-century kings and corporations alike is undoubted (Coleman, 1969).

The accumulation of money as capital is regarded by Marxists rather more than by Keynesians as one of the necessary conditions for the emergence of the capitalist mode of production. Marxists see the sixteenth century and early seventeenth as a period of primitive capital accumulation in Europe (Dobb, 1946, p. 209) and it is the concentration of money into a few hands through the influx of precious metals that they would regard as the essential contribution of foreign treasure to capitalism. The evidence cited is, first, the undoubtedly rapid development of industry in Britain in the last half of the sixteenth century (Nef, 1954, pp. 89–101), following the influx of gold and silver from the Americas; and, second, the major developments of the industrial revolution in England in the last half of the eighteenth century, following the victory of Clive at Plessey and the steady drain of tribute from India to Britain (Dutt, 1947, pp. 93–9).

Two such examples look convincing, but the mechanism by which the events are connected has been questioned. There is, in other words, no evidence that either the precious metals of the Americas or the tribute from India went into industrial investment in Britain. Most of it went into land and into great houses which the courtiers, aristocrats and nabobs of the times, who could get their hands on the loot, proceeded to surround themselves with. Marxists would be quick to add that the profits from human loot – the slaves taken from Africa to America, indentured labour from India and China – and more recently from inflow of interest and dividends in excess of capital outflows, have all added to the direct accumulation of capital in Europe. Such a transfer of wealth must have had some qualitative as well as merely quantitative effect. Capital investment in England in the 1760s is estimated at no more than £6 million–£7 million per annum and the annual tribute from India was at least £2 million (Mathias, 1969, table 2, p. 41). If sums of this order were not invested directly in industry, what was their effect? One answer of Keynes, perhaps not entirely serious, can be taken from his *Treatise on Money*:

The booty brought back by Drake in the *Golden Hind* (estimated at some £600 000) may fairly be considered the fountain and origin of British Foreign Investment. Elizabeth paid off out of the proceeds the whole of her foreign debt and invested a part of the balance (about £42 000) in the Levant Company; largely out of the profits of the Levant Company there was formed the East India Company; the profits of which during the seventeenth and eighteenth centuries were the main foundation of England's foreign connections (1930, pp. 156–7).

Thus Keynes calculated that at $6\frac{1}{2}$ per cent return per annum, and half of that reinvested each year, the £42 000 of 1580 should have amounted to £2 500 000 by 1700 – which was in fact about the value of the capital of the East India Company, Royal African Company and Hudson's Bay Company in that year – and to £4 200 000 by 1930 – which was again the approximate actual aggregate of current British foreign investments in that year. Forty years later in 1970 the figure should have risen to £15 000 million. It had. This tells us only that, in Myrdal's phrase, wealth attracts and poverty repels (Myrdal, 1954, p. 12). 'Unto him that hath shall be given . . .' It tells us only what advantages there were for Britain as the first industrial state. Winner takes all, and the devil take the hindmost, in a process of 'cumulative causation'. It does not tell us the relationship of such initial accumulations of wealth to the development of capitalism. Thus Keynes reminds us that it was not the absolute value of the bullion which mattered but the indirect effect on profit and enterprise.

The second and main answer of Keynes, therefore, although this was not perhaps a Keynesian answer in our sense, was that the inflow of precious metals raised prices (three-fold between 1520 and 1650) and by cheapening labour costs made possible exceptionally high profits (Keynes, 1930, vol. 2, pp. 152–63).[3] Against this view, Nef later argued that labour was dearer at least in England than had previously been supposed and indicated that improvements in industrial technology based primarily upon the necessity to go over from wood burning to coal were the cause of high profits. Nef adds a thoroughly underconsumptionist twist to his argument by commenting that 'the advantages which employers derived from hiring labour cheaply might have been offset by the reduction in the amount workmen could have spent on manufactured goods' (Nef, 1954, p. 133).

An apparently exogenous scientific factor like coal technology, taken together with the paradox that mercantilism as a system of economic administration of a Colbertian type was most written about in England and least practised (Hecksher, 1969, p. 23), fits well with a classical liberal view of the merits of free enterprise and free trade. But the Keynesians would argue that some increase in demand had still to evoke the new technology and the expansion of free enterprise. A more Keynesian view than that of Keynes in the *Treatise on Money* is to be found in the *General Theory* (1960, ch. 23). Here what he said was that the effect of the inflow of precious metals to Europe and the tribute from slavery and from India was to increase the circulation of money and reduce the rate of interest and thus elicit what Keynesians now call 'frustrated supply'.[4] The expenditure at home of merchants, slave traders and nabobs, on land and on great houses, not only helped to finance the agricultural revolution of England in the seventeenth and eighteenth centuries,

3. However, Keynes's argument was based on Hamilton (1929).
4. The phrase is that of J. A. Knapp.

which greatly reduced labour costs, but it also provided an important new market for industry. It is not for nothing that Mandeville (1934) extols the virtues of the rich in their conspicuous consumption ('private vices: public virtues'). Recent studies have shown the importance of the orders for livery for the servants of the great country houses and of the City merchants' houses too (Halstead, 1974; Hobsbawm, 1968, p. 30). Even more important was the stimulus of foreign commerce to ship building and the trades that depended on the overseas market.

It is possible that capitalism might have emerged in Europe without the aid of foreign treasure; the fact is that it did *not* emerge without it. A model of capitalist development without foreign treasure would have to suggest a source of sufficient circulating money to be accumulated as capital for the large-scale, highly capitalistic forms of manufacture which Nef described as emerging in Britain between 1540 and 1640 (1954, p. 95). This could have arisen from the exactions of a centralized state ploughed into industrial development. Government orders for armaments helped, but whatever else mercantilism meant it did not mean this, even in Colbert's hands. His bounties went to agriculture. [5] It could have arisen from the monetization of land, and this certainly took place before and during this period, from the dissolution of monasteries and land clearances for cash cropping by sheep farming. It could have arisen from increased profits on foreign trade through improved techniques of production rather than exploited slaves, and this also took place.

Increased profit from foreign trade and the monetization of land themselves involve an increased supply of money, and short of state credits, which again were not any part of mercantilism, this had to come from outside the area of capital concentration. In a nation state that was large enough, capital might have been accumulated in one part at the expense of other parts. England certainly developed at the expense of

5. Of course, the states that were 'late developers' in industrialization – Germany, the USA and Russia – all provided state funds for development but they were catching up on a capitalist economy that was already well established. See chapter 7.

Ireland and most of Scotland; the Northern States of the USA at the expense of the South. But is this not saying that an imperialist relationship was established between the developed and the underdeveloped parts? That it involved potential contradictions between cheapening labour costs and expanding employment and sales is a necessary part of the Marxist model. It need not mean that the attempt was not made by capitalists to do both and that this might indeed supply the dynamic of the system. It is of major importance for the argument between the Keynesian and Marxist views of this dynamic, that the Spanish, Portuguese and Dutch empires failed to generate industrial capitalism; while English merchants coming in late on the act bought themselves in by their sales of English manufactures as much as by their capture of Spanish gold or their monopoly of the slave trade. The implication is that mercantilist policies alone did not succeed in developing capitalism. For that a new class of industrial capitalists was needed and the incorporation of the plantation economies. This is the Marxist view and of course an ultra-Keynesian view would not be limited to an explanation in terms of mercantilist policies. The supply side of the Keynesian position on these matters still requires to be clearly articulated. However a start has been suggested (see Knapp, 1973, table 2, p. 36).

The importance of the slave trade for the development of British capitalism has been emphasized by several writers, and especially by Eric Williams. With a wealth of evidence he has established the stimulus that the 'triangular trade' between Britain, Africa and the West Indies and North America, gave to British industry.

The Negroes were purchased with British manufactures; transported to the plantations, they produced sugar, cotton, indigo, molasses and other tropical products, the processing of which created new industries in England; while the maintenance of the Negroes and their owners on the plantations provided another market for British industry, New England agriculture and the Newfoundland fisheries ... The profits obtained provided one of the main streams of that accumulation of capital in England which financed the Industrial Revolution (1964, p. 52).

The importance of these plantations for British economic development can hardly be exaggerated. British official trade statistics for this period are subject to major qualifications (see Deane and Cole, 1964, pp. 42–6), but we may take the official values as a correct indication of the *proportions* by composition and source of retained imports and of re-exports between the 1780s and 1840s.

The two major increases over this period were: in the first twenty years the imports of luxury consumption goods – coffee, tea, sugar, tobacco – and in the last twenty years the imports of raw cotton. Nearly the whole of these imports came from plantations in the West and East Indies, and at the end of the period from the plantation states of the USA. During the same period, with the exception of the war years, the prices of these imports were falling (Mitchell and Deane, 1962, table XVI.2; Deane and Cole, 1964, table 21), and this despite the mono-

Table 1 Imports into Great Britain, 1780s to 1840s, by source and composition (in £m official values)

Imports	1780–1784	1800–1804	1820–1824	1840–1844
total imports	11·5	30	33·2	68
re-exported	3·8	9·6	10	14
sources				
West Indies	2·7	8·0	8·0	(7·6)[b]
USA	0·1	2·0	3·7	(30)
Asia	3·3	5·5	6·7	(23)
composition				
all luxuries[a]	2·8	11·9	12·2	14·6
re-exported	?	4·2	3·3	2·7
all cotton	0·3	2·0	5·1	20·2
re-exported	—	1·0	1·1	3·0
other raw materials	2·5	6·6	8·0	19·3
corn	0·4	1·8	0·2	5·0

[a] Luxuries are items such as coffee, sugar, tea and tobacco
[b] Figures for import sources in brackets are for 1854, when total imports were £150 million; earlier figures are not available
Sources: Mitchell and Deane (1962, tables XI.2, XI.4, XI.10, XI.12)

polistic position of the importers, which raised prices in Britain by at least 20 per cent according to Sir Henry Parnell (Clapham, 1930, p. 328). The clearest example of falling prices is the fall in raw cotton prices from about £0·1 per lb in the 1780s to about £0·05 in the 1820s and £0·025 in the 1840s (Deane and Cole, 1964, tables 42 and 43, pp. 185–7).

To this we can add from Marx that in the cotton industry which became the heart of British capitalism 'the veiled slavery of the wage worker in Europe needed, for its pedestal, slavery pure and simple in the new world' (Marx, 1946, ch. 31). It is a striking fact of colonial history that slavery and other forms of indentured labour continued for so long. From the abolition of the slave trade in 1807, and of slavery in the British colonies in 1833, it was another thirty years before slaves were freed in the United States. In Cuba and Brazil and the Árab countries, slavery continued. Elsewhere forced and indentured labour took its place. Indians were brought to Trinidad and Guiana, to Ceylon, Natal, East Africa, Malaya, Fiji and Mauritius to work on plantations. Chinese were brought to Singapore, the West Indies, South Africa and British Columbia for mining and railway construction. Compulsory labour continued in Southern and in East Africa and especially in Portuguese Africa for railway building down to our own times (Knowles, 1928, pp. 170–201). As a source of the accumulation of wealth in Europe the employment of slaves overseas to replace a free peasantry finds few equals: and in defending that accumulation the recruitment of native troops under European officers, and especially the deployment by Britain of the Indian Army throughout Asia, became a prerequisite. Nor can we overlook the Nazi slave camps or the role of migrant labour as a 'sub-proletariat' in Europe today.

The concentration of wealth in Europe which was to divide the world for centuries between rich and poor areas had begun in the sixteenth century. The connection between imperialism as a system of plunder and the rise of capitalism cannot then be explained as a hangover of earlier social formations or earlier ideologies, nor as a result of mercantilist policies designed to achieve an inflationary inflow of gold. It is this connection between capitalism and imperialism as a system of exploitation that, on a Marxist view, lies behind the protected markets and capitalist employment opportunities that will be discussed in the next chapters. What we must add here is that the absence of outside sources of tribute, indeed the continuing outflow of tribute, makes the industrialization of the underdeveloped lands today all the more difficult. So hard is the road and so steep the climb up to industrial development that we shall find in a later chapter (12) even the Soviet Union preying upon the wealth of its neighbours; and similar, although weaker, attempts at the same game will be found in most of the underdeveloped countries which see that such opportunities exist. Those who look to the centres of capitalism from the underdeveloped and exploited lands can be forgiven for seeing only the predatory aspect of European domination, made all the more offensive by the cloak of an ostensibly Christian, civilizing mission to 'backward races', whose culture the Europeans could not understand and proceeded to destroy (Hodgkin, 1972, pp. 102–8).

Before we leave the subject of foreign treasure, however, we have to notice some more recent examples of plunder in the relations of capitalist states. Tribute in the form of a return on investments we leave to a later chapter; but the exaction of reparations in our own times, the recourse to slave labour and plunder by the Nazis, and the commandeering of scarce raw materials in recent years are appropriately examined here. The exaction of reparations by the Allied Powers after 1918 and 1945 are easily enough explained in terms of the emotions aroused in total war; and such an explanation fits neatly into the Schumpeter thesis of atavistic survivals. The fact, moreover, that after the Second World War the Soviet Union, which was not part of the capitalist system, took the largest share of reparations (having admittedly suffered the heaviest damage) appears to dispose of any association between capitalism and plunder of this sort, but may tell us much about the connection between economic development and plunder. Yet, the arguments of the Allies concerning the payment of reparations, especially after the First World War, and concerning the reduction of German heavy industry after the Second, do suggest major conflicts between the capitalist powers, for which an appeal to earlier social formations provides inadequate explanation.

It is the Marxist view that competition between rival capitalist powers is an essential element of imperialism and leads inevitably to wars. Certainly, it was not Germany or Japan, where, in Schumpeter's view, the nationalism and militarism of earlier social formations became inextricably involved in the establishment of capitalism, but Britain and the USA, where there was a close approximation to Schumpeter's 'pure' capitalism, which were demanding reparations. It is particularly striking that in the argument about reparations after the First World War it was not the classical liberal school that was arguing for their suspension but Keynes (1920, ch. 5). Even 'pure' capitalists were not above trying to get their hands on some plunder, and it was largely a political decision of capitalist governments to rescue Germany from Bolshevism that led to the Dawes and Young agreements. It was certainly a political decision of the United States after the Second World War, once more under the threat of communism, to lift reparations and the limitations upon German heavy industry and to finance economic reconstruction in West Germany. In this field neither the Marxist model nor the Schumpeter model seems to fit the facts very well, but Keynesian mercantilist explanations fit perfectly.

It is interesting to remind ourselves of what Keynes was saying at the time:

Just as the Allies demand vast payments from Germany and then exercise their ingenuity to prevent her paying them, so the American Administration desires, with one hand, schemes for financing exports and, with the other, tariffs which will make it as difficult as possible for such credits to be repaid. . . . Even the shipment to the United States of all the bullion in the world will be of no avail, nor the destruction of United States export industries and the shift of capital and labour to employment for the home market, for capital and labour are not so easily moved inside a nation let alone between nations. The division of labour is of historically long standing and cannot easily be changed (1932c, p. 57).

The tribute of the sixteenth century was not different; it left Spain enfeebled, while in England capitalism flourished. New markets were opened up for her industries not so much against payment in bullion but in exchange for the products of her trading partners. Tribute was an initial stimulus to England's economic development; it could not alone have sustained it, but it continued to strengthen it.

Slavery perhaps never quite died out and, as we suggested earlier in this chapter, was not confined at all to the less capital-istically developed lands like Arabia. Cases of the use of slaves have certainly been authenticated in quite recent years in Angola (Davidson, 1955, p. 190); and something near to slavery in Papua (Scarr, 1967) and in South Africa (Davidson, 1955, p. 125). The prison camps of the USSR are generally referred to as slave camps, but, since their aim is retributive rather than exploitative, they come in a different category. The revival of slave labour and plunder on a large scale by the Nazis in Germany in the 1940s does, however, raise a question about the relationship of German imperialism to German capitalism. Schumpeter (1955, pp. 92–5) argued that German im-perialism was accounted for precisely by the nationalist and militarist environment in which German capitalism emerged. In fact, however, the German army was opposed to the plunder and the use of slave labour (Davidson, 1950, p. 32). The force of German nationalism was indeed harnessed by the Nazis to their war chariot, and what Schumpeter calls 'the dark powers of the subconscious' (1955, p. 11) were indeed the basis of the Nazi appeal to the German people; but the German capitalists can-not be let off so lightly. It was they who put Hitler into power and they who organized the plunder and employed the slaves (Martin, 1950; Dubois, 1953). The fact that capitalists did behave like this does not allow us to argue that they had to do so. Yet one cannot easily escape the Marxist view that it was the competitive drive of German capital for markets, for colonies as fields of investment and sources of raw material that created Hitler, Frankenstein monster though he became for the German capitalists as well as for the rest of Europe. Individual capitalists tend sometimes to neglect both the economic interdependence of capital, upon which Schumpeter bases their lack of any 'class interest in forcible expansion' and equally the warnings of the mercantilists against cheap imports (1955, p. 75).

If we consider the current activities of large capitalist firms, there is growing exploitation of sources of scarce materials and growing rivalry actually to control them. The race for control over non-renewable and wasting mineral resources, including oil, leads to these being increasingly mined in underdeveloped lands, as the reserves in the more developed lands are used up (Jalée, 1967). Since the underdeveloped lands by definition have not yet been able to develop industries which could themselves make use of these minerals, extraction of their minerals for the benefit of the already developed lands is increasingly seen by the peoples of the underdeveloped lands as a form of plunder. By the time their underdeveloped economies are developed they fear the minerals will have gone. Yet because of the distortions which characterize underdevelopment these minerals may be all that they have to offer on the world market. As the Shah of Persia has put it, they may then determine at least to 'sell their heritage dear' and diversify their economies now while the mineral supplies last.

It is natural enough for any company and any government to wish to assure itself of continuing supplies of essential minerals, particularly if these look like running out.[6] But no situation could be less likely to lead to an 'essentially unwarlike disposition' than one in which the basic ingredients of capitalist production are running out; and it is just the minerals that go into making and propelling the motor car and the aeroplane, the very epitome of capitalist production, that are in question. There are many who would argue that, since the time when Staley (1935) first sought to answer Lenin's association of colonial wars with capital investment, there has been a growing list of examples of war-like moves by capitalist states to control raw material supplies (Caldwell, 1971). Certainly, the evidence

6. See the US International Development Advisory Board, 1951 Report and Commission on Foreign Economic Policy, *Staff Papers*, 1954, quoted in Magdoff (1970).

Table 2 Dependence of developed countries on imports of primary products from underdeveloped countries, 1962

Commodity according to degree of protection	Value in world trade ($m)	Imports in total consumption (percentage range) in USA	others	US consumption (as percentage of all consumption)	Imports from underdev. (as percentage of world imports)	Exports from underdev. (as percentage of all underdev. PP exports)
non-competing	4495	—	—	—	90	20·5
tropical products	3155				98	14·5
coffee	1737	75–100	75–100	34	99	8·5
cocoa	516	75–100	75–100	28	85	2·0
tea	466	75–100	75–100	5	94	2·0
bananas	376	75–100	75–100	7	96	2·0
spices	60	75–100	75–100	n.a.	70+	—
threatened by synthetics	1340	—	—		80	6·0
rubber	1011	20–50	75–100	36	76	4·0
copra etc.	168	75–100	75–100	8	99	1·0
jute	161	75–100	75–100	2	98	1·0
competing	42 025	—	—		45	79·5
unprotected	33 802	—	—		38	62·5
crude petrol	5736	10–20	75–100	36 }	93	26·0
petrol, products	3113	0–10	10–50		46	7·0
wool	1972	10–20	50–100	13	15	1·5
copper	1703	20–50	75–100	29	53	4·5
iron ore	1414	20–50	50–100	28	49	3·5
fish meal	803	10–20	0–20	7	43	1·5

timber	795	0-10	31[a]	49	2·0
hides	522	n.a.	n.a.	30	1·0
tin	265	75-100	26	75	1·0
bauxite	222	75-100	42	87	1·0
manganese	152	75-100	14	74	0·5
phosphates	188	40-100	32	65	0·5
others	16 917	exp.		17	12·5
zinc	—	10-20	26	30+	—
lead	—	20-50	35	30+	—
rice	—	exp.	1	40+	(2)
protected	8223			49	17
cotton	1424	exp.	20	61	4·5
meat	1268	n.a.	25	19	1·0
sugar	1139	50-75	10	78	4·5
wheat	1047	exp.	6	14	0·5
maize	880	20-75	34	20	1·0
tobacco	794	10-100	16	30	1·0
wine	559	n.a.	4	49	1·0
oil seed products	480	20-100	17	54	1·5
oranges	418	0-100	20	40	1·0
groundnuts	214	0-100	6	93	1·0
totals	46 520	—	—	44[b]	100

[a] US timber consumption includes pulp and newsprint
[b] Percentage of world imports of total underdeveloped imports
exp. = net exporter; n.a. = not available; P P = primary products; underdev. = all except Western Europe, U.S.A., Canada, Japan, Oceania, South Africa and Communist bloc.
Sources: United Nations (1964, tables 1.3 and 1.4); Oxford Economic Atlas (1972, Commodity and United States tables); Food and Agricultural Organization (1972, p. 64)

of increased United States industrial dependence on imports of key raw materials has been documented by successive Presidential Commissions from the 1950s onwards (Magdoff, 1970, pp. 45–54).[7] The chief commodities involved are tin, bauxite, manganese, nickel, chromium; but lead, zinc, iron ore and above all petroleum have been added to the United States' import list in the last two decades. To these one might add coffee, cocoa, tea, bananas and spices for each of which United States import dependence is high. Other industrial countries are dependent on imports for even more primary products, and for them a higher proportion of many of these come from *underdeveloped* lands.

A key feature of the table is the large share of the total world consumption of so many of these primary products that is accounted for by the United States. The extraction by the United States and by other developed countries of mineral and primary products from the whole world would not be regarded by classical economists as any sort of plunder, but rather as a rational exchange of staple products in a world division of labour encouraged by free trade. A growing threat of a scarcity of supply of any materials, moreover, could be expected to lead to a price increase in anticipation of shortages. Unfortunately for this comforting view, the bargaining position of the supplier of a single staple tends to be weak unless he has a monopoly and there are no substitutes; and long-term prospects of shortages do not have much influence on the short-term futures markets for commodities, unless governments start to build up strategic stock-piles against the day of scarcity. On a Keynesian view of bargaining power, increasing dependence of developed nations on imported materials should lead, nevertheless, to a strengthening of the position of the producers of these materials. There is little evidence that it has done so, at least until very recently.

There are two main pieces of evidence: the first is that, in fact, the prices of primary products, even of potentially scarce materials, have not been rising in relation to the prices of manufactures. We shall discuss this at length in the chapter on the

7. See Jalée (1967, pp. 110–11) for French experience.

terms of trade. Secondly, there is the evidence of continuous complaints over the underpricing of raw material exports from underdeveloped lands, compared with the prices realized by similar products from developed lands. There have been rumours of this in relation to some Latin American agricultural products, but the hard evidence comes from oil and iron ore prices obtained by Venezuela and from copper prices by Chile (Mikesell, 1971, pp. 106, 329, 371). The explanation given by the Marxists of these apparent acts of exploitation of under-developed lands is that such purchases are made through trans-national oil and mining companies, whose transfer pricing arrangements are extremely hard for governments of under-developed countries to control. The underdeveloped countries complain also of the overpricing of goods and shipping in their manufactured imports from developed lands, particularly in the case of aid-supported supplies.[8]

The case for recognizing a continuing element of straight plunder in imperialist economic relations is a strong one. But plunder impoverishes and may conflict with other capitalist aims. This is the element of truth in the classical view; and on a Marxist view also, the association of plunder with imperialism is only one aspect of the general tendency of capital to become centralized at the expense of the extremities. The large firm is only the most recent of the agencies in this polarizing process, which has over a long period of time involved the creation by capitalism of a quite artificial division of labour in the world. It is this that we must now try to comprehend.

8. Myrdal (1970, p. 339), quotes estimates varying from 20 per cent to 40 per cent overpricing of aid deliveries compared with the most favourable existing prices.

5 The World Division of Labour

Mercantilism was a system for ensuring a favourable national balance of trade, and thus a steady import of bullion, as well as monopoly profit for the merchants engaged in the trade. It was no less a system for establishing a particular division of labour between mother country and colonies. 'It was the intention in settling our plantations in America', wrote the English Commissioner for Trade and Plantations in 1699, 'that the people there should be employed in such things as are not the produce of England to which they belong' (Lipson, 1934, p. 173). If a national monopoly of the trade in those things could be won, as it was in sugar and tobacco, so much the better; but even without monopolies the colonies were worth while because the 'second great justification of colonies' for the mercantilist was that 'they could be constrained to buy English manufactures, and the whole trade be carried in English ships' (Pares, 1962, p. 421). Thus Cromwell's Navigation Acts of 1650–51 were followed by Acts of Parliament to restrict industrial development in the colonies – the Hatters Act, the Iron Act and later the Calico Act, as well as by Corn Bounty Acts and the Act of Limitation – forbidding the import of Irish cattle – to protect English agriculture. The North American colonies revolted against the system 150 years ahead of the Irish; outside North America, Britain's Colonial Empire established what was in effect an artificial world division of labour that has lasted down to our own times. If employment of cheap labour was a crucial element of early capitalist accumulation, how did it come to be perpetuated in a deep division between rich and poor countries?

Marx's characterization of this division of labour as 'suited to the chief centres of modern industry' follows a reference to

India. 'By ruining handicrafts production in other countries machinery forcibly converts them into fields for the supply of its raw material' (Marx, 1946, ch. 15, section 7). This is not tribute, but trade. After writing about the treasure transported from India to England in the eighteenth century, Marx goes on to write of the replacement of India's export of textiles by a steadily increasing import of textiles into India at the end of the century:

... the more the industrial interest became dependent on the Indian market, the more it felt the necessity of creating fresh productive powers in India, after having ruined her native industry. You cannot continue to inundate a country with your manufactures, unless you enable it to give you some produce in return. The industrial interest found that their trade declined instead of increasing (Marx, 1960).

For this reason, says Marx, the British industrialists set out to destroy the East India Company and to develop cotton and other primary products in India to exchange for their manufactures.

It is this integration of the world into capitalist relations of production, not just into capitalist market relations, that is central to Marx's view. It is the 'immanent necessity of this mode of production [i.e. the capitalist mode], to produce on an ever enlarged scale [that] tends to extend the world market continually, so that it is not commerce in this case that revolutionizes industry, but industry, which constantly revolutionizes commerce . . .' (Marx, 1909, ch. 20).

The neo-classical assumption is that the world division of labour is not artificial at all, but a natural consequence of the beneficial principle of specialization, achieved through free trade, while the Keynesians make no such assumption about free trade, which they regard as concealing a struggle for power between mercantilist states with very unequal bargaining positions. The Keynesians' question to the Marxists concerns the possibility that the impoverishment of one half of the world could ever have led to economic growth in the other half; their explanation for such growth *and* for the world division of labour being the special kind of mutual development of industrial centres and empty lands of European settlement, resulting from mercantilist policies that continued to be pursued throughout the nineteenth century. Marxists reply that this was one part only of a kind of dual economy established by industrial capitalism, in which economic growth in some areas did take place, albeit interrupted by cyclical crises, while other areas suffered underdevelopment; wealth in one part, poverty in another being inseparable aspects of capitalist growth.

While for the Marxists the division of labour was one 'suited to the chief centres of modern industry', for neo-classical theory it must carry an 'all-round advantage'. Just as each individual, by pursuing his own interest, so each nation, by developing its comparative advantage, ensures the best use of given resources. Those nations that failed to benefit from the freeing of trade in the nineteenth century must have either lacked resources or retained mercantilist and illiberal policies that excluded them from the general increase of wealth. It is from the time of Adam Smith that the great advance of those nations which adopted his policies can be dated; and *post hoc, ergo propter hoc*.

As Britain became the workshop of the world, so the rest of the world was free to supply Britain with raw materials and, after the repeal of the Corn Laws, with food as well. Moreover, provided that the overseas territory, colony or otherwise, could expand its 'staple' to offer in exchange, once the market was opened up, such countries as the USA could develop their own industries with British machinery, for which they could pay with food and raw materials. But that some trade actually expanded in this way does not demonstrate the advantages of free trade to all those taking part in it. European lands and lands of European settlement were developed; the rest, with the exception of Japan, were underdeveloped.[1]

The argument that both parties to trade exchanges must benefit is said to be based on Ricardo's law of comparative advantage (Ricardo, 1912, ch. 7). Ricardo was more cautious;

1. The use of the word 'underdevelop' as a transitive verb is Gunder Frank's and seems singularly appropriate to this artificially enforced division of labour.

he only said that the law indicated why foreign trade was advantageous even for a country which could produce all goods more cheaply than other countries. Some goods could still be produced in that country comparatively more cheaply than others. It would thus pay that country to concentrate resources on producing these goods and to import others. Each country should thus export those goods in which its comparative advantage was greatest. All that Ricardo's theory says is that the total output will be higher as a result of reallocating resources through foreign trade between countries which have different cost structures. It does not say how the extra output will be distributed between the (two) countries. This will depend on relative bargaining strengths and monopolistic positions and levels of employment in the two countries.

The assumptions of competition, and equally of similar income distribution inside the economies of trading partners, are quite unrealistic, but are necessary for differences in comparative costs to be reflected in differences in comparative prices. Ricardo based the argument on differences of land but the introduction of other factor endowments, and especially of technology, in standard foreign trade theory (Findlay, 1970), still leaves out the important fact that some endowments are historical. Both factors of production and the techniques of their utilization are what they are because of, amongst other influences, past trading relationships. Processes of cumulative causation are more likely to distort than to ease the specialization that free trade would indicate (Myrdal, 1954). As J. S. Mill noted 'the superiority of one country over another in a branch of production often arises only from having begun it sooner' (1880, p. 410).

The problem, indeed, for countries which had historically a narrow range of possible goods to offer on the world market has been that of their being able to change a division of labour once established. Free trade in manufactures made it especially difficult for a country, once committed to primary production for export, to develop a manufacturing capacity able to compete with established industrial centres. Yet the advantages of industrialization for any country were, and are, not only the possibility of diversification, so as not to be dependent on the vagaries of world prices for one or two crops or minerals, and on the monopolistic positions established by manufacturers in the world market, but also the general increase in productivity to be obtained from industrial mechanization.

There are very few areas of the world where output per man can be raised as high in agriculture as in industry, because of the limited extent of returns to scale in agriculture as well as because of the historically weak bargaining position of the many primary producers against the few manufacturing centres (Maizels, 1963, p. 24). Even the most richly endowed agricultural producing countries like Canada or Australia, where productivity in agriculture has been very high, have in fact today only a quite small proportion of their populations engaged in agriculture – 20 per cent in Canada, 10 per cent in Australia. Some mineral producing countries have raised productivity to high levels. Others, like the oil producers for example, have succeeded in establishing a near monopoly position over against the manufacturing centres.

Those nations are weak which are incorporated by capitalist development of only a narrow range of diversification into the world division of labour. Their weakness does not derive, however, from the poverty of their resources. There is no absence of raw materials of industry in those parts of the world that became underdeveloped.[2] On the contrary, the shortages were, and are if anywhere, in Europe, and this fact may indeed in part explain the outward drive of European adventurers over many centuries (Stamp, 1960, pp. 144–5; Kuznets, 1958, p. 139). The better explanation of this outward drive then, is that it was the East that once had the riches of which every European trader from the Greeks to the English went in search.

It is an important element, both of the liberal classical and the Keynesian approach to economic history, that most of the world is assumed to have been equally undeveloped up to about the beginning of the sixteenth century; it was then, on the neo-

2. This is the peculiar view of Professor Ritchie Calder, an otherwise well-informed journalist, who nevertheless seriously offers this as an explanation of what he calls the North–South gap (1961, pp. 165–6).

classical view, the freeing of English trade and industry from monopolies and royal restraints, that encouraged the development of capitalism in Europe (Knapp, 1973, p. 21). If endowments were not inadequate in the countries that did not develop, then on this view the cause of their failure to develop must have been their failure to adopt free trade. But the evidence suggests that all industrializing countries, including Britain, have rejected free trade and have, in fact, nurtured their infant industries behind protective tariff walls, and indeed maintained forms of protection for a long time thereafter.

In the Keynesian view such early protectionism indicates the respective roles of industrial capitalists and of a mercantile state in imposing it. According to contemporary writers the rationale for Britain's early protection of industry was the 'fear of goods'. A deep and disturbing doubt about disposing of their products drove the rising industrial capitalists to seek protected markets. Classical economics accepted that an increase in agricultural production would in good time produce an increased population to consume the extra supply; but the mercantilists felt unable to apply this law, as Say was later to do, to the corresponding growth of industrial production and industrial markets. Such doubts were carried over into English political economy and English economic policy, and continued to influence policy long after Adam Smith's attack on mercantilism in *The Wealth of Nations*.

This continuity of thought is the message of the researches of Semmell (1970). Indeed, he reminds us that, 'Even Adam Smith saw colonies and foreign trade as a necessary vent for surplus industrial production' (1970, pp. 9, 27–9), and Smith supported the Navigation Acts in the interests of self-defence. Schumpeter explained this by the early stage of capitalism in Adam Smith's time, and emphasized Adam Smith's debt to the French physiocrats who favoured employment of capital at home and especially in agriculture rather than in foreign trade (Schumpeter, 1954, p. 235).

Adam Smith had supposed that with trade freed and monopolies destroyed capital would be employed at home; and certainly throughout the eighteenth century Britain was a capital-importing country, especially of Netherlands' capital (Pares, 1962, p. 424). He had not, however, supposed that foreign trade would grow as it did; nor that the colonies should be retained and would continue to take such a large part of Britain's exports and supply so much of her imports. This was not at all part of his picture of foreign trade, giving only 'one half the encouragement to the industry or productive labour of the country as the home trade' (Semmell, 1970, p. 25). For Adam Smith it was only the merchant interest that profited from trade; industry profited from production at home and for the home market; though he never denied the importance of the foreign market, he did not regard it as essential. That expectation followed more naturally from those who still held the mercantilist fear of a glut of goods. Of these, Thomas Malthus became the leading exponent.

Malthus is best known for his belief that population would more than keep up with any growth of agricultural production, since less and less productive lands would be brought into cultivation. Paradoxically perhaps, Malthus also believed that a glut, either of goods or capital, was an inevitable result of increased investment in industry and commerce. Malthus, representing an older agrarian, if not feudal, pre-capitalist society, followed the physiocrats in arguing for slower industrial and commercial development, while home agriculture was allowed to catch up (Semmell, 1970, pp. 48–54). Malthus feared industrial gluts but did not at first argue for colonial trade. The agricultural interest was to be defended by protection of the old fields, not by extension to new. Malthus came to that later.

How was it that the colonies survived 'and 'Britain's foreign trade expanded so fast well after mercantilism was supposed to have died under the hammer blows of Adam Smith and his followers? Monopolies, they argued, raised both export and import prices; colonies did not provide the cheapest imports nor did they offer the best markets. The expansion of British exports to the United States after 1776 (year of the Declaration of Independence and the publication of *The Wealth of Nations!*) was proof of that. But the role of trade as a whole in the national economy grew steadily in the last quarter of the eighteenth century and the first quarter of the nineteenth, and Britain's colonial empire was considerably expanded despite the loss of the North American colonies. The Empire, moreover, took the greater part of the increased exports at the end of the eighteenth century, though the Empire share of Britain's trade levelled out in the early nineteenth century (see table 3).

That foreign trade was the 'engine of growth', as Nurkse called it (1961)[3] can be seen from the rise of exports from a sum equivalent to 7 per cent of the National Product to twice that proportion. This involved a new pattern of trade, exported manufactures from imported raw materials. While woollens comprised half of all exports up to the 1750s, and the main markets were then in southern Europe, the great expansion after the 1780s was in cotton goods and later in metal products, and the main markets in the American colonies and later in India. It is the succession of markets that is most striking (table 3). The trading of West Indies raw cotton, sugar and tobacco for English textiles, tools and hardware provided the first great new area of Britain's overseas trade expansion (Pares, 1962, p. 421). North America provided the second, but especially *after* the United States obtained their independence. The Southern states supplied England's raw cotton while the North took our manufactures. India provided the third market and, with its penetration, the destruction of the Indian hand-loom textiles industry. China and Southern America provided a fourth and a fifth. Each of these markets rose into prominence and declined in turn. They were to be succeeded later in the nineteenth century by expansion in Africa and Oceania. English manufactured goods and particularly textiles 'mopped up', so to speak, an existing market for handicrafts. In the case of some European countries and the USA this encouraged local capitalists to develop their own industries behind protective barriers, but in the case of what we now call the underdeveloped world, industrialization was held back.

Once British industry had been established as the 'workshop of the world', free trade would become the best way to

3. Nurkse was describing economic development outside Europe and his thesis will be subjected to criticism later in this chapter.

Table 3 Direction and composition of Britain's foreign trade, 1710–1914

Commodities and direction	1710s–1730s	1740s–1760s	1770s–1790s	1800s–1820s	1830s–1850s	1860s–1870s	1880s–1890s	1900s–1914
average annual value (£m)								
exports	5.5	10	12	40	70	220	250	380
re-exports	3	4	5	10	12	55	65	90
net imports	7	8	15	50	90	260	420	560
exports as percentage of GNP	7	8	10	14	16	20	19	20
commodity shares (%) of exports								
woollen goods	72	45	40	12	10	13	9	6·5
cotton goods	0	2	12	50	40	34	28	27
iron and steel	3	5	9	3	10	12	12	11·5
coal	2	2	4	1·5	3	5	7	10
other	23	46	35	33·5	37	36	44	45
direction of exports incl. re-exports (%)								
N Europe	46	34	25	25	23	22	20	19
S Europe	35	44	25	13	17	16	16	16
N America	7	10	25	30	20	17	16	12
other America	8	8	13	20	18	11	11	10
Asia	2	2	10	10	15	20	22	22
Africa	2	2	2	2	4	6	6	10
other	0	0	0	0	3	8	9	11

direction of exports excl. re-exports (%)

Empire								
Dominions	—	—	5	6	12	14	16	17
India	—	—	8	8	10	11	12	11
other colonies	—	12	12	16	8	7	6	7
total	7	20	25	30	30	32	34	35

share in textile exports (%)

India	—	—	—	10	15	20	20	25
other Empire	—	—	—	14	8	11	16	19

share in iron and steel exports (%)

India	—	—	—	14	5	7·5	9	16·5
other Empire	—	—	—	16	15	20	26	34

Iron and steel includes rails, cutlery and other hardware

Dominions are Canada, Australia, New Zealand and South Africa before and after Dominion status was achieved

Trade with Ireland is excluded throughout the table, but accounted for about 10 per cent of Great Britain's exports up to 1804

Source: Mitchell and Deane (1962)

perpetuate Britain's industrial monopoly. This was Marx's view, but it is equally the Keynesian view based on the concept of a 'disguised' or 'reluctant' continuation of mercantilist policies (Knapp, 1956–7; Robinson, 1962, pp. 62–6, 87–8). The classical economists like Ricardo and James Mill, while they accepted Say's Law of Markets, in effect relied on an expansion of Britain's exports to maintain the law. The only limits to economic expansion for Ricardo were the diminishing returns from the land. 'If food and other raw produce could be supplied from abroad in exchange for manufactures', he observed, 'it was difficult to say where the limit is at which you could cease to accumulate wealth and to derive profit from its employment' (Sraffa and Dobb, 1951, vol. 4, p. 179). Ricardo therefore, supported, indeed inspired, the reduction of duties on imported corn, although he did not go so far as to believe that they should be abolished. Others went further.

In the campaign to repeal the Corn Laws, however, those who took the most radical line were 'far from being devoted to the Cobdenite ideal of a pacifistic cosmopolitanism and were ready to follow up vigorous language by vigorous action when the expansion of British commerce was at issue' (Semmell, 1970, p. 151).[4] This is the first major argument of Semmell in defence of the concept of 'Free Trade Imperialism'; the second will be dealt with in the next chapter. Semmell makes the interesting point that the radical free trader, Joseph Hume, who hotly defended the Opium War in China in 1840 and the Punjab War in 1849, had seen service with the forces of the East India Company in the Mahratha Wars, from which he retired in 1808 with a fortune of £40 000. This might be regarded as evidence for the Schumpeterian thesis of pre-capitalist survivals in an age of developing capitalism, but the 'Indian' officers – those who had served in the British East

4. Semmell's book is used here to make the free trade imperialism case, but it is only fair to record, as he does himself, that the origin of the phrase goes back to Gallagher and Robinson (1963, pp. 1–15), and that this was subsequently developed by Winch (1965). The origin of the concept goes back still further to Knapp (1956–7), and Durbin and Knapp (1949).

India Company – were excluded from Army commands elsewhere by the aristocrats like Lord Raglan in recruiting for Crimea (Hibbert, 1961). Their origin was frequently in the company's counting houses (Woodruff, 1953, p. 89).

Where then did the pressure come from in Britain for free trade and the ending of colonial monopolies? The usual answer is to point to the Manchester School of businessmen. It was in fact Josiah Tucker, Dean of Gloucester, in 1783, and not Disraeli or Cobden, who first used the phrase about the colonies as a 'millstone about the neck of this country, to weight it down' (Semmell, 1970, p. 8). He was then referring to North America, and that is the sense in which the Cobdenites of the Manchester School (and Disraeli also) used the phrase. They certainly meant to be free of the settlements of Britons in North America (and Oceania) who had such costly requirements for defence and the supply of capital. Nobody, however, proposed that British forces should be pulled out of India; for there the forces were financed by the Indian people and guaranteed important markets and sources of raw materials for Britain. The clearest vision of a free-trade Britain as Workshop of the World without the need for colonial rule was revealed to a Whig MP in the Corn Law debates in the House of Commons in 1846. Semmell quotes this gentleman describing free trade as the 'beneficent principle by which foreign nations would become valuable colonies to us, without imposing on us the responsibility of governing them' (Semmell, 1970, p. 155).

There seemed to be no doubt, however, about the views of early British capitalists on the ways in which government should establish and maintain free trade. Pressure was brought to bear upon Canning by the Manchester Chamber of Commerce to recognize the new republics of Latin America in 1824 and to sign free-trade agreements with them. In the Treaty of Nanking in 1842, which opened the ports of China to foreign trade and conceded Hong Kong to British rule, the same Chamber had been joined by the City of London to give Palmerston support. Semmell quotes many other examples (chapters 6 and 7) and before him Gallagher and Robinson (1963) had claimed the Manchester School as promoters of

Britain's 'informal empire', if not of her formal one. The pressure behind the anti-Corn Law campaign could not have been better expressed than by the Prime Minister, Sir Robert Peel, himself a Lancashire manufacturer, in moving their repeal:

During the war we commanded the supply of nations. Now England was encountering difficulties. The continuance of England's manufacturing and commercial pre-eminence, however, might be ensured by cheap and abundant food which would promote the increase of British capital by which we can retain the eminence we have so long possessed (Semmell, 1970, p. 150).

It was a view of a 'cosmopolitan trading association' but 'subject to our controlling power' as the *Economist* so nicely put it at the time (Semmell, 1970, p. 150).

The classical liberals are seen here in their moment of victory; but the facts, first of the role of exports in the economy and of the direction of those exports and, second, of the actions taken to establish a special kind of free trade that maintained Britain as workshop of the world because of her head start over all others, tell against their liberalism. As Alfred Marshall admitted, and Robinson has reminded us of this confession from a neo-classical economist, free trade was 'believed in only by those who will gain an advantage from it' (Robinson, 1966b, p. 24; 1962, pp. 65–6).

We are not saying that there was a divorce between political practice and economic theory, such as Schumpeter would have us expect from the survival in Britain of a feudal military class in positions of political power. There was indeed such a survival, but Adam Smith's precepts were obeyed. Long before Corn Law repeal, in fact, Pitt's foreign trade policy with the USA, with France and with Ireland (though he was defeated on the Irish Bill) was as liberal as Smith could have wished. It was indeed piloted by Smith's followers (Semmell, 1970, pp. 30–40). Customs duties were reduced and the Navigation Acts modified. By the 1820s Huskisson had modified most of the restraints on colonial trade and on manufactured imports and had even introduced a sliding scale for duties on corn imports.

Monopolies were ended, even that of the great East India Company, first in India and then in China. Free trade maintained the division of labour once it was established between manufacturing centres and primary producers; it continuously reinforced the strength of the most industrially advanced producers, according to the Marxists. But why the need for the navy, the occupation of naval bases and the expansion of the Empire right through the first half of the nineteenth century? Knowles (1928, pp. 10–15) called this 'the period of continental inland expansion' that followed the 'Empire of Outposts' and opened up the continents of America, Africa, Australia and India. Table 4 shows the extent of this expansion before 1870 during the very years of the dominance of the free-trading, and ostensibly anti-colonial, manufacturing interest.

The explanation for this world-wide naval and military presence is, on the classical view, as expressed by Schumpeter, that it was a hangover of pre-capitalist, militaristic social formations in England. For the Keynesians it may be inferred that it represents pieces of *ad hoc* and, possibly largely unconscious, mercantilist state policy, having the welcome effect of opening up new markets for export and new lands for settlement. The Marxists regard the show of force as a necessary part of colonial exploitation, especially the exploitation of India as that vast continent was opened up to the depredations of the British during the nineteenth century.[5] In fact, the navy as well as the army was run down by Parliamentary neglect, but the lessons of Crimea and of the Indian mutiny at about the same time were quickly learnt and the army in India being financed from India never suffered from parliamentary economies (Woodward, 1938, pp. 259–61), nor from aristocratic domination. Contemporary opinion in the middle of the nineteenth century was deeply divided about the advantages of empire, by which, as we have seen, was meant in general the colonies that were to become self-governing (Bodelsen, 1960, ch. 1).

5. The first Indian Famine Commission report was made in 1878 following a steady increase in famines, as more land was turned over to raw material production for export and as food was increasingly exported. See Dutt (1947, pp. 105–6).

Table 4 Occupation dates of British possessions, to 1869

Before 1700	1700–1815	1815–1869
1583 Newfoundland	1704 Gibraltar	1817 Ascension
1607 Virginia	1713 Nova Scotia	Tristan da Cunha
1609 Bermudas	1732 Georgia	1818 Rajputana
1612 Surat	1757 Bengal	(protectorate)
1620 New England	1763 Windward Isles	1819 Singapore
1625 Barbados	Anderman Isles	South Shetlands
1629 Bahamas	1765 Falkland Isles	1820 Port Elizabeth
1632 Leeward Isles	1775 South Georgia	1824 Malacca
1638 British	1784 Chagos Isles	Brisbane
Honduras	1785 Penang	1826 Burma (North)
1639 Madras	1788 Lord Howe Isles	1829 Swan River
1651 St Helena	Botany Bay	1834 Mysore (India)
1655 Jamaica	Sierra Leone	1836 Adelaide
1661 Cape Coast	1790 Pitcairn Isles	1839 New Zealand
Bombay	1791 Chatham Isles	Aden
1662 Fort James	King George Sound	Assam
1663 Carolina	(Albany)	1841 Hong Kong
1670 Hudson Bay	1792 Laccadives	1842 Natal
	Malabar	Sarawak
	1793 Seychelles	1843 Sind (India)
	1795 Cape of Good Hope	1846 Labuan (Borneo)
	1796 Maldives	Punjab (India)
	Ceylon	Kashmir
	Guiana	1852 Pegul (Southern Burma)
	1797 Trinidad	1853 Norfolk Isles
	1800 Malta	Berar (India)
	1801 Hyderabad (India)	Bhonsla 'slands (India)
	1803 Tasmania	1856 Oudh (India)
	1806 Auckland Isles	1857 Cocos Isles
	1807 Heligoland	1861 Lagos
	1809 Ionian Isles	1866 Malden Isles
	1810 Mauritius	1867 Bahrain Island
	1811 Macquarie Isles	1868 Basutoland
	1814 Victoria (as it came	
	to be called)	

Sources: Brampton (1938); Muir and Philip (1929)

The main support for retaining the dependencies proper came from the radical, Charles Dilke, who had the closest association with industry through his friend Joseph Chamberlain. 'Were we to leave India or Ceylon, they would have no customers at all,' he wrote, 'for, falling into anarchy, they would cease at once to export their goods to us and to consume our manufactures' (Bodelsen, 1960, p. 67).

To decide between the Keynesian and the Marxist view, we have to decide between the relative importance of the self-governing lands of European settlement and of the colonies, especially India, between the relative importance of expanding export markets and of obtaining cheap raw material and food imports. In this difference at least one Marxist, Rosa Luxemburg, is claimed for the side of the Keynesians (Luxemburg, 1951, p. 28). Her explanation of capitalist expansion was based upon the supposed breakdown of realization in extended capitalist reproduction (p. 352). Her emphasis on markets for exports of goods has a very mercantilist ring to it, but Luxemburg's picture of capitalism assimilating non-capitalist social organizations included not only the capture of markets but the extraction of raw materials and the exploitation of fresh sources of labour (p. 366).

The rise in Britain's exports was even more striking in the middle of the nineteenth century than at the beginning (see table 3). This did not result in an export surplus on the foreign trade account, as mercantilists might have hoped, but trade was perhaps, nevertheless, an 'engine of growth' (Nurkse, 1961, p. 284). It is certainly a fact that, in the period of most rapid industrialization of every capitalist state, exports have risen as a share of the national product (Kindleberger, 1958, ch. 14). The United States is sometimes regarded as an exception to this rule, but in fact, exports rose from an average 6 per cent to 7 per cent of total private production in the 1840s and 1850s in the USA to over 10 per cent in the 1870s, and, although they fell back to 8 per cent in the 1880s, were nearer 10 per cent again in the 1900s (US Department of Commerce, 1952, pp. 14, 243–5). This all appears to give powerful support to a mercantilist view, such as the Keynesians would put forward.

Britain provides the classic example of export-led growth in the nineteenth century, but Japan, Sweden and Denmark after 1880, Switzerland, the Netherlands and Canada from 1900 to 1913 are all quoted by Kindleberger in the same sense (1958, pp. 245–6). Moreover, world trade grew twice as fast as industrial output between 1840 and 1870 and significantly faster between 1880 and 1913, and this has led one economist to speak of trade as 'a handmaiden of growth' (Kravis, 1970). In the recessions of the 1870s and 1930s, by contrast, trade grew slower than output. Many countries enjoyed increased trade without industrialization taking place – India is the obvious example – but expanded exports can be a necessary condition for industrialization without being a sufficient condition. The argument that followed Nurkse's proposition of the theory that trade was an 'engine of growth' concerned the demand of already industrialized countries for the exports of under-developed countries. This, Nurkse suggested, had been high in the nineteenth century, and accounted for the economic growth of the USA, Canada and Australia, but was low today and could not be relied on any longer as an engine of growth for the currently underdeveloped countries. This strengthens the Keynesian type argument that the first industrialized countries could grow, *for a time* at least, just because they pre-empted the markets of the rest of the world. The Marxists would agree, but insist that the turning of the rest of the world into cheap primary producers was equally important.

It is further evidence of the role of exports for capitalist industrialization that, by contrast, the Soviet Union and China embarked upon industrialization without any increase in the place of foreign trade in their economies (Baykov, 1946). Even the Eastern European countries' industrialization has involved only moderate increases. Among these countries, and contrary to capitalist experience, industrial output has grown consistently faster than exports (see table 5). These are all countries where industrialization has been achieved with state capital accumulation and not with private capital. It appears that there is no other form of capital accumulation that has achieved industrialization except either state capital accumulation or private capital accumulation *plus* expanded exports.

The fact that exports grew faster than the increase of manufacturing output in capitalist countries in the 1950s–1960s, after the inter-war years of stagnation, just as it had in the previous period of rapid growth earlier in the century after the stagnation, at least in Britain, of the 1870s–1880s, certainly suggests a

Table 5 Industrial output and trade in capitalist and communist countries, 1928–1970 (1938 = 100)

Country	Industrial output volume					Manufactured exports volume				
	1928	1938	1953	1960	1970	1928	1938	1953	1960	1970
Capitalist										
all	105	100	210	280	485	112	100	175	290	720
USA	100	100	280	350	540	120	100	190	330	600
EEC	90	100	150	240	440	125	100	150	360	970
Germany	80	100	180	330	565	160	100	120	295	710
France	110	100	115	180	315	210	100	220	430	1000
Italy	92	100	160	290	550	—	100	140	390	1500
UK	80	100	150	178	232	110	100	175	200	325
Japan	55	100	100	250	365	140	100	80	195	780
Communist										
all	—	100	175	390	840	—	100	160	350	800
China	—	100	—	(400)	(800)	—	100	(130)	(240)	(250)
USSR	30	100	250	540	1260	—	100	180	360	850
E Europe	—	100	—	310	700	—	100	160	340	780
total	—	100	205	375	715	115	100	170	315	750

Figures in brackets are estimates
Sources: GATT (1958); UN (1972b)

connection between economic growth and expanding foreign trade. The new forms of mercantilism today actually involve the old aim of an export surplus, above all in the case of the most rapidly growing economies, West Germany and Japan. Robinson defines the new mercantilism as a situation where:

... the total market does not grow fast enough to make room for all, each government feels it a worthy and commendable aim to increase its own share in world activity for the benefit of its own people ... everyone is keen to sell and wary of buying. Every nation wants to have a surplus in its balance of trade. This is a game where the total scores add up to zero. Some can win only if others lose. The beautiful harmony of the free-trade model is far indeed to seek (1966b, p. 10).

Common markets, she goes on to say, serve to combine the strength of a group of nations in competition with the rest of the world. The process is cumulative. 'Investment in the strong country brings technological progress, which improves its competitive position and makes its balance of trade all the stronger, while the weak country slips into stagnation' (p. 17).

Among developed industrial countries themselves this process has led to deep antagonism and even war; between the developed countries and the rest of the world it leads to the polarization of development and underdevelopment. As Keynes commented about an earlier mercantilist system:

> Never in history was there a method devised of such efficacy for setting each country's advantage at variance with its neighbour's as the international gold (or formerly, silver) standard. For it made domestic prosperity directly dependent on a competitive pursuit of markets and a competitive appetite for the precious metals (1960, p. 349).

Moreover, as Robinson goes on to show, colonial investment provided the underdeveloped world outside the developed countries with one or two commodities for export, and, as this put them in a weak bargaining position, the prices of these were held down, while industrial prices drifted up. The Keynesian view is a hard-headed one of a situation of cumulative inequality. But it is quite different from the Marxist view of capitalist incorporation and retention of wider and wider areas of the world economy, although Robinson comes near to this in seeing economic aid as 'being aimed to perpetuate the system that makes aid necessary' (1966b, p. 25). Much aid is certainly given in the form of export credits (OECD, 1970a, pp. 176-7). Thus a quarter of United States manufactured exports, including a quarter of iron and steel products, in the 1960s, were financed by aid and nearly a third of United States agricultural exports (Magdoff, 1970, pp. 131-2). In Latin America, 'according to the State Department ... the United States has been able to protect its share (of the trade of the industrial countries) and even increase it at the expense of the other industrial countries' (Magdoff, 1970, p. 135). But to put too much emphasis on this is to see only the inter-imperialist rivalries and miss the source of imperialism. Another US State Department report, quoted in the same work, goes to the heart of the matter:

> So our influence is used wherever it can be and persistently, through

our Embassies on a day-to-day basis, in our aid discussion and in direct aid negotiation, to underline the importance of private investment (Magdoff, 1970, p. 728).

Robinson sees a snag in the process. 'There will still be a deflationary kink in a financial system, in which every country likes to gain monetary reserves and hates to lose them' (Robinson, 1966b, p. 15). Governments today, at least in large developed countries, can take measures to check deflation from going too far, but how was expansion achieved under mercantilist policies at the beginning of the nineteenth century? John Knapp believes that it was the wide scope of mercantilist policies that raised the inducement to invest – wage policy, acceleration of technical progress, military expenditure in commercial wars, the opening up of empty lands to European settlement, as well as the regulation of the balance of trade to achieve a surplus and the import of gold (Knapp, 1956–7). The import of gold came *before* the main years of Britain's industrial revolution and the opening up of empty lands, mainly *after* the middle of the century; but military expenditure did provide a strong incentive to invest, and deflationary policies did follow the end of the Napoleonic wars. 'Holding a static conception of the total economic resources of the world, commercial wars were inevitable'.[6] The essence of the argument is that only successful mercantilist policies lead to economic expansion, and then only within limits that are normally narrow. Britain was singularly successful.

The export surplus provided a means both to increase foreign investment and indirectly to induce home investment through lower interest rates (Keynes, 1960, p. 336). The mercantilists feared goods and believed that a nation without an adequate stock of money must sell cheap and buy dear. In fact, there was not an export surplus during Britain's industrial revolution. If such mercantilist views had persisted, it seems unlikely that the growth of capitalism in Britain and throughout the world would have taken place. The import of gold provided a crucial stimulant to Britain's economic growth, but the old colonialism had to be destroyed for a new colonialism to be

6. Keynes, quoting Heckscher (1960, p. 348).

established; and this involved cheap exports and also cheap imports. Other states pursued mercantilist policies in the eighteenth century, but only in Britain did industrialization take place. The Marxists would argue that the difference was that an industrial-capitalist class emerged in Britain.

This industrial-capitalist class had, from its very relationship with its technology, to aim to sell cheap as well as to buy cheap; and, by contrast with the mercantilists, it saw the economic resources of the world dynamically. This is the essential difference between the old colonialism and the new, between merchant and industrial capitalists. Keynes himself pointed out that in Spain there was an excessive abundance of precious metals, excessive, on his definition, in relation to the wage unit (1960, p. 337). But this is only half of the story; the other half is that Britain had a new capitalist class with a new technology capable of reducing wage costs per unit of output. Spain did not. The Keynesians see the role of state policies as a crucial element in capitalist expansion, or decline, both when openly mercantilist and when ostensibly liberal economic policies are pursued. This in itself is not necessarily in conflict with the old established Marxist view of the state. In the Marxist view the state is seen, not as a neutral arbiter of different interest groups, but as the agent of the most powerful group; this by the first quarter of the nineteenth century was beginning to be the industrial capitalists. The functions of the state are regarded as not only repressive and ideological, but as conformative, that is to say in shaping (or attempting to shape) what would otherwise be conflicting interests.[7] It is part of the Keynesian argument that in the mid-nineteenth century, British state intervention in the conformative sense, at least in overseas affairs, was much more far-reaching than the classical liberals or even Marx would have allowed (Knapp, 1973). Marx in his journalistic writings was well aware of such intervention, but evidently wished in his theoretical work to discover what were the tendencies of capitalism within a self-regulating system. Marxists would now see the state in the nineteenth century as an

7. For a development of this definition at length, see Barratt Brown (1972b, ch. 3).

extremely active agent in economic affairs on behalf of the industrial capitalist class (Murray, 1971a).

In the Marxist view, Keynes's own emphasis on the regulation and control by mercantilist policies of the trade balance is wrong; first, it underestimates the new technology and the new class of industrial capitalist that were together involved in a new mode of capital accumulation;[8] secondly, the development of primary production overseas becomes for the ultra-Keynesian a matter of national power relationships and a special geo-political condition of European settlement of empty lands, rather than of capitalist incorporation of overseas primary producers, including plantation economies, in a special division of labour; and thirdly, the failure of other nations like India or China to develop is explained by Keynes in terms of Indians' preference for hoarding and not of their transformation and underdevelopment by capitalism.[9] In the last chapter the plantation colonies were seen as an essential element in capitalist development, and this cannot be either pushed back into the pre-capitalist era nor subsumed with either earlier gold imports or later opening up of empty lands for European settlement. The incorporation of India and large parts of Latin America, and later of Africa, into the capitalist economy on a similar basis to the plantation colonies is simply not explained by Keynes's own appeal to mercantilist state regulation, if it is only supposed to operate on the balance of trade. The Corn Laws and Navigation Acts were not repealed until 1845 and 1849, and colonial preferences continued for a while, but the foundation of the colonial monopoly was slavery (Clapham, 1930, p. 398).

It is a major element in narrowly political theories of imperialism to see capitalist expansion in terms of interstate rivalries, without seeing that the rivalry was fundamentally about the compulsions of competitive capital accumulation

8. Contemporary followers of Keynes would be in agreement with the Marxists here.
9. Keynes's contemporary followers would agree in not emphasizing hoarding, but otherwise do not appear to have developed a clear, agreed and systematic common view of underdevelopment.

(Fieldhouse, 1973, pp. 3–9). Even the 'ultra-Keynesian', Knapp, who defines mercantilism as 'the system of nationalistic regulation of economies which is designed to advance a particular state's economic, political and military power in competition with rivals' (1973, p. 19), omits to emphasize these compulsions. Correspondingly, in a chart which gives his view of economic history, he summarizes the condition of the underdeveloped countries since the fifteenth century as 'stagnation because of peripheral location in relation to actual capitalist development' (1973, p. 21), rather than seeing that the advances of prosperity that would have occurred in the now underdeveloped world were aborted by the impact of the now developed world upon them. What the capitalists in Britain, and later in other countries, wanted from the rest of the world they made plain enough. Thus, the President of the Manchester Chamber of Commerce in evidence to a Parliamentary inquiry in 1840:

In India there is an immense extent of territory, and the population of it would consume British manufactures to a most enormous extent. The whole question with respect to our Indian trade is whether they can pay us, by the products of their soil, for what we are prepared to send out as manufactures (Dutt, 1947, p. 105).

Knowles has summarized the result: 'The colonization of continents really rested on the market obtainable for the goods which could be produced in far interiors . . .' (1928, p. 13) and in relation to India she concluded:

The importance of India to England in the first half of the nineteenth century lay in the fact that India supplied some of the essential raw materials – hides, oil, dyes, jute and cotton – required for the industrial revolution in England, and at the same time afforded a growing market for English manufactures of iron and cotton (1928, p. 305).

This transformation of India from a manufacturing country into 'the agricultural farm of England', as another witness at the 1840 Parliamentary inquiry put it, is regarded by Marxist writers as the source of India's underdevelopment (Dutt, 1947, p. 104).

For Keynes himself, however, the explanation is different:

The history of India at all times has provided an example of a country impoverished by a preference for liquidity amounting to so strong a passion that even an enormous and chronic influx of the precious metals has been insufficient to bring down the rate of interest to a level which was compatible with the growth of real wealth (Keynes, 1960, p. 336).

Contrary to the charts of the 'ultra-Keynesians', the wealth per head of the present underdeveloped lands, not only in India, but in China, Latin America and Africa, was higher than in Europe before the seventeenth century and fell *pari passu* as wealth grew in capitalist Europe.[10] The two events were connected, on the Marxist view. The underdeveloped lands are not just undeveloped, but in a special condition of underdevelopment. Vents were closed, to use the ultra-Keynesians' terms (Knapp, 1973), for export of finished products and opened for primary products; and the structure of colonial production changed from independent village agriculture and handicrafts to plantations of slave and indentured labour, and this not in India only but in Latin America and Africa too.

A modern Marxian like Robin Murray sees the state performing a very much wider range of services for industrial capital, not only today but throughout the development of capitalism, than is allowed for in Keynes's view of the impact of mercantilist regulations (let alone in neo-classical theory), and one of them is precisely the provision of inputs which we have just been considering – labour, land, capital, technology and infrastructure (Murray, 1971a, pp. 15–18). This, then, ranks in importance with the guarantee of property rights and the measures of economic liberalization, which neo-classical economists emphasize.

There is no consensus of economists about the causes of economic growth, and in particular about the rapid and sustained growth that creates an industrial revolution. On classical theory, real wages can always absorb new productive capacity,

10. The evidence for India is summarized in Barratt Brown (1970a, pp. 28–31); for Latin America in Frank (1969a, pp. 29–33); for Africa in Davidson (1969, pp. 211–17). Knapp's chart (1973, p. 21) shows them all at the same level up to the sixteenth century.

which depends on supply only (Marshall, 1920, p. 372). On the neo-Keynesian view, investment must be just sufficient to generate demand capable of absorbing new productive capacity (Harrod, 1939) and is more important than the regulation of effective demand, both internally and in external relations, which Keynes himself emphasized. Marxists will be particularly interested to see how far the emerging ultra-Keynesian theory, when it is more articulated, will come to endorse Marxist emphasis on supply and technology. On the Marxist view, investment depends on the going rate of accumulation among competing capitalists, which technological advances make possible, subject to periodic crises of realization because of disproportional growth. When we apply these theories to industrial growth in the period of an industrial revolution itself, the problem to be explained is how a sufficient proportion of an economy's current output can be reinvested without, in the long run (cyclical crises apart) the economy running into a condition of excess capacity to produce, in relation to the capacity to consume, at profitable prices for the producers. This is where an export surplus achieved by mercantilist policies in the past, and recently also in the case of West Germany and Japan, resolves the problem, at least for one country or one group of countries at the expense of others. There are other ways in which foreign trade, on the Marxist view, solves the problem of 'long-run development bottlenecks', as Kalecki has called them (1971). The Marxists would claim that one of the chief ways is by cheapening imports as well as expanding exports.

Although the cheapening of imports has created recurrent problems for British exporters as a result of impoverished overseas markets, it appears to have been an essential element in Britain's economic growth. Cheap labour both at home and overseas was the predominant feature of the period of the industrial revolution. The Keynesian question concerning who then provided a market for the expanded output, before the economic development of empty lands, has to be answered by the Marxists in terms of a dual economy. All countries that have undergone the capitalist process of development seem to have passed through a stage of dual economy. This consists of sectors and areas of high productivity with high profits (rates of profit), and high wages providing expanded markets, on the one hand, and sectors and areas of low productivity with low wages and low profits (rates of profit) providing a mass of surplus (profit), on the other. The two parts are insulated from each other by limitations on the movement of labour, through slavery, indenture and other artificial restraints including restrictions on educational opportunity. Disraeli's novel *Sybil – The Two Nations*, written in the 1830s, reveals most of these restrictions.

It is not necessary that all markets should grow for Say's Law to be fulfilled, but only that some should, i.e. those catering for the products of the main investments of new capital. These have changed throughout the history of capitalism: first, the products of slave plantations, then of the cotton textile industry, then of railways and iron and steel, then of electrical machinery and the motor car and today of all the varied products of the giant trans-national company. Other markets may be depressed and decay, but the producers for them must continue to supply a surplus of capital for the advanced sector, unless the state steps in by taxation of the rich to support this. The danger to sustained expansion inherent in such a dual economy is of cumulative polarization of wealth and poverty; and this is a problem which exercises some Keynesians as well as Marxists (see Knapp, 1969). Here, on the Marxist view, lie the causes of cyclical crisis and of long-term stagnation until technological advances, holding forth the promise of new levels of productivity, serve to revive the inducement to invest. Keynes provided no theory of the long-run inducement to invest, and his successors' work on this is still in its infancy.

A brief review of the statistical evidence available for the period of Britain's industrial revolution provides some material which seems relevant to any systematic tests of the rival views which may come to be undertaken. The increases in imports during this period were noted in the last chapter – first, the increase in luxury imports in the twenty years before the Napoleonic wars, then, after the wars, the increase in imports of raw cotton and other raw materials; and with these increases in volume, evidence also of reduced prices despite the continuation of monopoly profits on most of this trade, averaging perhaps as much as 25 per cent up to the abolition of the monopolies in the 1840s. Now, in table 6 we can see that Britain's gross terms of trade fell steadily from the 1750s to the 1800s as the volume of imports rose continuously faster than the volume of exports.

After the Napoleonic wars, by contrast, export volumes in Britain's trade rose faster than import volumes and export prices fell faster than import prices, so that the terms of trade moved against Britain for the whole period of the 1800s to the 1840s. None of this looks like the result of typical mercantilist policy; nor does the chronic, and rising, deficit on the balance of trade. These deficits were covered by income from invisibles; but until the 1850s imports of gold were small and the balance on current account each year allowed for a slowly accumulating balance of credit abroad (see table 7). The 'other services' shown in table 6, which covered so much of the deficit on trade, consisted of 'profits on foreign trade', estimated by Imlah for most years at 5 per cent of the value of all imports, exports and re-exports, and of 'insurance and brokerage', likewise estimated for most years at $2\frac{1}{2}$ per cent. Taken in conjunction with the importance of the re-export business, and with the main direction of exports and re-exports to the European market, the picture of a dual world economy clearly emerges. In a sense all Britain's international business consisted of some kind of re-exports, of imported raw materials refined and processed, or just warehoused for auction on the London commodity markets, and then resold. Cheapening imports and cheapening processes of manufacture were equally important.

Despite money-wage increases, between the 1750s and the end of the century, real wages fell by about 30 per cent in London and ended at about the same level in Lancashire after some improvement in the 1780s. Money wages rose again in the Napoleonic wars, but prices moved ahead of them to bring down real wages still further. There has been much argument with Hobsbawm's view that the living standards of the

British people probably deteriorated rather than improved in the years between 1790 and 1850 (Hobsbawm, 1964, pp. 64–104). Certainly, it worsened during the ten years to 1815; how much it recovered thereafter with money wages falling by about 20 per cent and domestic prices by about 40 per cent is hard to judge since there are several different series of statistics involved (Mitchell and Deane, 1962, tables XII.1a and 1b, XII.2). According to Hobsbawm, the 1830s saw 'hopelessness and hunger and discontent', 'falling real income per head', and much anxiety among businessmen about 'the rate of their profits and the rate of expansion of their markets' (1968, pp. 55–6). Yet, industrial output continued to rise in Britain after the setback of the 1820s with rising exports and imports; and the fall in import prices, almost as fast as in export prices, must have greatly contributed to Britain's continued economic growth. Between 1814 and 1830 the prices of imported commodities were halved; during the 1830s they rose slightly again, but fell sharply after 1844. Over the whole period prices of domestic commodities, after a 50 per cent fall between 1815 and 1820, remained relatively stable until there was a new sharp fall in 1849–50 (Mitchell and Deane, 1962, table XVI.1b). And this cheapening of imports was based largely on plantation labour and its extension from the West Indies to India and South America, and well before the opening up of empty lands for European settlement.

Rapid economic growth implies a high rate of investment which must be at the expense of consumption, or at least of increases in consumption. Hobsbawm has estimated that, 'Not until the 1830s and 1840s did gross capital formation in Britain pass the 10 per cent threshold . . . regarded as essential for industrialization today' (1968, p. 57), and much less than the 'late developers' have needed to catch up with Britain. The 7 per cent or so of Britain's national income, which was invested in the decades before the 1830s had, however, to be found almost entirely from the ploughback of profits, since the rich landlords and monopolists provided a market, but did not invest in industry. The profit for reinvestment had to come from the industrial workers, so that our dual economy model has to

Table 6 Britain's trade balance, 1750s to 1850s, terms of trade and industrial index, 1800s to 1850s

Periods	Exports	Net imports	Balance	Services			Index of prices			Gross terms of trade	Industrial index
				Ships	Property	Other	Exports	Imports	Net		
Official trade values (£m annual averages)											
1750–1759	8·7	8·3	+0·4	—	—	—	—	—	—	98	—
1760–1769	10·0	10·6	−0·6	—	—	—	—	—	—	89	—
1770–1779	9·3	11·8	−2·5	—	—	—	—	—	—	80	—
1780–1789	10·9	15·8	−4·9	—	—	—	—	—	—	82	—
1785–1794	14·2	19·5	−5·3	—	—	—	—	—	—	79	—
1795–1804	22	24·3	−2·3	—	—	—	—	—	—	78	—
Computed values (£m annual averages)											
1796–1800	33	37	−4	—	—	—	349	182	192	76	—
1801–1805	40	48	−8	—	—	—	381	198	198	65	11
1806–1810	42	54	−12	—	—	—	364	205	177	69	12·5
1811–1815	43	50	−7	—	—	—	336	215	156	88	13·5

1816–1820	41	50	−9	10	1·7	9	261	174	150	88	15·5
1821–1825	38	46	−8	9	4·2	7·5	207	134	154	82	18
1826–1830	36	49	−13	8	4·6	7·3	168	113	149	76	21
1831–1835	40	53	−13	9	5·4	8	146	115	127	95	25
1836–1840	50	74	−24	11	8	10·7	144	121	119	90	29
1841–1845	54	71	−17	12	7·5	10·7	116	104	111	106	35
1846–1850	61	88	−27	14	9·5	12·7	108	94	114	94	41

National Income: in 1801 = £232m; in 1811 = £301m; in 1821 = £291m; in 1831 = £340m; in 1841 = £452m; in 1851 = £523 m

Other services = profits on trade and insurance

Prices: net = net terms of trade, i.e. export prices/import prices (1880 = 100)

Gross terms of trade = volume of exports/volume of net imports (1880 = 100)

Industrial index = Hoffman's index including building, reworked for 1880 = 100

Sources: Imlah (1958, tables 4 and 8); Mitchell and Deane (1962, tables XI.1, XI.14 and table X.15)

be modified to allow for low wages even in the high productivity sector. Investment could not have been realized and growth maintained without the wealth of the merchants and the plantation owners, both based on slave labour, and the artificial division of labour established with the colonies, to provide the market for British manufacture. 'Late developers' that did not have colonies had to rely on accumulation from their own agricultural and pre-capitalist sectors; and this applies equally to countries with non-capitalist social systems which have entered upon the hard road of industrialization. Marxists have tended to evade this problem, and the earliest Marxist to explain the meaning of the 'iron-heel of primitive accumulation' was murdered by Stalin (Preobrazhensky, 1965, pp. 83–91). It is in its resolution of this problem that the dual economy evolves – in the artificial division of labour inside and between countries, that has survived with all its concomitant burden of human suffering down to our own times.

6 Extending the Field of Capitalism

Economic growth of individual capitalist economies has been strongly associated with an expansion in the role of foreign trade in the economy and particularly with the expansion of exports of manufactures in exchange for primary products. It might still be argued in accordance with the classical liberal model of political economy that this was a temporary phenomenon, appearing at the emergence of each new capitalist economy or at the recovery of war-devastated economies like Japan and West Germany, but that the normal 'pure' development of capitalism required no territorial expansion. If the main direction of British exports throughout the nineteenth century was to the colonies, this might have been only because the colonies already existed and there were non-economic ties that kept them associated with the homeland. Then it might still be only a hangover of militarism that extended Britain's imperial bases. Thus, the expansionist and protectionist measures of the United States and of Germany in establishing themselves as capitalist powers were regarded by Schumpeter as temporary and likely to be reduced, when the economic position of these powers became more firmly established in the world economy (Schumpeter, 1955, p. 77). There has been little sign of this happening.

In this chapter we consider the fact that not only colonial trade but colonial settlement was associated with the rise of capitalism in Britain and particularly with the supposedly anti-colonialist free-trade period of the mid-nineteenth century. This is the second strand of Semmell's development of the thesis of Britain's 'Free Trade Imperialism' (Semmell, 1970). This is equally the central point of the ultra-Keynesian explanation of the long boom of the nineteenth century

(Knapp, 1973). It is a striking fact, which Semmell has stressed, that some of the leading advocates of free trade, including Corn Law repeal in the first half of the nineteenth century, were also advocates of colonial settlement. Not only the new whigs like Brougham but many of the radicals supported Gibbon Wakefield's programme of 'systematic colonization'. For this they became known as Colonial Reformers, and not because they were anti-colonialist. These men did not include Joseph Hume, the leader of the Parliamentary radicals, who probably had the best claim to be one of Schumpeter's survivals from an earlier social formation. Hume was moved by an orthodox Ricardian fear of 'capital loss' from investment at home to propose investment in the colonies. The others – Buller, Molesworth, Grote, Rowland Hill – saw the colonies as new fields for employment both of capital and labour. In this they were supported by Malthus and, following him, by Tories like Peel's Under-Secretary for Colonies, Wilmot-Horton. For them the colonies, and by this they meant Canada, Australia and New Zealand, could provide precisely the new lands where the diminishing returns from agricultural expansion could at least be postponed (Semmell, 1970, p. 104). James Mill thought he knew what they were up to – the Empire was 'a vast system of outdoor relief for the Upper Classes'. Yet Mill and his son were converted to the Wakefield programme precisely as the alternative to the old colonial system (Semmell, 1970, p. 109).

For Marx the most obvious illustration of the extension of capitalist relations of exploitation was the existence of colonies. Their development was the clearest case of the imposition of the capitalist mode of production upon the pre-capitalist. 'Where the capitalist regime,' as Marx put it, 'comes into collision with the resistance of the producer who, as owner of his own conditions of labour employs that labour to enrich himself instead of the capitalist,' (Marx, 1946, ch. 33) there slavery and other forms of forced labour are introduced, or land prices are raised by government purchase and by 'systematic colonization', to supply the landless wage labourers for capitalist exploitation. A special form of colonial society emerged, which Marx first identified in Ireland (1946, ch. 25, section 5.4), where capitalist and landlord (both often absentees) made common cause with the independent peasantry to exploit either the indigenous people or the imported servile labourers. A major neo-Marxist explanation of imperialist acts has been the pressure of colonial settlers to extend or retain the servile labour at their disposal (Emmanuel, 1972a).

On the neo-classical view, colonies of settlers are but extensions of the free market economy to outlying areas when diminishing returns are experienced at the centre. The use of force may be needed, in the first place to extend the market economy, and colonial rule thereafter, to reduce the risks involved for traders; but the benefits of trade diversification, and of the expanded scale of operations, supposedly provide gains for all from the freeing of the market (Hicks, 1969, pp. 55–8). In the Marxist view, if land is cheap, the extension of capitalist relations is not made possible simply by the process of liberalizing the market. Land has to be made artificially dear by state action. Slavery appears then not as a 'relapse' to a pre-capitalist formation, but as an essential element in capitalism in certain conditions.

For the Keynesians, Robinson accepts the Marxist view from Hill (1967), that,

Landless and dispossessed countrymen and artisans ruined by competition from the factories were driven by necessity to become wage earners (1970a, p. 62), [but goes on to say that] development of the New World, revolutionary improvements in transport and in manufactures to trade for agricultural products, provided an ample supply of food. This is a piece of history that will not repeat itself (1970a).

It is this very special moment in history when new lands were opened up by a 'disguised form of European mercantilism' that the Keynesians believe to have been the explanation of the abnormally rapid expansion of wealth in the nineteenth century (Knapp, 1949). These were the special conditions which overcame the normal reluctance to invest and the preference of owners of wealth for liquidity. But were these then specific to industrial capitalism as a mode of production, as the Marxists see it, or, according to the Keynesians, a chance combination of factors that worked on unchanging modes of human behaviour in any money economy, the desire especially of capitalists 'to consider themselves gentlemen' (Robinson, 1970a, p. 67)? A brief look at the men involved and at what was said at the time about early colonization may help us to judge.

Malthus and the Tory agricultural interest pressed for colonial settlement, but 'systematic colonization' was not just a question of developing new lands to put off the evil day of Malthusian overpopulation. New opportunities could be created for labour to be employed profitably by capital. As Marx comments at the end of volume 1 of *Capital*, Wakefield gave the game away. Capital accumulation depended on ex-propriated labourers (Marx, 1946, p. 739). Early settlers in the colonies, including convicts released after their sentences were completed (and Wakefield was a quite unrepentant advocate of slavery 'where land was cheap') (Semmell, 1970, p. 111), tended to take up the free land available after the indigenous population had been wiped out and to develop it to the profit of none but themselves. By bringing all land under the ownership of the Crown, or of private companies operating as Crown Agents, as Wakefield proposed (1834), and by selling it off 'at a sufficient price', bond slavery would be unnecessary, capital could profitably emigrate, and local agriculture be placed upon its most productive footing (see Semmell, 1970, p. 83).

In his *Notes on Adam Smith's Wealth of Nations* (1835), Wakefield accepted Smith's belief that 'the competition of capitals' tended to drive down the rate of profit. This thesis Mill also accepted, Marx was to develop, and the Marxists to incorporate as 'the drive for capital exports' in their model of capitalist imperialism. The central argument was that land was as essential as capital for the employment of labour; for land was the 'field of employment of capital itself', the surplus of agriculture, the basis of the division of labour and of capital accumulation (see Semmell, 1970, pp. 84–5). This made good sense in the empty lands of the Southern hemisphere. Profits and wages did not, as Ricardo supposed, regulate each other. High profits *and* high wages were possible if the *field* of investment were extended. This combination already existed in the United States and could be enjoyed by British capital and labour through complementary trading of English manufactures for American food and materials. The same principle could be applied to new fields of development in the colonies. 'The mere division of produce between capitalists and labourers is of very small moment when compared with the amount of produce to be divided' (see Semmell, 1970, p. 90).

In other words, Wakefield and the Colonial Reformers were arguing for an extension of the area of capitalism. This was no survival of pre-capitalist ideas and formations. What was driving Wakefield and his followers was the fear of social revolutions in a period of capitalist stagnation and slump in Britain (the late 1820s and early 1830s) and of revolution in France. Wakefield asserted that the Constitution established under the Reform Act of 1832 'will not last'. The working class was determined to have universal suffrage, and 'if it were to come to a trial of strength between the two parties in open warfare (which God forbid!) the result must inevitably be favourable to the great majority' (see Semmell, 1970, p. 88). Colonization was thus to be an outlet for the unemployed and an opportunity for raising wages and profits at home through new openings for capital investment (Marx, 1951, part 2, ch. 17).

Palmerston and others, including Alexander Baring of the banking family, had the wit to notice that the Colonial Reformers were all themselves involved in land speculation in the colonies. 'Those persons who have engaged in land speculation in our Colonies preach Emigration upon a large scale as a cure for all our domestic evils, because at all events it would probably help them to turn their lands to good account' (see Semmell, 1970, p. 121). In fact, Wakefield's companies failed in Australia and New Zealand, but this was not for want of trying. For the failures Wakefield blamed the Government, which resisted the Colonial Reformers' pressure for a measure of self-government in the colonies (Semmell, 1970, ch. 10). This was resisted, in part because of the state expenditure involved, in part because of Cobdenite pressure from those humanitarians and missionaries who interested themselves in the rights of the aborigines, whom only the Mother Country seemed prepared to defend (Semmell, 1970, pp. 120–29), and largely because Wakefield did not get the wage labourers he needed.

There were many successors to Wakefield who were to carry on his campaign, notably Robert Torrens (1844), an ex-Colonel of marines, who carried forward mercantilist arguments into the campaign against the Corn Laws. Torrens, noting the falling terms of trade of Britain's manufactured exports against her imports of food and raw materials (this continued fairly steadily from the 1820s to the 1850s), and fearing competition from other capitalist states, advocated reciprocity in trade agreements. It was only the 'colonial markets in which we could not be met by hostile tariffs of foreign rivals'. Britain's prosperity could not be arrested by such tariffs 'if England would establish throughout her widespread empire a British commercial league – a colonial *zollverein*' (see Semmell, 1970, p. 194). In this Torrens anticipated by sixty years Joseph Chamberlain's proposals for imperial preference. The argument for protection failed, but colonization went ahead.

The strong opposition of the Cobdenites to Torrens and to the radical Colonial Reformers, despite their support from the Mills, does suggest that those capitalists with colonial interests might have been atypical. Indeed, it is the central argument of the supporters of the Schumpeter neo-classical view that these men were colonials themselves with a special interest in colonial investment. This accords with the theses of Gallagher and Robinson (1963), and of Emmanuel too (1972a), that most of the pressure for imperialist expansion came from the periphery and not from the metropolis. Certainly it is true that Wakefield and Buller had colonial interests and Torrens spent some time in Australia. The fact is, however, that investment in the colonies steadily increased. In the 1850s about a half of British foreign investment was in Europe, a quarter in the USA and another quarter roughly equally divided between Latin America and the Empire. Investment in Latin America in the 1820s had proved disastrous but railway investment in the

1850s and 1860s profitably opened up trade in Argentine wheat and meat, Brazilian coffee and Chilean copper (Rippy, 1959, pp. 17–35). Investment in United States' railways boomed in the 1850s and in the years after the Civil War (Clapham, 1930, vol. 2, pp. 234–41).

By 1870, however, 36 per cent of British overseas capital was in the Empire and nearly half the annual flow was going to the Empire (see Barratt Brown, 1970a, table 2, p. 110). The big expansion of investment in the Dominions came in the 1870s. India provided the main opening for British capital in the late 1850s and the 1860s in the railway building programme that followed the Mutiny. Till then the plantations in India had developed slowly, except in producing opium for China (Greenberg, 1951, ch. 5). India had mainly been a market for British cotton textiles, which involved for India an import surplus. With the opening of the Suez Canal in 1869, India became a major source of food and raw materials for Europe – tea, wheat, oil seeds, cotton, jute – and a location for investment, not only in railways and canals, but in cotton mills and jute mills. An Indian surplus was built up and this paid for the annual interest on the 'Home Debt' – a sum of £30m – which had been brought into existence between 1857 and 1860 and was to grow steadily thereafter (Jenks, 1927, pp. 223–4; Saul, 1960, pp. 188–94).

The search for land for profitable investment of capital had spread from Europe to the European settled colonies, to Latin America and to India. India had always been the core of the Colonial Empire: first, when empire meant plunder, secondly, when it was seen primarily as providing a market for manufactures and, finally, as a source of raw materials and investment income. We earlier quoted Marx in the *New York Daily Tribune* articles of 11 July 1853: 'The more the industrial interest became dependent on the Indian market the more it felt the necessity of creating fresh productive powers in India after having ruined her native industry' (1950). Plantations of tea as well as cotton and jute were established in India, often with planters from the West Indies (Buchanan, 1934, pp. 34–40). Plantations sometimes involved taking away land from food crops; sometimes, by irrigation or by clearing of forest, new land was brought into cultivation.

The great expansion of imports into Britain in the 1850s and 1860s was made possible by overseas investment of British capital in railways and ports and shipping. Imports rose by 1870 to the equivalent of nearly a third of Britain's national income with exports rising in line. What made possible this export of British capital in the second half of the nineteenth century was the steady accumulation of surpluses on the balance of foreign payments; and this was not after the 1820s the result of a favourable balance on goods and services; it was the result of the accumulation of interest and dividends from past investment. Where had this accumulation originated (see table 7)?

By 1854, according to Imlah's estimates, Britain's accumulated balance abroad stood at £235m. A gross figure might have been nearer £280m. The whole of this sum had been accounted for by the balance on interest and dividends over the period after 1815. According to one estimate, the accumulated British foreign credit was made up in the 1850s as 35 per cent in European government securities, 12 per cent in French and Belgian railways, 13 per cent in Latin American public issues and 15 per cent in private issues not defined by area (see Imlah, 1958, p. 68). By 1870 the total credit had risen to £700m and 36 per cent was in the empire, 17 per cent in the USA and only 25 per cent in Europe and 10 per cent in Latin America (Feinstein, 1960). Since we know that there were heavy losses in Latin America, these figures suggest that profits were made in Europe and the funds *switched* to the Empire and in part to the USA. Two-thirds of the Empire investment was in India, one third in the self-governing colonies, that is to say in what came to be called the Dominions. Between 1850 and 1870, then, in the heyday of British capitalism, the opportunities for investment in the Empire were evidently attractive.

The Keynesian view of the special geo-political conditions that induced investment seems at first sight to be justified. But it must be noticed that the overwhelming share of the investment was in India. This was not an empty land nor was its wealth

Table 7 Balance of payments and capital export, UK, 1815–1913, by 15-year periods (£m)

Period	Merchandise (including ships)	Gold and silver	Services	Net balance on trade and services	Balance on interest and dividends	Total credit abroad	Cumulative credit abroad at end of period
1815–1830	−149	−16	+213	+48	+53	111[a]	111
1831–1845	−271	−4	+245	−30	+104	74	185
1846–1860	−435	−26	+467	+6	+189	195	380
1861–1875	−943	−78	+1193	+172	+513	685	1065
1876–1890	−1550	−11	+1405	−156	+1026	870	1935
1891–1905	−2280	−68	+1520	−828	+1535	707	2642
1906–1913	−1103	−46	+1176	+27	+1321	1348	3990
1815–1913	−6731	−249	+6219	−761	+4741	3990	3990

[a]Total includes £10m investment prior to 1815
Source: Imlah (1958, table 4)

increasing. Investment *in* India was entirely financed *from* India. Exports from India exceeded imports by some £4m a year in the 1850s and from this excess the 'tribute' to England, as the 'Home Charges' were still called at that time, was financed (see Dutt, 1947, p. 110, quoting Colonel Sykes, director of the East India company in 1848). These were then reinvested in government guaranteed railway stock at home and abroad and in Indian and other overseas commercial stocks.

If Indian investment was self financing, then the switch from European investment to the colonies and the USA becomes more important, and the Keynesian argument is strengthened. It cannot, however, be overlooked that India was providing to Britain a steady flow of tribute and after the 1860s India was Britain's main supplier of cotton as well as of tea and jute and of large proportions of Britain's rice and wheat imports. Britain's relationship with the self-governing colonies was evidently different. These were the empty lands of European settlement whose development is regarded by the Keynesians as so important for Britain's economic growth.[1] The Marxists will also insist that the openings for British capital investment were more important than the markets for British manufactured goods.

It is the Keynesian view that there were very special geo-political factors at work. The argument is that these comprised the relative technical, economic and military strengths of the densely populated north-west of Europe, and particularly of Britain, and the relative weakness of the native populations of North and South America and Oceania, which held great areas of land with rich natural resources very thinly settled. 'The "vast secular boom" of the nineteenth century consisted essentially of people moving out of Europe and into the New World' (Knapp, 1956–7). Britain's adoption of free trade, combined with the export of men and of capital, enabled Britain particularly, and other European countries later and to a lesser degree, to enjoy the benefits of this great opening up of new lands. Despite free trade, the whole process involved a

1. It should be said that I adopted the same view in my book *After Imperialism*, 1963 edn, p. 448. I have subsequently modified my views.

concealed form of mercantilism in the extensions of colonial rule, which are described as 'Free Trade Imperialism'. It is a most attractive thesis for the Keynesians, since it fits so neatly into their view of normal stagnation from the normal weakness of the inducement to invest, overcome only by special conditions encouraging the incentive to invest.

Table 8 Migration to lands of European settlement, 1846–1940 (millions of persons)

Years	Total	Emigration from			
		UK	Spain and Portugal	Germany and Austria	Others
1846–1850	0·5	0·2	—	0·2	0·1
1851–1860	2·2	1·3	0·05	0·65	0·2
1861–1870	2·6	1·6	0·1	0·7	0·2
1871–1880	3·1	1·85	0·15	0·75	0·35
1881–1890	7·0	3·25	0·75	1·8	1·2
1891–1900	6·2	2·15	1·0	1·25	1·8
1901–1910	11·3	3·15	1·4	2·6	4·15
1911–1920	7·6	2·6	1·7	0·9	2·4
1921–1930	6·6	2·15	1·6	1·1	1·75
1931–1940	1·7	0·25	0·2	0·2	1·05
total	48·8	18·5	6·95	10·15	13·2

Years	Total	Immigration to				
		USA	Canada	Argentina and Brazil	Australia and NZ	Others
1846–1850	1·6	1·25	0·25	—	—	0·1
1851–1860	3·4	2·6	0·3	0·05	0·05	0·4
1861–1870	3·4	2·3	0·3	0·2	0·2	0·4
1871–1880	4·0	2·8	0·2	0·5	0·2	0·3
1881–1890	7·5	5·2	0·4	1·4	0·3	0·2
1891–1900	6·4	3·7	0·2	1·8	0·45	0·25
1901–1910	14·9	8·8	1·1	2·45	1·6	0·95
1911–1920	11·1	5·7	1·1	2·0	1·0	1·3
1921–1930	8·7	4·0	1·0	2·15	0·7	0·85
1931–1940	1·9	0·5	0·1	0·6	0·1	0·6
total	62·9	36·85	4·95	11·15	4·6	5·35

Other emigrants included nearly 10m Italians, 2m Russians, 1m Swedes and ½m Poles. Other areas of immigration included Cuba 1m, Uruguay 6m, South Africa 0·3m, other African States 1·5m. One main difference between the figures for immigration and for emigration is caused by negroes and Latin Americans entering the USA

Source: Woytinsky and Woytinsky (1953, tables 34 and 36)

There are three elements in the thesis – the emigration of labour, the development of the wealth of empty lands and the extension of colonial rule to guarantee the investment. All these, and not just free trade, are said to account for the continuing incentive to invest and for the expansion of wealth at home in Britain. There is no doubt about the scale of emigration (see table 8). For many years in the middle of the nineteenth century 150 000 emigrants were leaving Britain each year mainly for the United States, but some for the British colonies (Thomas, 1954). There can be no doubt either about the potential wealth of these empty lands. In terms of land area, although some of it is barren, the United States, Canada, Australia, New Zealand, South Africa and the main lands of European settlement, comprise over a fifth of the earth's land surface while containing even today less than 7 per cent of the population (5·5 per cent in the USA alone). In terms of food supplies and raw material resources, by 1870 nearly all of Britain's food and two thirds of her raw material imports were coming from the USA and the dominions, about a half in both cases from the USA. Nor can there be any doubt about the extension of colonial rule in the decades prior to 1870 (see table 4).

We examine the relationship of capital export and imperialism *after* 1870 in a later chapter; here we can note how the settlement of empty or cleared lands by Europeans, and mainly at first by British kith and kin, before 1870 expanded the field of capitalist development. Far from the home economy being able to absorb the surplus of both capital and population in the mid-nineteenth century, outlets were needed the world over. The same result followed, whether we accept a Marxist or Keynesian view of the causes.

What is still in doubt is that the direction of investment was primarily to these empty lands or that it led in all cases to economic development. We have already seen that India was the major area of British investment prior to 1870 and India did not develop; indeed, India became underdeveloped as tribute was extracted, as the handcraft industries were destroyed and as land was switched from food production to export crops.

Latin America also received much British investment at the beginning of the century and again in the 1860s, especially in Argentina after the law of 16 November 1863, which guaranteed payment in sterling in London on all public bonds (Ferns, 1953). But Latin America too became underdeveloped. These two cases greatly weaken the Keynesian argument that it was the real development of empty lands with European settlers and capital that provided the incentive for continuously expanded investment in the nineteenth century.

British capital certainly did encourage development, first in Europe, then in the United States and then in the dominions, but not in India or Latin America. India was not, of course, an empty land, and investment was internally financed, although the dividends returned to Britain; and that was cause enough for underdevelopment. It has been argued that the return to Britain on capital invested in Argentina was very high and the same point is made about investment in the USA:

The net stock of foreign indebtedness of the United States rose from $200m in 1843 to $3700m in 1914. But the net long-term borrowing of the United States, to the tune of $3 billion between 1850 and 1914, was throughout either matched or exceeded by net payments of interest and dividends amounting, in total, to $5·8 billion over the period (Knapp, 1957, p. 433).

Despite the payments of debt on foreign loans, mainly provided by Britain, the United States developed economically by leaps and bounds. Australia and Canada had also to pay heavily in dividends and interest on the capital borrowed from Britain. Australia was, for most of the nineteenth century, having to devote one-third of all her export earnings to debt payments (Butlin, 1964). Yet still these lands were developed. Why?

It could be that British emigrants were in themselves better colonizers than the Spaniards, Portuguese and Italians who went to Latin America. The British did have some important advantages. Above all, they came from a capitalist Britain and not from a feudal Spain or Portugal. Because the colonials were 'kith and kin' with the suppliers of capital, and because many settlers took capital as well as skills with them, they established capitalism.[2] A figure of £70–£80 per head for British emigrants has been suggested by Clapham (1930, vol. 2, p. 492). Moreover, the inflow to the UK of dividends and interest from the colonies of European settlement was probably not so great in relation to the outflow as in the case of India, Latin America or the plantation colonies. There was another factor that kinship provided. British colonials obtained political independence; and the granting of self government (within limits set by defence considerations and the requirements of sterling reserves for currency issues) permitted the dominions, like the USA before them, to impose tariffs on imports of British manufactures and to build up their own processing industries. In fact, the ties of British capital for long limited what the dominions could develop on their own. Only the competition between US and UK capital in Canada and later in Australia led to the opening up of today's full range of dominion industries. For over fifty years from the last decade of the nineteenth century, there was practically no *per capita* economic growth in Australia; but prior to that time there is no doubt about the record of growth (Butlin, 1964).

There was something else that was shared by all the lands to which British capital was exported that could account for the incentive to invest besides their emptiness and their potential riches. This something is central to the Keynesian view; it is the state guarantees of the investment. But these were the guarantees of local governments. In India and in Latin America governments provided such guarantees no less than in the British Colonies. In fact, in Argentina and in the USA, although British government guarantees did not exist, local legislation established state support, especially for railway undertakings, in the shape of guaranteed profits and land grants (Ferns, 1953).[3]

2. I have emphasized the importance for the development of Britain's empire of the 'outsiders', the proto-industrial capitalists of the seventeenth century in my book, *After Imperialism*, 1963, pp. 31–8.
3. The fact that these guarantees did not discriminate in favour of British traders, and that there was much competition between European and United States traders, does not derogate from the value of the stimulus to foreign capital, as Platt seems to argue, see Owen and Sutcliffe (1972, pp. 306–7).

As well as donating the land – 160 million acres on either side of the railroad lines – the United States government actually built many of the railroads and handed them over to private companies (Russell, 1914).

The amounts of capital required were considerable, both for the infrastructural development – of railways, ports and communications – to make possible the transport of primary products back to Britain, and for the tools, wire fencing, agricultural machinery, house building and furnishing hardware, which settlement and the production of an exportable agricultural surplus implied. Sums of the order of £80m a year were raised on the London capital market in the early 1870s (Simon, 1967). Some of these funds may have become self-generating through plough-back in the territory itself; most funds were found from reinvestment by shareholders of their earlier investment income. Rentiers wanted security, whether there was a small percentage or not above the normal rate of capital return at home (Feinstein, 1960). This was particularly true of Scottish investors (Bailey, 1966, pp. 61–9). State guarantee of the investment was crucial, and the Marxists and Keynesians will agree on this point. But the Marxists will see it as one aspect only of capitalist assimilation of these areas.

Given the high proportion of losses (Saul, 1960, pp. 65–6; Rippy, 1959, pp. 17–35) and failures early in the nineteenth century in developing overseas primary production, even where there were state guarantees behind the investment, or at least state protection of the general climate for private capitalist enterprise, it seems unlikely that, without protection amounting to incorporation, capital on such a scale would have been ventured. Indeed, state support for British capital was really only 'available either in the USA, the dominions and other colonial territories, or in territories like those of Latin America, which had government trading agreements with the British and protection from the British navy.

Could British capitalism, then, have developed in the nineteenth century, first, without an extension of the area of capital investment beyond Britain and, secondly, without that extension being protected by some degree of imperial rule? The first does not necessarily imply the second; the United States was almost as important for British investment as the Empire up to 1870. In fact, for twenty-five years after the repeal of the Corn Laws, British agriculture supplied nine-tenths of the nation's food. When, in the 1870s, the iron ships and the completion of railway and port building in North America brought a flood of prairie grains to Britain, the wheat acreage at home was cut back (between 1874 and the end of the century it was halved) and land under cultivation in Britain fell steadily (from 17 million acres to 13 million between 1874 and 1913). Even if home production could have been expanded rather than contracted, it is difficult to believe that prices would not have risen. Today, with the most modern methods of production, subsidies are still required to protect British agriculture.

Other imports could hardly have been substituted by home production. Imports of tin and lead and other minerals came in to Britain to replace depleted home supplies. By the end of the century iron ore imports were supplementing poorer home ores. Cotton and tea continued to be major imports; with the rise of the motor industry, oil, copper and rubber were added and, as standards of living rose, tropical and sub-tropical fruits completed the list (Schloete, 1952, p. 51). It was not only, however, that British capital was needed to develop these overseas products, but that the opening of the British market both encouraged their production and, in exchange, enabled British industry to raise its productivity by expanding its scale of production through sales to wider markets overseas. We must not exaggerate. Europe continued to take as much of British exports as the Empire right up to the 1920s.

For Britain, with limited land area and raw material resources (apart from coal), the development of overseas sources of food and raw materials was a necessary corollary of industrialization. Behind the opening of British markets to the produce of the rest of the world and through the establishment of free trade, we have seen the state guarantees for the migration of capital and capitalists overseas, either under colonial rule, or under relations of informal imperialism in South America, or under state-financed capitalism in the USA. This can be viewed as a form of mercantilism, however disguised. Free trade meant the opening up of the markets of the whole world to British manufactures; but free capital movements opened the world to British capital and this was more important. Those countries which won their political independence could protect their infant industries against free trade and develop their own economies. On the Marxist view, their incorporation in the capitalist mode of production was as important as the expansion of empire. In fact, the governments of the Latin American states were so dominated by ruling groups that depended on pastoral or mineral exports to Britain (Ferns, 1960, pp. 487–91), and on British and, later, on United States support for their rule, that they made no attempt to break out of the artificial division of labour into which they were cast.[4] Others were held by British capital just as securely in that artificial division of labour which we have described, where the British Navy protected the capital invested in that form of primary production to which their most accessible natural resources assigned them.

The role of protection in the process of industrial development is the subject of the next chapter. The conclusion of this chapter must be that the neo-classical view of free trade as the generator of economic development through free movement of capital as well as goods, to the benefit of both parties to the exchange, is quite untenable outside the lands of European settlement; the Keynesian view can be accepted of the incentive to invest in empty lands, but this must be modified to allow for the investment in India and for the world-wide penetration of British capital, far beyond the Empire and well before 1870.

This last is what is emphasized in the Marxist view of the pressure of Britain's capitalists in the mid-nineteenth century, to use the artificial world division of labour, which they had already created, to extend the sway of their capital with the aim of exploiting cheap labour and cheap land the world over. In this process capital accumulation was confined primarily to the original centres, but, wherever independent capitalists

4. The implications of this today are discussed in chapter 11.

could establish themselves, new centres developed with new polarizing effects on the distribution of wealth. Such effects have no place in the neo-classical model, and, if this had been only for the capitalists to 'consider themselves as gentlemen' or from the capitalist 'animal spirits', as the Keynesians would have it, I find it hard to believe that the process would have gained the dynamism that it did and involve the whole world in capitalist rivalry, when the sway of Britain's capitalists was challenged by others. The fact is that Britain's era of free trade cannot be separated from the economics of imperialism.

It is an extraordinary *bouleversement* that at the end of his study of British 'Free Trade Imperialism' in the first half of the nineteenth century, Semmell comes down in defence of Schumpeter's neo-classical model of imperialism. The failure of Schumpeter to 'see the possibility of a free trade imperialism' is pardoned by Semmell because of his need in the twentieth century to defend free trade, 'embodying the soundest international morality under attack by a racist (*sic*) neo-mercantilism, and classical economics condemned by a new school of historical economists' (Semmell, 1970, p. 221). Free trade imperialism is then explained by Semmell on Schumpeterian grounds, as deriving from assumptions that were a survival

from the agrarian era of relative scarcity, which constituted the entire past of the race, and from the economic analysis of the age - of mercantilism which had preceded it. The persistence of such assumptions were undoubtedly more understandable at a time when the enormous powers of the new industrialism had not been fully displayed (Semmell, 1970, p. 221).

This is simply to accept what has to be proved, that the new industrialization could have displayed such enormous powers without the help of free trade imperialism. It is not true that only pre-capitalist economies and economics indicated gluts, as Semmell avers. There were periodic slumps every six or seven years from the time of the industrial revolution right through the nineteenth century, as Beveridge long ago showed (1902).[5]

5. For a table of slumps and booms from 1822 to 1960 see Barratt Brown (1970a, table 3, p. 76).

That these involved a glut of goods was observed and well understood by politicians and economists at the time, and not only by Karl Marx. What Semmell's study has shown is precisely that.

The very success of capitalist industrialization in Britain, and the enormous power it developed, has been found in the last three chapters to have been attributable to the accumulation of treasure and the use of slave labour, to an artificial world division of labour and to the extension of the area of capitalism, which imperial expansion made possible. Whether there was some other, slower way, according to Fieldhouse's dictum (1967, p. 188), by which the process could have been accomplished cannot finally be decided until we have looked both at the protection of privileged markets and at the mechanism of private capital accumulation involved in the export of capital after 1870. The fact remains that this was the way it was accomplished in Britain, and in Britain not just as one of many capitalist nation states that industrialized but as the first nation state to succeed in that long and difficult process.

7 Protection and Preference

Marx saw protection as:

an artificial means of manufacturing manufacturers, of expro-
priating independent labourers, of capitalizing the national means
of production and subsistence, and of forcibly abbreviating the
transition from the mediaeval to the modern mode of production
(1946, p. 782).

When this was done, free trade removed the challenge to the
hegemony of industrial capital from an older, agricultural
interest, cheapened the cost of labour and opened a wider
field for the division of labour and the accumulation of capital:
'from the moment that dependence on the world market is
established, there is already more or less dependence upon free
trade' (Marx, 1935c, appendix).

In introducing Marx's *Address on the Question of Free Trade*,
from which this passage comes, Engels spelt out the Marxist
view:

Under capitalist conditions an industry either expands or wanes. A
trade cannot remain stationary; stoppage of expansion is incipient
ruin; the progress of mechanical and chemical invention, by constantly superseding human labour, and ever more rapidly increasing
and concentrating production, creates in every industry a glut both
of workers and capital, a glut which finds no vent anywhere because
the same process is taking place in all other industries. Thus the
passage from a home to an export trade becomes a life and death
question for the industries concerned . . . (Marx, 1935c, p. 176).

Schumpeter answered this argument directly on behalf of the
classical economic view. Goods that were not offered abroad
would, he says, 'be offered at home, in general affording the
same employment opportunities to the workers and in addition

cheapening consumption . . .' and if 'the industry in question is expanding beyond economically justifiable limits . . . it is in the interest of all productive factors, excepting only the cartel magnates, for capital and labour to move into other industries, something that is necessary and always possible' (1955, p. 86). This is Say's Law with a vengeance and assumes not only effective demand, required, in the Keynesian view, to meet capacity at home, but a rate of accumulation from competitive home investment that, on the Marxist view, could be expected to come up against problems of capitalization on account of overproduction. Engels had gone on to say that:

Germany turned protectionist [in industry and agriculture] at a moment when more than ever free trade seemed a necessity for her . . . the exportation of German manufactures was carried on at the direct cost of the home consumers . . . this absurd system of protection to manufacturers is nothing but the sop thrown to industrial capitalists to induce them to support a still more outrageous monopoly given to the landed interest (Marx, 1935c, pp. 186–7).

The classical argument for free trade neither proved that the advantages of free trade were equally shared between trading partners, nor that under conditions of monopoly and monopsony free trade was generally advantageous. None of the assumptions are realistic – perfect competition and full employment, immobility of capital and labour between countries (and perfect mobility *inside* the countries), imports and exports balanced by price movements, static conditions of resources, of technical knowledge, of population and of capital stock.

The advantages of free trade for Britain, once established as the most technically advanced industrial country, were very great in widening the market for British manufactures and encouraging in exchange the development of primary production overseas. To break out of this artificial division of labour, other countries were forced to interfere with free trade; and their politicians and economists had to challenge free trade theory. Alexander Hamilton, the American federalist, in his *Report on Manufactures* published in 1791, not only looked back to the mercantilists but forward to Frederick List, the theorist of the Prussian *zollverein*, in expanding the argument for the protection of infant industries into advocacy of a national economic policy (Schumpeter, 1954, pp. 504–5). Even the neo-classical economist, Alfred Marshall, in an appendix to the *Principles of Economics*, as we saw earlier, conceded that List had 'showed that in Germany, and still more in America, many of its indirect effects [i.e. those of free trade] were evil, and he contended that these evils outweighed its direct benefits' (see Robinson, 1962, pp. 65–6). This is a very mercantilist view, as Keynesians would recognize.

In fact, however, the tariff surrounding the Prussian *zollverein* was quite moderate – about 10 per cent on most manufactures, although some industries like iron and textiles were more protected (Henderson, 1962, pp. 57–8). It was not until after 1870 that German protection was increased. Similarly, after the initial protection of industry in the United States, the long period of Anglo-American free trade only ended with the Civil War. In both cases industry was established in an expanding and protected home market. By 1870, however, German and American industry were coming out into the world market to challenge Britain as the workshop of the world. They adopted protectionism once more as their weapon and the tariffs they established were this time high (Clapham, 1930, vol. 2, p. 247). French and other European manufactures were acting in the same way, and Engels noted that even Manchester's Chamber of Commerce was turning protectionist in the 1880s; but he concluded that Britain's competitors would have to 'fight the fading industrial monopoly of England with its own weapon, free trade' (Marx, 1935c).

Engels' argument comes near to that of the classical economists; this was that an older agricultural interest had combined with a popular conviction that industrial production was to be preferred, and had brought about policies which were, in fact, against the public interest. This is still the argument of the neo-classical economists, that vested interests get the ear of undemocratic governments, and that political parties in a democracy bow to the irrational preferences of the electorate. This is why industrial countries will only bargain one tariff reduction for another, despite the fact that under free trade theory all reductions of tariffs are supposed to be beneficial.[1] Thus, too, Schumpeter associated imperialism in Britain with Disraeli's need after the 1867 Reform Act to catch the votes of the newly enfranchised workers by the appeal to national greatness and to a national unity which overcomes class divisions.

Imperialism became a 'catch phrase' – in Schumpeter's words 'arousing the dark powers of the subconscious' (1955, pp. 11–13). Schumpeter's proof, that Disraeli spoke but did not act, is refuted by his purchase of the Suez Canal shares and support for the 'prancing pro-consuls', Sir Bartle Frere in Africa and Lord Lytton in India. Even the title granted to Victoria in 1876, of Empress of India, was no mere symbolic gesture; it was part of a policy of establishing indirect rule through Indian Princes in those parts of India that had not been annexed to the Empire. British exports to the Indian market grew rapidly in the railway building and irrigation programmes that followed in the decade after the Indian Mutiny of 1857 (Macpherson, 1955). Economic and political motives cannot be easily separated.

The Keynesian view of protection is that this was the policy into which national governments were forced if they were to induce investment. The equilibrium of free trade doctrine could be reached, and generally is reached, at levels of employment well below the optimum. Protection is at least one way of maintaining effective demand through its encouragement of the inducement to invest. This was the 'element of scientific truth' which Keynes identified in the mercantilist doctrine (1960, p. 335).

After Britain all countries that successfully industrialized their economies did so behind the protection of tariff walls. As a matter of fact the early English manufacturers also benefited from protection both of the home market and of the colonial market. Once they had achieved a competitive manufactured product, free trade was expected to sustain their supremacy.

1. This is the explanation which Johnson (1972, p. 99) puts forward, in answer, he says, to the persistent questioning of Knapp, the Keynesian economist.

Newcomers would have to protect their 'infant industries' as even the free traders conceded; and indeed the 'infant industry' argument can be extended to a whole economic environment where external economies become possible (Scitovsky, 1936, p. 358). Giving up this protection, however, when the young industries grew up proved to be difficult. Indeed, United States, German and French industry not only raised their tariffs higher when they first met the competition of Britain head on, but continued to maintain high tariffs and other restrictions on imports a hundred years after their industrialization was established.

The arguments for protection after the stage of 'infant industry' development are not all related to forms of imperialism (see Beveridge, 1931) (all types of protection are referred to here as tariffs, including quotas and other forms of discrimination):

1 Tariffs for revenue purposes. These have a long history; a tax on goods entering a state being an easy tax to collect and unlikely to be resisted by its citizens. For the classical economists this is the main rationale of tariffs (see Hicks, 1969, pp. 82–5; Schumpeter, 1955, p. 89).

2 Tariffs for bargaining against the tariffs and 'dumping' of other states. The effect of these, on classical theory, should have been to reduce tariffs as a whole, but this had not happened.

3 Tariffs for correcting the balance of trade. These persist, although classical theory assumes that gold movements working on internal prices would ensure such correction without state intervention.

4 Tariffs for balancing foreign capital movements, so that the whole foreign-payments account may be in balance without general deflation or competitive devaluations. Classical theory assumes no movement of capital between countries, although in the nineteenth century this was considerable.

5 Tariffs for obtaining the guaranteed home markets necessary for large-scale production; this is basically the infant industry argument.

6 Tariffs for enabling preferential treatment to be offered to those trading partners who will guarantee preferential markets in exchange; this on classical theory only limits the division of labour to certain trading partners, but customs unions have nonetheless received the support of free traders (see Meade, 1956, pp. 29–40).

7 Tariffs for protecting particular industries of supposedly strategic national importance, e.g. agriculture or computer manufacture; this is the non-economic argument that neo-classical theory permits.

8 Tariffs for maintaining high wages and full employment where tariffs are combined with controls over movements of labour; classical theory assumes full employment and labour immobility between countries, but these assumptions are equally unrealistic.

It is the last three aims of tariffs that may be associated with imperialism – in imperial preference and protection and in an artificial world division of labour. The sterling area, dollar area, franc zone, Japanese co-prosperity sphere and EEC associated territories are all examples of privileged and protected trading arrangements. Capital and labour movements will be considered in the next chapters. Here we look at preferential markets for goods in relation to two questions: (a) of the neo-classical economists: if free trade really encourages the maximum total benefits from the most efficient resource allocation, why the persistence of protectionism? (b) of the Keynesians: was this the result of disguised mercantilist policy or, as the Marxists would say, of industrial capitalists' expanding operations?

According to Schumpeter these aberrations from 'pure capitalism' occurred because of the social formations from which capitalism was born in these countries, with militaristic and nationalistic elements involved, and because of the neo-mercantilist role of the state in setting these new capitalist formations on their feet (Schumpeter, 1955, pp. 64–70). What, then, was the pre-capitalist formation in the United States? Presumably, the slave economy of the South. But this was defeated by the Northern States which owed their foundation to English capitalism (Lawson, 1950, part 6); and it was *after* this defeat that tariffs were raised most sharply. The best example of such a pure capitalism outside the textbooks of classical economics is in the General Agreement on Tariffs and Trade, signed by the main capitalist powers in 1943 as part of the Bretton Woods agreement. New tariffs were outlawed and in subsequent GATT negotiations, particularly the so-called 'Kennedy Round', tariffs have been reduced and other discriminatory international trade measures modified. This was seen as the dawn of a new era of free trade:

The general direction of international action is comparatively clear; a more equitable division of the benefits of trade, by continuing efforts already begun, to regulate the production and marketing of raw materials, so vulnerable to the forces of the free market, and by a planned international programme of the capital development of backward areas, to help, among other objectives, to sufficiently diversify undeveloped economies so as to enable them better to meet market fluctuations. Fairly immediate steps, on a global basis, must be taken if catastrophe is to be avoided, and if the great goal of the political economists, a universally beneficial international division of labour, is to be more equitably achieved (Semmell, 1970, p. 229).

This is Semmell writing at the very end of his book on free trade imperialism; but these are hopes, not actualities; and they sound more like Keynesian economic management on an international scale than classical liberal theory. According to the latter, high incomes should spread automatically, without state intervention, through trade from one area to another according to factor price equalization under conditions of free trade. But free trade as a basis of equality of opportunity has never existed; it certainly does not exist today.

Even the founders of the European Economic Community, which was to be devoted to 'the progressive abolition of restrictions on international trade',[2] found it necessary to maintain a wall of tariffs around the Community not lower than the arithmetical average, and that much higher than the weighted

2. Rome Treaty Preamble (1957).

average, of the individual national tariffs that preceded it (GATT, 1958, p. 115). The Common Market has indeed much in common with the Prussian *zollverein*, which replaced earlier free trade policies by a protectionist ring encircling a wider area (Henderson, 1962). In table 2 we saw the very small proportion (about one-sixth), of the exports of underdeveloped countries which were not in competition with the products of the developed countries, and which were frequently sold in protected markets.

One of the main protected industries, if not the main one, in the Common Market and in other developed capitalist countries is, in fact, agriculture; in underdeveloped countries it is industry. Is this just a question of 'balance' as Johnson (1972, p. 101) suggests? This might be for strategic self-sufficiency, against the threat to food supplies in time of war, or to protect agricultural employment. Since any form of protection must be assumed to raise the price of the protected product, and thus to raise home costs, such protection cannot be in the general economic interest of industrial capitalists, but they could have a political interest in supporting their agricultural population. Most governments of capitalist states have been formed by conservative parties that united the interests of capital owners and of the peasantry. Industrial workers tend to give their support to Labour or Socialist parties which present varying degrees of challenge to private capital ownership. The evolution of a working-class, Tory voter in Britain implied a special response of British capitalists to the absence of a British peasantry (Harrison, 1965, ch. 3).

This is not quite the same argument as Schumpeter's when he appeals to pre-capitalist agrarian interests to explain distortions from pure capitalism. It might be seen by a Marxist rather as a necessary capitalist strategy in the general conflict between capital and labour. Such an argument is also strengthened by the strongly labour-protective bias in the protection of non-agricultural industries in developed capitalist states, since these other industries are in fact mainly labour intensive. While, therefore, Johnson's argument is not supported by the facts of non-agricultural protection, an ultra-Keynesian view of mercantilist policies, designed to strengthen the state, is confirmed.

One of the troublesome problems for classical economic theory, which accepts that factor endowments determine the flows of international trade, has been the 'Leontieff paradox'. This was so called from the discovery by Leontieff (1953), that the United States with the richest capital 'endowment' in the world apparently exported *labour*-intensive products and imported *capital*-intensive products.

Several explanations were offered of this seeming paradox, with corresponding answers given (Findlay, 1970, pp. 94–105):

1 US labour might be superior in productivity to others, even at the same capital per head; but there was no evidence that it was superior at the same capital–labour ratio.

2 Similarly, there might be a human factor involved in the higher skill of the US labour in the export industries; but estimates of such differences did not show these to be large.

3 US patterns of consumption involved more capital-intensive goods than those of other countries; but it was found that in fact at higher standards of living more labour-intensive goods are consumed.

4 Leontieff had not compared US exports with US imports but with US import-competing industries, i.e. US substitutes introduced in place of imports. US imports, by contrast with such substitutes, were relatively labour-intensive; much doubt however, remained about the evidence for this.

5 US imports might require capital-intensive substitutes because the US was deficient in certain natural resources, particularly certain minerals, and these should be excluded from consideration, because they represented scarce 'land' relative to capital *and* labour; when these were excluded, the paradox disappeared; but so in a sense did the whole of classical theory, since this treats factors of production as being analytically isolable rather than bound up in complicated relations of complementarity.

The simple explanation of the paradox, which seems to have escaped the neo-classical economists, was that labour-intensive industries in the USA were being protected. This was pointed out by Travis (1964) with a wealth of supporting geometry and statistics. Yet in 1970 a standard economic text on trade and specialization (Findlay, 1970), from which the above paragraph is summarized, could discuss at length the Leontieff paradox without referring either to Travis or to protection. Such is the effect of separating economic and political factors. Once the political element was admitted to economic analysis, it was not difficult for Travis to construct a trade model for the USA and other developed economies based on the assumption of maximum protection for their labour-intensive industries and to find that it fitted with their commercial practice. If industries are grouped as Travis suggested, not only into primary products and manufactures but into final and intermediate sectors, four groups emerge, as in table 9. Intermediate primary production – agriculture, coal, mineral and oil extraction and electric power – is the most land-intensive but is also found to use most direct capital in proportion to direct labour.[3] Final manufactures use the least land *and* the least direct capital to direct labour; and are the most protected by the commercial policies of the developed states, which specifically discriminate between raw materials, partly processed manufactures and finished manufactures with successively higher levels of *ad valorem* duty.

Agriculture is the odd man out, even though agricultural protection is largely effected through subsidies and other non-tariff restrictions, which would not show up in the table. In the USA agriculture is highly capital-intensive but the farm vote remains an important political factor. In UK agriculture today there is nearly the same level of capital intensiveness as in industry, and the farm vote is relatively unimportant; but in France and Japan, and even in Germany, labour-intensive agricultural techniques survive, and with them the importance of the peasantry in national politics. Travis neglects this political argument and puts forward an economic argument of very

3. This is truer in the United States than elsewhere, having thicker seams of coal. European mining, and especially coal mining, has been traditionally more labour intensive, but modern mechanization is altering this.

Table 9 Import duties according to production sector for five countries, 1950s or 1960

Industry and group	Average level of import duties (% ad valorem)				
	US 1960	UK 1958	Japan 1960	Germany 1953–1955	France 1953–1955
intermediate primary	2	0	0–5	—	—
food	1	0	} 4·5	25	23
agricultural materials	18	0		6	8
intermediate manufacturing	6	10	13–20	—	—
chemicals	24	15	—	13	19
final manufactures	20	20–33	8–33	13	18
food products	12	—	—	—	—
clothing	32·5	26	—	13	26
final primary (tertiary) services	0	0	0	0	0

UK figures are not averages but the most common level. German and French 'agricultural materials' include minerals apart from fuels
Source: PEP (1959)

doubtful validity to explain the place of agriculture in the economies of the developed countries. This is that the 'most favourable agricultural land lies between the thirtieth and fiftieth parallels . . . good agricultural land is virtually a North American and Western European monopoly' (Travis, 1964, pp. 242–3), i.e. of the most developed countries. Even if the first statement were correct, we must include Argentina, Uruguay, South Africa, Southern Australia (including nearly all of New South Wales and Victoria), New Zealand, much of Eastern Europe and Western Asia and North Africa, and, if not the whole of China, most of the Yangtse valley plus Manchuria, all of which lie between these latitudes. Moreover, to exclude from 'good agricultural land' the Ganges plain, the Punjab and the river valleys of Burma, Thailand and Indo-China, none of which lie between the thirtieth and fiftieth parallels, seems peculiarly perverse.

Travis thus refers back to the arguments of the physiocrats, à la Schumpeter, to explain the protection of agriculture in what he calls the 'landed nations' of North America and Western Europe. The underdevelopment of the rest of the world is supposedly due to their poor land. Agriculture and raw-material production only *appear* to be labour-intensive because the 'non-landed nations must employ nearly their entire labour force in an attempt to secure food' (1964, p. 245). The situation is aggravated today, Travis concludes, by the protectionist policies of the 'non-landed nations' in restricting the import of capital-intensive heavy manufactures that would enable them to develop their own labour-intensive industries. 'Only landed countries can industrialize through protection,' he concludes, 'because only they can afford it.'

Thus, trade is a 'vent for surplus', in Adam Smith's phrase – a surplus of labour – paradoxically in the richest lands, but because of faulty policies of a protectionist nature there is no corresponding surplus to exchange arriving in the poorer lands. This fits well with Myint's thesis (1958, p. 317), that there were once unused resources of land and labour in the poorer lands lying idle for want of trading opportunities. These were developed by trade, primary products being exported and in exchange manufactures imported. Since, however, there was no intersectoral shift of resources in the poor country, what happened was the destruction of handcrafts and the specialization of the economy on production of raw materials and food, partly for home consumption and partly for export. As populations grew, then, without land-saving technical progress, the exportable surplus of food was used up. This seemed the more likely to be true because these countries were assumed to be agriculturally poor. Handcrafts, which might have formed the basis for new labour-intensive products to sell to the developed countries, had been destroyed; and sales from labour-intensive industries were obstructed by the commercial policies of the developed countries.

This last line of argument has a strong element of truth in it. Although attempts have been made through UNCTAD to reduce the rich countries' tariffs applied against the industrial products of the poor, and even to give them preference, the results so far have been limited. Even the EEC's apparently generous offer in 1971 of free movement of certain goods into the Community from poor countries was limited to the ceiling of total imports of these goods as of 1968, and exempted textiles which form the largest potential manufacturing export of the poor countries.[4] Keynesian measures of world-wide demand management have been conspicuously rejected by the rich countries at UNCTAD Conferences (Kaldor, Hart and Tinbergen, 1964, vol. 2).

The theses of Travis and Myint bear some resemblance to those Keynesian views concerning the importance of geo-politics and 'vents' for surplus. It still leaves the relationship only half explained; the underdeveloped world is not, in fact, short of good agricultural land, the developed capitalist world is not so self-sufficient in natural resources and Travis has a footnote in his book that concedes this (1964, p. 244). The incorporation into the capitalist world, not only of North America but of Argentina, South Africa and Oceania, was precisely to develop their lands. Finally, it is not only these countries, but Japan, the USSR and Eastern Europe, also, which have industrialized behind protective barriers, and China is in process of doing so.

It remains unexplained why labour could not be used inside the capitalistically developed lands without the protection of their labour-intensive industries against labour-intensive products from outside, and why, in addition to duties on labour-intensive imports, and imports competing with labour-intensive industry, a whole battery of protective measures grew up as capitalism in the developed countries evolved monopolistic tendencies. For protection of the home market has as its corollary a monopolistic position for national capital in the home market. The larger the market, of course, the more firms it has room for. Schumpeter thought there were very definite diseconomies of scale as firms increased in size, so that economies of scale would not lead to one or two firms in each industry (Schumpeter, 1955, p. 88). This is almost precisely what it has led to. The introduction of computers has greatly increased the span of control of one individual, but the trend was there before the computer. Even though falling short of full monopoly, oligopoly and oligopolistic competition have not produced the kind of free market conditions which Schumpeter predicted as typical of capitalism and guaranteeing its peaceful

4. For a fuller discussion of this see Barratt Brown (1972a, pp. 137–56).

development. 'In particular, the rise of trusts and cartels – a phenomenon quite different from the trend to large-scale production with which it is often confused – can never be explained by the automatism of the capitalist system.'

If monopolistic practices, especially in exporting, cannot be explained directly by the large scale of production, they can be explained indirectly by the large scale of finance required for such production. In a competitive world market the protection of large investments was bound to become a necessity. This was the argument of the Marxist, Rudolf Hilferding.[5] National economic development for those countries that would succeed Britain in industrialization required state support for monopolistic positions for national industries, first, in the home market, and then, in export markets. Hilferding may have exaggerated the role of the banks, but the integration of the state and industry through the mediation of the bankers into a conscious policy of capitalist expansion was true of Germany and of other continental European countries and even of America (see Cole and Deane, 1965, pp. 17–20; Landes, 1965, p. 576).

Such policies are easily accepted by the Keynesians as examples of mercantilism. They had been foreshadowed by Friedrich List and were widely accepted as forms of neo-mercantilism in the 1880s. They were probably inevitable for any 'late developers', but had obvious implications of rivalry between states. International cartel agreements to divide up the world's markets served only as a temporary truce in a continuing war, which Hilferding believed would certainly lead to military conflict. Hilferding saw this primarily as a struggle for protected fields of development, not just for markets, as Rosa Luxemburg saw it; and the development which Hilferding identified was the actual capitalist development going on in the lands of European settlement, not the extraction of raw materials from lands that remained underdeveloped.

Control over competition in the home market by way of financial associations can be discovered in the early trusts in the

5. Hilferding's argument is fully summarized and criticized in Sweezy (1942, pp. 258–69, 294–306).

USA that led to the Sherman anti-trust act of 1890, in the network of *Kartelle* in Germany in the 1880s and in the terminable associations of manufacturers in Britain of the same period. All writers on monopoly attribute this to the attempt at this time to establish monopolistic positions in face of increased international competition, and associate it with the movement for national protection in the home market (Clapham, 1930, vol. 3, pp. 221–36; Macrosty, 1907, p. 23; Moody, 1904).

What, then, was the reason for the failure of the campaign for tariff reform and imperial preference in England at the beginning of the twentieth century? This failure suggests a very lively sense of the advantages of free trade, not only benefiting England but also perhaps those countries which found markets in Britain in the second half of the nineteenth century and thus earned foreign exchange with which to advance their industrialization. If the countries that failed to industrialize were not so poorly endowed as Travis asserts, then they must have suffered from some special internal problems of development. Argentina might be taken as a test case. The countries settled by capitalist 'kith and kin' did develop industrially, and the British economy did appear to benefit at least as much from their successful development as from Argentina's or India's failure. In other words, despite the protection that the dominions applied in order to nourish their infant industries, British economic development, far from suffering a setback from the competition of new industrial centres, appeared to benefit from it. The fact was that Britain's exports to these developing countries grew as fast as they did to those that were not developing, even though the former were protecting their own industries (see table 19). This would seem to be the main reason for Britain's continuing free trade policy right up to the 1930s, and long after the ending of her monopoly of trade as the world's workshop. Was it justified, and how was it justified at the time? Were there not other colonial advantages which the Marxists would wish to assert?

The answer to the questions raised may best be examined by noting the forces that lined up in Britain on either side of the tariff reform controversy at the beginning of the twentieth century. Already in 1844 Robert Torrens, fearing the 'hostile tariffs of foreign rivals' had, as we saw earlier, proposed 'a British Commercial league – a Colonial *zollverein*', with a system of imperial preference, and called for a statesman to carry forth this programme. Over fifty years later the statesman appeared in the person of Joseph Chamberlain, and the programme was almost the same, falling short of full *zollverein*, a common external tariff and common tax system being by then regarded as impossible to impose upon self-governing dominions. In the meantime, the 'hostile tariffs of foreign rivals' had indeed challenged Britain's foreign trade. The United States market declined after the 1860s from taking a share of nearly one fifth of Britain's exports to a figure of less than one tenth. United States' and German steel, moreover, was being dumped in the British market, as a result of the protectionist policies of these countries; and to this British steelmakers could not retaliate. The free entry of North American grain was providing a larger and larger proportion of Britain's food consumption at the expense of British agriculture, yet British manufactures had no reciprocal advantages in the North American market.

Chamberlain, the Birmingham radical social reformer, had joined the Tories with the great Whig landlords against Gladstone's proposed Home Rule for Ireland. He not only represented the Midlands engineering industry but he had a direct interest in the colonies through his shares in the Royal Niger Company and his friendship with Rhodes, and had chosen to be Colonial Secretary when he entered Lord Salisbury's government in 1895. In 1902 he called the self-governing colonies together at an Imperial Conference and, although he failed to obtain their assistance towards the cost of imperial defence, he won support for a system of imperial trade preference. The small duty on corn introduced in 1901 by Ritchie, the President of the Board of Trade, was designed only to collect revenue to help pay for the Boer War, but it was seen by Chamberlain as a thin end of a larger wedge. When the duty was withdrawn in 1903, Chamberlain resigned from the Cabinet to stump the country for a programme of tariff reform that would unite the empire, provide the revenue for social reform and protect British steel and agriculture.

It was not difficult, then, for Chamberlain to win the support of the squirearchy in the House of Commons. Smaller landowners like Walter Long, a later Colonial Secretary, and Henry Chaplin were active members of the Tariff Reform League. But some of the great landlords hesitated. Cavendish reneged on earlier promises to Chamberlain (so much for the Schumpeter thesis in this instance!). The leaders of heavy industry – mainly in steel – gave the most consistent support, especially Sir Vincent Caillard, Chairman of Vickers, but they included also the Chairmen of Armstrong Whitworth, of Bessemer and of Guest Keen. Chamberlain had the 'jingo' press behind him led by Arthur Pearson, and even *The Times* carried the articles by Hewins that inaugurated the campaign. Hewins, who had devoted his life to the study of mercantilism, was Chamberlain's chief academic adviser, and resigned from his directorship of the LSE to become Secretary of the Tariff Commission and, in effect, Chamberlain's right-hand man; but he had allies also among the economic historians, Professors Cunningham and Ashley and in Professor Mackinder, the geographer. Chamberlain even had the support of social reformers like Charles Booth and could rely on the Liberal Imperialists led by Lord Rosebery for friends in the Opposition camp. It sounds an impressive list, and yet, although at one stage Balfour's Cabinet agreed by a large majority to give the colonies preference on a one shilling Corn Duty, Chamberlain failed.

It may be that some of these allies were doubtful assets. It can be argued even that the labours of Hewins, a social *parvenu*, a Catholic and an inveterate intriguer, were actually counterproductive.[6] His campaign was nevertheless the first to be conducted in British politics with statistics effectively deployed (though Chamberlain tended to make his up) and with serious academic research going into the work of the Tariff Commission. Much of the fire went out of the campaign, moreover, with Chamberlain's stroke in 1905, after which he took little

6. This is the view of Peter Lowe with whom I have been associated in the study of the Hewins Papers in the Sheffield University Library. Much of this paragraph is based on these papers as well as on Hewins's own autobiography (1929).

part in public life, although he did not die until 1914. However that may be, it was another thirty years before another representative of Midlands Steel should carry imperial preference.

Chamberlain's appeal was, first and foremost, to the British worker, and if it failed we must understand why. Social imperialism appeared to be a powerful force. It had been exploited by Bismarck in Germany as Chamberlain had observed, presumably because workers in Germany had actually benefited from protection. Why not in Britain? Import duties, said Chamberlain, were to be used to finance old age pensions and increased public services. The repatriation of profits from overseas in the 1880s and 1890s was widely understood to have expanded the home market. The Fabian imperialists not only believed in 'the "Socialist" goal of breeding an "imperial race"' but were ardent 'neo-mercantilists' in the Keynesian sense of believing in the management of the economy to maintain full employment. Tariffs were an essential part of that management, although the Fabians pulled back at the prospect of food taxes replacing income taxes, since this would mean putting the costs of social reform upon the people themselves (Semmell, 1960, pp. 138–40, 164–5).

The difference between Britain and Germany was that Britain already had the colonies, with their protected markets and preferential opportunities for investment, and Germany had not. What more could Chamberlain add to the support for employers and workers in British industry that they did not already enjoy? They had the markets *and* the imperial interest to overlay class divisions. Social imperialism in Germany was connected with the demand for colonies and not with protection, even for export industries, which had proved a poor weapon in the years of depression after 1873. The fact that this demand was regarded by Bismarck, according to his son, as a 'concern for domestic politics' has been seen as strengthening the case for non-economic explanations of imperialism (Wehler, 1972, pp. 79–92). Further strength is adduced from the claim of President Cleveland that United States expansion in Latin America was not a question of foreign policy, but 'the most distinct of home questions' (Wehler, 1972, p. 87); and similar statements can be quoted from Napoleon III and from Russian statesmen in the 1890s (p. 91). Wehler, from whose work these references are taken, makes it clear, however, that the origin of social imperialism, at least in Germany, was economic – not just the depression of the early 1880s, but the general 'unsteadiness' and 'unevenness of economic growth' which made 'rational business calculation impossible' (p. 76). He quotes the comment of the French Ambassador in Berlin as typical of German decision-makers in the mid-1880s: 'Overproduction drives Germany to seek the acquisition of colonies' (p. 80).

Who then, in Britain, was opposed to Chamberlain's campaign? The Cobdenite liberals were marshalled in all their fury with the classical economists, Professors Marshall, Cannan, Edgeworth, Pigou and Clapham behind them. Many industrial traders still saw their strength in a market of the whole world and were content with their privileges in the non self-governing colonies. India alone was still taking a sixth of Britain's exports. These industrialists included the coal owners, the cotton industry and shipbuilding and engineering employers, who also enjoyed the advantages of cheap German and American steel. The Trades Union Congress supported them and, perhaps most important, the City of London threw in its great weight against Chamberlain. As Keynes, in his essay on *The Economic Consequences of the Peace* (1920, pp. 9–10) was to emphasize, the 'now almost unrecognizable internationalization of the economy', that existed prior to the First World War, was still a reality. British capital abroad no longer depended on manufacturing industry's exports. It derived from the income of past investments which was then applied to the promotion and management of foreign loans, to brokerage and insurance and the issue of bills to finance the world's trade. British finance had then no need to cultivate the lesser field of empire, when the whole world was still open to it, when the London capital market was preponderant and when sterling was as good as gold.

Britain before 1914 was still far behind her rivals – the USA and Germany – in the development of monopolies. This development was to follow in the 1920s. Marx (1935c) had insisted from the 1840s that free trade and not protection was of the essence of British capitalism. Schumpeter built this view into his model of 'pure capitalism'. Yet the world in which British capital was operating was increasingly a world of monopolies, trusts and cartels. Hewins always insisted that tariff reform did not mean protection but rather a preferential system of Empire free trade. Given the historic links of Britain with the self-governing colonies, and the direct British control exercised over the non self-governing colonies, such a system almost existed *de facto* without new institutions or imperial preference. By contrast, Germany and the United States had to fight their way into the world market. Monopolies and trusts at home, cartels and concessions and colonies overseas were used to this end and forced Britain, in response, to extend the territory of her empire in the last decades of the nineteenth century. Protection and preferential markets may be seen economically, then, as a product of inter-capitalist competition. This is our understanding of mercantilist policies, as they were developed in the nineteenth century.

Control over raw-material sources became increasingly at the end of the century a key element in the integrated operations of trans-national companies. It was sought on strategic grounds by the states in which those companies were based. The vertical integration of the oil companies with state support, as in the case of the British Government's purchase of shares in Anglo Persian oil, provides only one example among many. It is worth reminding ourselves here that in the 1930s the argument between the 'haves' and the 'have nots' was not an argument between rich and poor countries but was an argument between Britain and France and the USA on the one hand, Germany, Italy and Japan on the other, i.e. among already developed capitalist states. What the first had, and the second had not, was colonies and privileged markets and sources of raw-material supplies.

The Keynesian model of a disguised mercantilism provides a partial explanation of most of the facts of Britain's nineteenth-century development, just as open mercantilism explains the growth of her rivals. It does not explain the failure of Chamberlain's campaign for imperial preference, which should surely have succeeded on a Keynesian view, unless it is said that disguised mercantilism did not need to be revealed openly. The fact is that mutual preferences in the trade with the dominions, just those empty lands of European settlement, upon whose development the Keynesian argument depends, failed. This suggests not only that in Britain finance had attained a certain hegemony over industrial capital, as Keynes himself supposed, and as Robinson insists (1966b, p. 20), but also that the integration of the labour of the nonself-governing colonies, and even of the dominions, amounted not only to a market relationship but to a productive system.

Chamberlain introduced Chinese coolie labour into the South African goldfields, and near slave-labour continued to be employed in them thercafter (see Barratt Brown, 1970a, p. 167). Such labour provided little or no effective demand for British exports, but the surplus accruing to British capital was increased. The first years of the twentieth century saw the rapid development of overseas mining and plantations to meet the needs of the motor car for tin, copper, rubber and oil as well as the growing consumption in Britain of sugar, tea and coffee. With this followed colonial port and railway building. Indentured Indian labour was imported into Malaya, the Straits Settlements and Ceylon as well as into Assam, Trinidad, British Guiana, Jamaica, East Africa, Mauritius and Fiji (Knowles, 1928, pp. 182–201). Whether this seemed to be more important to British industrialists than the development of the Dominions, it was certainly so regarded by German, Dutch and American industry in this period (1928, p. 178).

Apart from the direct colonial rule established by Britain throughout the nineteenth century, and by other European countries and the USA at the end of the century, it is possible to identify spheres of influence in other nominally independent countries. These can all be measured in terms of shares of the metropolitan countries' exports of manufactured goods against imports of mainly primary products and shares of the metropolitan countries' exports of capital. In table 10 we can see the association in both trade and investment of Britain with the Empire, of the USA with Canada and Latin America, of Germany with Europe, of France with her colonies (and especially with Africa), of Japan with non-British Asia and of the Soviet Union with Eastern Europe. There is a marked change in the 1960s, with the emergence of a new trend of increased trade and investment between the developed capitalist countries themselves at the expense of their old relationships with the underdeveloped areas. A major reason was the sharp decline in the share of primary products in world trade (see chapter 9).

Protection and preference have been essential factors in the development of national centres of industry wherever these have been achieved by capitalism. Where, however, one state like Britain in the first two-thirds of the nineteenth century, or the USA after 1940, had overwhelming economic superiority, then free trade was nationally advantageous for it. New competitors had to cut into the game by claiming their own preferential spheres of influence. Even then the protection of agriculture and of labour-intensive industries at home became politically essential to support the full employment of industrial workers at home and to retain the support of the conservative farm vote. That capitalism failed in the absence of protection to maintain full employment in industrially developed economies has still to be explained. The thesis of 'landed' nations has been found to be inadequate. They should have found it easiest to develop without protection and did in the end find ways to manage their economies with minimal protection. Such protection has to be explained within the capitalist system and not, *pace* Schumpeter and the classical liberal economists, as a hangover of an earlier mercantilism. It has much more in common with Keynesian economic management within the nation state. Why then, have Keynesian measures of demand management not been applied on a global basis? The Marxist answer is that the competitive drive for accumulation of private capital cannot be so rationally controlled. Competition compels the search for preferential positions. But that is the subject of the next chapter.

Table 10 Chief foreign markets and location of foreign investment for certain countries, 1770s to 1970s

Years	Main areas of exports (%)	Main areas of capital investment (%)
Great Britain		
to 1770s	Europe 75–80, N and C America 15–20	capital imported
1800–1820s	Europe 40, N and C America 40	Europe 30
1830–1850s	Europe 40, Empire 30	Europe 25, USA 30
1860–1870s	Europe 40, Empire 33	Europe 20, Empire 40
1900–1910s	Europe 35, Empire 35	Empire 50 (Dominions 30), Latin America 25
1920–1930s	Europe 38, Empire 43	Empire 60 (Dominions 35)
1950–1960s	Europe 30, Empire 45	Empire 60 (Dominions 40)
1970	Europe 45, Empire 25	Empire 50 (Dominions 45), Europe 20
USA		
to 1870s	Europe 60–70, Latin America 25	capital imported
1870–1880	Europe 80, Latin America 10	capital imported
1900–1910s	Europe 70, Latin America 15, Canada 15	capital imported
1920–1930s	Europe 45, Latin America 15, Canada 15	Latin America 42, Canada 27, Europe 20
1950–1960s	Europe 33, Canada 20, Latin America 20	Latin America 35, Canada 30, Europe 25
1970	Europe 35, Canada 22, Asia 24	Europe 50, Canada 30, Latin America 12
France		
1890s	UK 30, other W Europe 40	Europe 39, Russia and Turkey 32
1910s	UK 20, other W Europe 40	Europe 29, Russia and Turkey 32, Colonies 10
1920s	UK 15, other W Europe 40, Colonies 30	Colonies 70
1950–1960s	W Europe 33, (EEC 26), Colonies 30	Colonies 80

Germany

1890s	UK 20, other W Europe 33	capital imported
1910s	UK 15, other W Europe 30, non-industrial 28	Africa?
1920s	UK 10, other W Europe 35, non-industrial 31	capital imported
1950–1960s	W Europe 45 (EEC 28), non-industrial 29	non-industrial 70

Japan

1910s	USA 30, Europe 20, non-British Asia 34	capital imported
1920–1930s	USA 40, non-British Asia 40, British Empire 20	
1950s	USA 15, British Empire 45, non-British Asia 35	
1970	USA 30, British Empire 30, non-British Asia 25	export credits to underdeveloped countries

Russia, USSR

1913	UK 18, Germany 30, other Europe 27	capital imported
1920s	UK 28, Germany 21, other Europe 15	
1930s	UK 27, Germany 10, other Europe 19	
1950s	East Europe 57, China 18, other Asia 7	
1960s	East Europe 56, China 6, other Asia 8	
1970	East Europe 53, China 5, other Asia 9	

Sources: see table 17 and Barratt Brown (1973)

8 Capital Export

The Marxist argument that replaced Marx's own insistence on free trade as the main form of capitalist expansion, was the thesis of capital export to protected areas providing the basis of imperialism as a new stage of capitalism. The surplus of capital in the most advanced industrial countries led to the search for new profitable opportunities for accumulation overseas. The new stage of 'monopoly capitalism' was reached sometime after 1870 and the great expansion of European colonies thereafter was to be explained from this conjuncture. The idea of a major turn after the 1870s to foreign investment seemed plausible in view of the expansion of overseas investment at the end of the century, first of English capital and secondly of other European capital. This was well documented at the time especially in England, thanks to Sir Robert Giffen's studies which Hobson drew upon in his work on imperialism (1938, pp. 61–3). Subsequent studies have shown that Giffen even underestimated the increase in British overseas investment in the two decades after 1880 (Imlah, 1958, p. 78). The process, moreover, continued after the turn of the century with other European countries joining in, so that a recent estimate showed that all European foreign investments had been raised from about six to forty-four billion dollars between 1874 and 1914. Roughly three quarters were British in the first year and 40 per cent in the last year, France and Germany by then accounting for respectively 10 per cent and 12·5 per cent, Netherlands, Switzerland, Belgium and the US for most of the rest (UN, 1949).

Although the absolute amounts added to capital stocks abroad grew with each decade, and new countries were increasingly involved, the most rapid rate of growth was, never-

Table 11 European countries' foreign investment stock, 1854–1914 ($m)

Year	Britain	France	Germany	Others	Total (approx.)
1854	1100	—	—	—	1200
1862	1900	—	—	—	2000
1874	5000	1000	—	—	6500
1885	7000	3500	—	—	12 000
1900	11 000	5600	1450	4000	22 000
1913	18 300	8700	5600	11 400	44 000

Sources: Imlah (1958, table 4); Feis (1930); UN (1949)

theless, in the 1860s and early 1870s, and accounted for largely by British capital.

The idea of a new stage after 1870 was so easily accepted because for many reasons 1870 seemed to be a turning point in the nineteenth century and especially for Britain. The great depression that followed 1874 brought to an end a period of fifty years of almost unbroken boom (Ensor, 1936, p. 136). Industrial output in Britain never grew as fast again although the growth of the real national product recovered at the end of the century[1] (and again in the 1950s). In fact, this implied a growth in service industries as living standards rose, but for manufacturing industrialists it seemed a period of disaster. Prices and profits fell continuously for almost twenty years, and the causes were examined by no less than three great Commissions of Enquiry into the Depression of Trade and Industry successively in 1886, 1887–8 and 1894–7. Competition from the United States and Germany had not only reduced Britain's position as workshop of the world but was making inroads into the British market itself. The conclusion, and not only of Marxist historians, was that after 1870 British capital

1. See Deane and Cole (1964, tables 73, 74 and 77), which use Feinstein's figures (1961), and which really settle the argument between Coppock and Phelps-Brown concerning the dating of Britain's economic 'climacteric' in favour of the latter's choice of the 1890s and not the 1870s. See Phelps-Brown and Handfield-Jones (1952) and Coppock (1956).

was forced into mergers at home and investment in the empire overseas (Dobb, 1946, p. 311).

The association between empire building, capital export and the new monopolistic practices in industry – all following upon the great depression of the 1870s – had, then, an obvious plausibility. Hobson, looking back at the turn of the century, and considering the causes of the Boer War and the scramble for African colonies, found the 'tap-root of imperialism' in the congestion of capital looking for profitable investment opportunities overseas after the concentration of industry had reduced opportunities at home (Hobson, 1938, ch. 6). Lenin, on the basis of Hobson's work and of Hilferding's study of finance capital, developed the concept of imperialism as a higher stage of capitalism (Lenin, 1933; Hilferding, 1923). The main objective of the export of capital was, in Lenin's view, the winning of what he called 'colonial super-profits'. The desire for capital export arose not so much from a failure of consumption at home to grow, as Hobson suggested, but from competition between rival capitalist states for control over markets and raw material sources overseas.

Capital export might simply have been the result of growing shortages of primary products at home (Fieldhouse, 1967, p. 188); but Hobson insisted that it was the maldistribution of income in Britain that led to excessive savings and inadequate consumption and drove capital to find new opportunities overseas (1938, p. 83). Hobson believed that capitalist states could redistribute income more equally, if the state was prepared to guarantee a return to capital inside as well as outside the home market (1938, p. 105). Lenin had no such illusions, but saw capital export in terms of cheap land and cheap labour to be exploited, and opportunities for 'finance capital to spread its net over all countries of the world' (1933, ch. 4), as 'monopoly capital' became increasingly centralized.

For Hobson, as for Hilferding, the role of the state was crucial in assuring the incentive to invest. That is, of course, a very Keynesian view of the matter and in absolute contradiction to the classical liberal view according to which no such intervention should have been necessary. But the Keynesians have raised some crucial questions about the meaning to be assigned to capital exports (Knapp, 1957, p. 132). In chapter 6 we noted that the surpluses on Britain's annual current balance of payments, which represent net capital exports, arose in the ninety years after 1825 not from the trading account in goods and services, but from partial reinvestment of interest and dividends due to British citizens (see table 7). Knapp, taking the hint from Keynes's estimate of the 1913 value of Drake's Treasure at compound interest, makes the point that during the forty year period between 1874 and 1914 – which was the heyday of foreign investment – 'the total of the estimated capital exports (of Britain, France and Germany) roughly equalled their aggregate income from the investments'. 'The average annual income,' he adds, 'was about 5 per cent' (Knapp, 1957, p. 438).[2] As Knapp emphasizes, it was a *partial* reinvestment of income over the whole period from 1815 to 1914. After 1825, income generally exceeded reinvestment, although there was a twenty-year period between 1855 and 1875 when it fell below. These were the years of most rapid overseas accumulation. Between 1875 and 1914 there was, in effect, no capital export overall. There was, however, once more, a steady switching of income from one area into investment in another.

Knapp concludes that capital exports were not so much financing a real transfer of goods and services as a steadily rising indebtedness in the borrowing countries. To the extent that this was so, capital exports did not then represent real assets but only paper assets. This is confirmed by the fact that about half of British overseas capital investment consisted of loans to governments or to mixed public and private enterprises. Moreover, 70 per cent of the total was for social overhead capital, i.e. railways, public utilities and other public works which frequently had government guarantees (Simon, 1967, p. 42). Nearly all of French and German capital exports consisted of government to government loans (Thomas, 1967, p. 11), although it was at the turn of the century that German electrical firms began to establish subsidiaries in other European countries (Feis, 1930, p. 78).

2. Knapp is using figures from the United Nations (1949, p. 1).

Table 12 Growth of UK and French capital abroad, 1815–1913 (annual averages, absolute increase and percentage compound increase by decades and rate of return on UK capital)

Decade	UK capital			French capital	
	Absolute increase £m	Compound increase (%)	Average rate of return	Absolute increase (billion francs)	Compound increase (%)
1815–1825	88	26·0	4·6	—	—
1826–1835	43	3·9	3·5	—	—
1836–1845	42	2·7	4·5	—	—
1846–1855	64	3·0	4·7	—	—
1856–1865	241	7·0	5·0	—	—
1866–1875	575	8·0	5·1	5[a]	4·0
1876–1885	432	3·4	4·7	5[b]	3·0
1886–1895	698	3·9	4·7	8[c]	3·4
1896–1905	447	2·0	4·3⎫	17[d]	3·5
1906–1913	1348	5·3	5·0⎭		

[a] 1869–1880
[b] 1880–1890
[c] 1890–1900
[d] 1900–1917

Rate of return is calculated from interest and dividends as a percentage of accumulated capital abroad in the middle of each period
Sources: Imlah (1958, table 4); Feis (1930, pp. 23–4)

Capital export between 1874 and 1914 did not consist primarily of investment overseas by increasingly monopolistic industrial combines. The connection between 'finance capitalists' and governments in Lenin's thesis could still suggest a reason for infrastructural development to secure privileged markets and sources of raw materials, and indeed to provide a generally favourable climate for the remaining proportion of overseas investment in the extractive, manufacturing and commercial activities of large companies. Moreover, where the exports of borrowing countries were reduced in value (and probably in volume) by conditions of slump in the lending countries, the continuation of a given level of imports and of savings by the borrowing countries might require further borrowing from abroad. Hence in Knapp's argument there was 'excess borrowing' during this period, due to a failure not of domestic saving but of domestic lending in the borrowing countries, either because of the undeveloped state of the banking system and capital market in these countries or because of 'a tradition that capital should come in from abroad' (1957, p. 436).

Knapp's argument is designed to show that there is little evidence for a real transfer of resources needed for growth in developing countries. The example that he gives of the capital movements between Britain and Argentina shows the huge size of the 'excess borrowing' (1959, pp. 593–6). Only a third of the sum provided by British loans to Argentina in the 1880s was needed to cover Argentina's foreign payments deficits in those years. The rest financed the local costs of railway and port building, thus greatly increasing Argentina's indebtedness. According to another calculation, 'Argentina's exports expanded six times between 1881–1885 and 1910–1914, whilst imports expanded five times and foreign debt service eight times' (Ford, 1958, p. 589).

Such excessive flows of capital suggest not only the dependence of underdeveloped primary producing countries on the level of economic activity in the more developed industrial countries, but also a certain pressure of savings in the latter for investment opportunities. None of the income from overseas *needed* to be reinvested overseas. Most of the capital exports from Britain consisted of the portfolio holdings of rentiers. The most obvious explanation for increased foreign investment would be a higher rate of return. In table 12 we saw that the average return on all British overseas investment was around 5 per cent. By contrast the yield on consols shown in table 13 was not much over 3 per cent in this period, following the same course of fall and rise. The rate of profit on industrial capital at home stood at a much higher figure, despite its steady fall after 1874. Rates of return overseas could not then have been the attraction.

The aim of such holdings was security of income. It was easy for rentiers to buy stock through solicitors and bankers; and the British capital market was well organized and strongly oriented towards foreign stocks. Indeed, they formed the very

Table 13 National income, investment and rates of profit, Great Britain 1865–1913

Period	National income (£m)	Investment percentage of national income			Yield consols (100 = 3·2%)	Percentage rate of profit on industrial capital	Percentage of share profit in industrial income
		Foreign	Home	Total			
1865–1869	845	4·5	6·2	10·7	102	16·5	46
1870–1874	1060	6·9	6·4	13·4	100	18·6	47·7
1875–1879	1080	2·4	7·7	10·2	98	15·2	43·4
1880–1884	1140	5·0	5·7	10·8	93	14·7	42·6
1885–1889	1215	6·5	3·8	10·3	92	15·0	42·2
1890–1894	1360	4·7	4·2	8·9	88	13·5	37·8
1895–1899	1560	2·7	5·9	8·6	82	15·2	40
1900–1904	1720	2·2	8·2	10·4	88	12·7	39
1905–1909	1880	6·7	5·2	11·9	90	11·9	39·4
1910–1913	2120	9·3	4·1	13·4	101	12·1	40·2

Source: Feinstein (1960; 1961; 1972)

heart of the operations of the City of London (Brown, 1965, p. 56). Apart from the premium that made these stocks attractive to the issuing houses, they had a government guarantee whether from Indian, colonial or foreign governments. Most German and French capital exports of this period were also state guaranteed or state issues, so that even where the state did not provide direct protection for capital at home, it did provide or obtain this protection abroad.

It is in the years between 1880 and 1894, and again after 1905, that we have to explain why British investors chose to invest abroad as much as or more than at home. Some foreign issues were certainly made more attractive because of the premiums at which they were issued. But how far were the two types of issues – foreign and home – seen as real alternatives? The waves of foreign and home investment appear to alternate – foreign investment ahead in the early 1870s, 1880s and early 1890s and 1910s, home investment ahead in the 1870s, late 1890s and 1900s. But these alternations have to be understood both in relation to the amplitudes of *total* investment – high in the early 1870s, low in the 1880s, lower still in the 1890s and high again after 1905 (see table 13) – and in terms of the type of investment involved. Rentiers who invested abroad were not apparently attracted by investment in home industry (Feinstein, 1960). To the extent that they switched from home to foreign investment and back, they were moving between one set of government stock or government guaranteed stock and another. The home issues that rentiers went for were railways and local government stock. Industry at home raised its funds, *not* through the Stock Exchange, but by reinvestment and local borrowing. The risks of industry were not for the rentiers.

The main additions to home investment when they came were occasioned by local authorities borrowing to meet the new responsibilities laid upon them by the Education, Housing and Public Health Acts of the 1870s (Feinstein, 1960). Overseas investments, as we have seen, were in railways and other public utilities in the USA, in Australia, in Latin America and in India – most of them Government loans or loans carrying government guarantees. When even governments overseas failed to redeem their promises, the rentiers lost money and were scared away until memories were dimmed and new expectations aroused. The very heavy outflow of capital in certain years could be absorbed in the national balance of payments over the long period because, despite failures and excess lending, development did take place in some countries overseas and investments did then begin to pay (Ford, 1965, p. 22). Not all the failures took place at the same time; accumulation was continuous.

For this reason, it appeared to Cairncross that the big waves of investment overseas could perhaps be explained by movements in the terms of trade – as overseas prices rise, overseas investment should rise; as home prices rise, home investment should rise (1953, p. 208). But the facts are otherwise. According to Thomas, 'The three major surges in foreign investment between 1860 and 1913 shared one common feature: in the second half of the boom when capital exports were at their heaviest and moving towards the peak, the terms of trade were moving sharply in favour of Britain, i.e. 1868–72, 1883–90 and 1910–13' (1967, p. 27). Movements in the terms of trade have therefore to be seen as 'a consequence of the fundamental forces at work rather than a causal factor'. What were these forces? If full employment were assumed at home and abroad, shifts of investment could be seen, as the neo-classical economists see them, in terms of changing return to capital, when techniques of supply and consumption patterns of demand change. But the Marxists and Keynesians cannot assume that Say's Law operates and that new technology is necessarily applied.

There were potential alternative investment opportunities at home arising from new technology – in the development of the electrical industry, for example, in which British capital was exceedingly slow to engage. This is not the place to examine the long time-lag in Britain between the fundamental discoveries and their application in industry but the lag seems to have arisen out of the historical conditions of capitalist accumulation – the small family firms, the existence of vested capital in existing technology, the unpreparedness of rentiers to risk their capital in industry at home and a general lack of initiative in third- and fourth-generation family firms where technical and financial management had become separated (Bernal, 1953, ch. 6). This was an aspect of the continued small scale of British industrial enterprises. The monopolies and large-scale industrial units of Lenin's essay were not to emerge in Britain until the 1920s. Although they did exist in the USA and in Germany much earlier, these countries were also exporting capital by the end of the nineteenth century.

The export of capital is closely associated with the export of capital goods. These became increasingly important in Britain's total exports. Between 1850 and 1890 textiles fell from 63 per cent to 43 per cent of the total; metal and engineering products rose from 18 per cent to 25 per cent (E. A. G. Robinson, 1954, p. 540). It appears (Ford, 1965), that in Britain between 1870 and 1913 exports as a proportion of imports moved very closely in line with the long waves of foreign investment. If Say's Law operated, exports could be expected to lead to investment by creating the necessary surplus on the balance of payments. In fact, the evidence is to the contrary. When the deviations from the long waves are examined it is found that British investment overseas *followed* fluctuations in Britain's exports and in world trade by one or two years. Cyclical movements in incomes and employment in Britain had as their main immediate cause the fluctuations in exports; there is no similar correlation with changes in home investment. Ford concludes that, since a certain value of investment going abroad would be expected, at least in the short run, to raise home employment and incomes by less than a similar sum invested at home, 'a considerable part of *ex ante* overseas lending was financed from idle holdings so that exports rose by more than the initial fall in home spending, if any, and transmitted expansionary force to incomes' (Ford, 1965, p. 29). This would be amplified by the general upsurge of overseas activity encouraged by the increased overseas lending (Brown, 1965, p. 53). The direction of investment at home into industry or development by local authorities, and abroad into mining and industry or development by foreign governments, cannot, therefore, be separated from the overall rate of accumulation (on the Marxist view) or the overall level of savings (on the Keynesian view).

As a criticism of the Marxist view, it might still be asked why British exports of goods did not expand faster over the whole period 1870–1914, especially the export of capital goods. For, on the Marxist view, it is the overproduction in the capital goods industries which would be typical of a chronic crisis of capital accumulation; the main element in the decline in Britain's share of world exports after the 1880s was, in fact, in capital goods. In the 1880s, however, Britain was already exporting about 44 per cent of her output of manufactures. This proportion fell in the 1890s but rose again from 42 per cent to 45 per cent between 1899 and 1913. For Britain to have maintained her share of world exports would have meant her exporting as much as 60 per cent of her manufactured output. As it was, nearly all the increase in manufactured output between 1910 and 1913 went to export. A more rapid shift in commodities from textiles, coal and iron to engineering and electrical goods, and of markets from less developed to more developed countries, might have increased Britain's exports further, but for the general declining competitiveness of British industry (see Brown, 1965, pp. 47–50). The Empire was taking, in 1913, 44 per cent of textile exports and 42 per cent of Britain's capital goods exports compared with only a third of each in the 1870s (see table 18 and Schloete, 1952, Appendix, table 22).

The question remains whether investment in new industries at home to replace the declining staples of textiles and iron-ware grew so slowly because capital was attracted abroad, for reasons associated with an earlier imperialist stage of the economy, or whether the export of capital was the result of failing opportunities for investment at home. Industrial profits in Britain were falling after the mid 1870s (see table 13). In competition with foreign producers, export prices fell even faster than import prices until the 1890s (see table 14). Home costs also fell with import prices, but real wages, even allowing for heavy unemployment in 1879 and in 1884–1886, were stable

Table 14 Movements of unemployment, wages and prices, UK, 1860–1914 (index base, 100 = 1913 or 1914)

Period and position in cycle	Unemployment rate	Money wages index	Real wages index	Retail prices index	Wholesale prices index	Import prices index	Export prices index
1860 top	1·9	58	51	113	113	140	114
1862 bottom	8·4	(59)	(52)	(113)		132	120
1866 top	3·3	66	58	114	113	152	141
1868 bottom	7·9	(65)	54	(117)		145	126
1870	3·9	66	60	110	103	139	120
1872 top	0·9	(73)	(65)	(116)		138	135
1874	1·7	80	70	115	114	135	129
1877	4·7	77	70	110	103	130	110
1879 bottom	11·4	(72)	(71)	(102)		114	100
1880	5·5	72	69	105	96 ·	120	103
1882 top	2·3	75	73	102		116	101
1885	9·3	73	81	91	83	102	90
1886 bottom	10·2	72	81	89		95	86·5
1890 top	2·1	83	93	89	82	97	91
1893 bottom	7·5	83	94	89		92	86·5
1895 bottom	5·8	83	100	83	68	82·5	79
1899 top	2·0	89	104	86		85·5	83
1900	2·5	94	103	91	85	91·5	95
1904 bottom	6·0	89	97	92		89	87
1905	5·0	89	97	92	81	89·5	87
1906 top	3·6	91	98	93		93·5	92
1908 bottom	7·8	94	101	93		94	93
1910	4·7	94	98	96	91	99·5	93
1913 top	2·1	99	97	102	100	100	100
1914	3·3	100	100	100			

Export prices in 1900 and 1901 were exceptionally high; money wages here do not allow for unemployment; allowing for unemployment, real wages fell sharply in 1879 and 1884–1886 and slightly in 1892–1893. The unemployment rate is for trade unions making returns; wholesale prices from Rousseau index; figures in brackets from Wood (1909)
Sources: Bowley (1937, p. 30); Mitchell and Deane (1962, table II.3, XI.15, XVI.3 and XII.1.B and C)

in the 1870s and rose steadily thereafter to the end of the century.

One explanation for failing investment at home is that given by Rostow (1948, pp. 103–7), that labour saving investment was the cause of competitively reduced profits and falling effective demand (see Saville, 1954). But the level of home investment was low throughout the 1880s and early 1890s, and unemployment was not particularly high except in the depression years of 1878–1879, 1884–1887 and 1892–1894. On a Keynesian view, rising real wages at home during this period should have encouraged home investment. That they did not do so until the end of the century, when investment in dwellings and local authority schemes made up some 40 per cent of the total (Sigsworth and Blackman, 1965, table 4), suggests rather a Marxist explanation of the failure of capitalization. The very fact that real wages were rising, largely as a result of growing trade union strength in the 1870s and 1880s (Pollard, 1965), while prices were squeezed by developing foreign competition, implies just the type of capitalist contradiction of falling profit rates despite rising demand, such as Marx foresaw.

By the 1880s, the unprofitability of *past* investment in Britain combined with the overseas orientation of the capital market to lead to future prospects at home being ignored. Hobson's emphasis (1938, pp. 362–3) on the possibility of increasing consumption at home, which was in part realized in the late 1890s by local authority investment, and still more in the twentieth century by extended 'welfare state' investment, assumed that there was a profitable domestic alternative to overseas investment. John Strachey, writing some fifty years later, also associated 'The End of Empire' with the rise of welfare state expenditure at home. To the extent that this was paid for by taxation of the rich, it had, he believed, corrected income distribution (1959, ch. 5). But the tax system even after the First World War was not particularly progressive (U. K. Hicks, 1938, p. 269) and overseas investment has continued into our own times. Marxists saw the distribution of income as determined, not so much by bargaining about the share of wages from existing production levels as by the required long-run rate of accumulation. Overseas investment looked to most capitalists to be a necessary part of their portfolio *in spite of* rising demand at home.

Even if the Marxists' case stands, that there was a plethora of capital looking for investment opportunities at a certain stage of capital accumulation in Britain and in other capitalist countries, there are certain awkward questions for those who follow Lenin to answer about the timing of capital exports and imperialist expansion, about the direction of capital exports as between colonies and independent countries and about purely political pressures behind imperialism both at the centre and from the periphery in the period we are studying.

The question of timing

There are three major changes of trend which occurred in the last quarter of the nineteenth century which Lenin's argument associates together. Each is given by Lenin a quite different date and not necessarily the right one (1933):

Development of the monopoly stage of capitalism

In the last quarter of the nineteenth century this monopoly of England was already being undermined (p. 57). . . . The apex of pre-monopoly capitalist development . . . was reached in the period between 1860 and 1880 (p. 71) . . . 1876 – a date happily chosen, for it is precisely at that time that the pre-monopolist stage of development of Western European capitalism can be said to have been completed in the main (p. 73). . . . An enormous 'surplus of capital' accumulated in the advanced countries (p. 57). . . . The old capitalism . . . is passing away. A new capitalism is succeeding it (p. 38).

Macrosty, Moody and Clapham all put the date for this development in the 1890s with the emergence of Lever Bros, the Salt Union, Coats Paton and other giants. Large factories were still the exception in Britain in the 1860s and family firms were only slowly replaced by joint stock companies after the Companies Act of 1862 (Dobb, 1946, pp. 264–5).

Export of capital

'The export of capital did not develop formidable proportions until the beginning of the twentieth century' (Lenin, 1933, p. 58); this is Lenin's summary of a table which, however, shows British capital exports growing by decades: *fourfold* between 1862 and 1872, by 50 per cent in the next decade, doubling in the next decade, increasing once more by 50 per cent to 1902 and by another 50 per cent to 1914; French capital exports moving from a much lower base roughly in line with British; German capital exports leaping up after the turn of the century (compare table 11).

Colonial expansion

On this Lenin is categorical; 'For Britain, the vast increase in colonial conquests fall between 1860 and 1880, and the last twenty years of the nineteenth century are of great importance. For France and Germany it falls precisely in those last twenty years' (1933, p. 71).

Hobson, in his work on imperialism, marks the years 1884–1900 as being the period of intensified 'expansion' of the chief European states (Lenin, 1933). Lenin's figures here need little correction and are summarized in table 15.

In the case of colonial expansion by the European powers the absolute additions were largest between 1876 and 1900; additions after 1900 were slight; but the fastest rate of growth was in the decade or so *prior* to 1876, once more primarily of British possessions. Lenin (1933, p. 71), however, concludes that, 'It is *precisely after that period* [his italics referring to the period between 1860 and 1880] that the tremendous "boom" in colonial annexations begins'.

The fact is that expansion of both territory and capital exports occurred simultaneously for Britain in the 1860s and for France in the 1870s–1890s while German territorial expansion *preceded* her capital exports. Moreover, the greater part of British expansion of both territory and capital exports took place *before* the 'monopolistic stage' that followed the great depression (Gallagher and Robinson, 1953, pp. 1–15). There was evidently no turning point in the 1870s, for Britain at least, when competitive capitalism supposedly began to change into monopoly capitalism. The extension of British rule in India occurred mainly before the 1870s (see table 3). The scramble for Africa, however, did take place after the 1870s, adding huge extra territories with quite small populations to the British Empire. What cannot be denied is the involvement of other, mainly European, nations in colonial expansion after

Table 15 European colonial possessions, area and population 1830–1914 (area in million square miles, population in millions)

Year	British		French		German		Russian		Others		Total foreign possessions		Total home European states		Total world	
	Area	Pop.	Area	Pop.	Area	Pop.	Area	Pop.	Area	Pop.	Area	Pop.	Area	Pop.	Area	Pop.
1830	?	126	—	—	—	—	—	—	—	—	—	126	6·7	250	52	1050
1860	2·5	145	0·2	3·4	—	—	—	—	—	—	2·7	148	6·7	270	52	1180
1876	8·7	252	0·4	6·0	—	—	6·6	15·9	2·8	24	18·5	298	6·7	300	52	1250
1900	12·6	367	4·0	50·0	1·0	14·7	6·6	20·0	4·0	59	28	511	6·7	400	52	1610
1914	13·1	393	4·1	55·5	1·1	12·3	6·6	33·2	4·1	74	29	568	6·7	445	52	1656

UK possessions here include Canada and other Dominions throughout and also protectorates totalling 3·6 million square miles and 56 million people in 1900. The figure for British colonial possessions in India in 1860 is almost certainly understated. Semi-colonial countries like China, Persia, Turkey and the Latin American states were excluded
Sources: Hobson (1938, pp. 17, 20, 23); Lenin (1933, pp. 71–5); Supan (1906, p. 254); Morris (1900, vol. 1, p. 415; vol. 2, pp. 84–7, 304); Woytinsky and Woytinsky (1953, table 14; 1955, tables 234 and 235)

1880. Table 16 gives the picture which complements table 4. We must conclude that there was some association in time between the export of capital and the process of industrial concentration at the end of the nineteeth century but that colonial expansion mainly preceded both rather than following after, as Lenin suggested. Indeed, Britain, the country with the largest empire, was the last to experience the full process of merger and combination and to adopt protective policies. If Lenin's thesis of a new imperialist stage of capitalism dating from the 1880s does not fit the facts, this might only be because capitalism in Britain had never been anything else than imperialist and newly emerging capitalist nations were bound to follow suit.

The question of investment in colonies

To sustain the Marxist thesis, which relates colonial expansion to openings for a surplus of capital, as well as for a surplus of goods, it would still be necessary to show that the direction of capital exports was to the colonies. Lenin, while conceding that French and German capital was invested mainly in Europe, gave figures to suggest that 'the principle spheres of investment of British capital are its colonial possessions, which are very large in America (for example Canada) and also of course in Asia, etc' (1933, p. 59). Certainly the share of the Empire in British overseas capital was increased between 1870 and 1890 to about half of the total (see table 17). But this is to include the self-governing dominions of the British Empire with the colonies. If the two are separated, the great increase of British capital investment in these years was in the dominions. The share of India was reduced. At the same time, while the share of Europe was also sharply cut back, that of Latin America was extended. These swings of direction of investment in the 1880s are quite marked and became stabilized thereafter until the sales of British-held United States stock in the First World War and its replacement by still further dominion and colonial investment by Britain in the 1930s. What all this means, in the light of the fact that British capital exports did not exceed income from overseas, is that income from past

Table 16 Colonial possessions of European powers acquired after 1870

Britain pre 1870, Africa only[a]

Bathurst
Sierra Leone
Cape Coast Castle
Gold Coast
Lagos
Cape Colony
Mauritius
Perim Island

---

post 1870

1874	Fiji	1888	Christmas Islands
1876	Sokotra		Fanning Island
1878	Cyprus		Cook Island
	Walvis Bay		Brunei
1878–1903	Baluchistan	1890	Uganda
1881	North Borneo		Zanzibar
1882	Egypt		Nyasaland
1883	Papua	1892	Gilbert Islands
	Federated Malayan	1898	Wei-hai-wei
	States	1899	Tonga Isles
1884	Somaliland	1900	Transvaal
1885	Kenya		Orange Free State
1885–1890	Rhodesia	1901	Niue
1886	Nigeria	1914	Samoa
	Kermadek Isles		S W Africa
	Burma Occupation	1917	Palestine
	completed	1918	Tanganyika
	Ashanti		Transjordania
1887	Zululand		
	Tongaland		
	(Protectorate)		

France pre 1870, Africa	*post 1870*	
Algiers	1830–1902	Algeria
Senegal	1843–1880	Tahiti
Guinea	1881	Tunis
St Marie	1889	Austral Isles
Reunion		French West Africa

Table 16 – *continued*

France pre 1870, Africa		post 1870	
Obock		1893	Cochin China
Slave Coast		1897	Madagascar
			French Congo
			Dahomey
			Morocco
		1898	Kwangchow
		1884	Tongking
			Amman
		1904	Cambodia

Russia pre 1870		post 1870	
1801	Ukraine	1881–1884	Russian sphere in
1815	Finland		Persia
	Poland	1898	Port Arthur
	Baltic States	1900–1905	Manchuria
1854	Crimea	1939	Poland
1858	Amur		Finland
1860	Vladivostock		Lithuania
1864–1868	Turkestan		Latvia
			Esthonia

Japan		Germany	
1895	Formosa	1871	Alsace Lorraine
1905	Port Arthur	1888	Tanganyika
	Kurile Isles		S W Africa
	Sakhalin		Togo
1910	Korea	1898	Kiaochow
1937	Manchuria		Cameroons
1938	China	1935	Saar
1942	SE Asia	1938	Austria
		1939	Czechoslovakia
USA			Poland
1867	Alaska		Denmark
1898	Philippines		Norway
	Guam	1940	France
	Puerto Rico		Hungary
	Hawaii	1941	Yugoslavia
1917	Virgin Isles		Roumania
1944	Okinawa		Bulgaria
			Greece
			Russia

Italy		*Belgium*	
1911	Libya	1879	Belgian Congo
1919	Istria		
1920	Dalmatia		
1926	Albania		
1935	Abyssinia		
1940	Greece		

[a] Pre 1870 British annexations are shown in table 4
Source: Brampton (1938); Taylor (1965)

investments in Europe, in India and to a lesser extent in the US, was switched after 1880 into investment in the dominions and Latin America, mainly in fact Argentina, (see table 17).

Such a switch was indeed a major one. It might be expected that this concentration of investment in the 1880s on relatively independent lands of European settlement would be found to have been associated with rising shares of trade with them. But Britain's trade pattern seems to have been firmly established already by 1870 and the changes thereafter were quite small until the 1930s. Extra investment in developing lands could still have been required to maintain this trade pattern.

Opening up fields of development overseas was an essential aspect of the growth of British capitalism in the first half of the nineteenth century. The extension of this process in the second half of the century, with especial concentration on Latin America, was not, therefore, a new phenomenon. And if the new areas of development were not colonies ruled directly by Britain, they were not wholly independent states either. British power in the dominions was not equalled in the Latin American republics but it was still very great. Despite the objections of Ferns (1960, pp. 487–91) and others, the evidence adduced by Furtado (1965, p. 47), Frank (1969a, p. 281), and Griffin (1969) does suggest that British economic, military and political power were used to influence the lines of development of the economies of Latin America and to protect British investments there. Government guarantee covered more than three quarters of British investments in 1890, since nearly a half were direct

Table 17 Area pattern of British exports (*E*) and imports (*I*) of goods, and investment of capital (*C*), 1860–1970 (figures are a percentage of totals)[a]

Areas	1860–1870			1881–1890			1911–1913		
	E	*I*	*C*	*E*	*I*	*C*	*E*	*I*	*C*
British Empire total	32	23	36	34	22	47	36	24	46
Canada	4	3	2·5	3	4	13	5	4	13
Southern Dominions	10	6	9·5	13	6·5	16	13	9·5	17
India[b]	10	8	21	12	6·5	15	12·5	7	10·5
other[c]	8	6	3	6	5	3	5·5	3·5	5·5
Latin America	12	11	10·5	11	5	20	12	10	22
USA	13	15	27	14	22	22	9	18	19
Europe	39	41	25	36	42	8	36	40	6
other	4	10	1·5	5	9	3	7	8	7
total	100	100	100	100	100	100	100	100	100

Areas	1933–1935			1955–1959			1970		
	E	I	C[a]	E	I	C	E	I	C[e]
British Empire total	43	35	(59)	44	37	60	25	27	56
Canada	5	9·5	(17)	6	8	14	3·5	7·5	12
Southern Dominions	16·5	12·5	(20)	18	13	25	10	5·5	30
India[b]	9·5	5·5	(14)	6	4·5	4	5	1·5	6
other[c]	12	7·5	(8)	14	11·5	17	6·5	12·5	8
Latin America	9	13	(22)	5	8·5	11·5	3·5	4·0	8
USA	6	11	(5·5)	8	10	6	11·5	13	11
Europe	38	36	(8)	29	28	8·5	46	41	14
other	4	5	(5·5)	14	16·5	14·5	14	15	11
total	100	100	100	100	100	100	100	100	100

[a] Export and import figures are average flows over the period. Capital investment figures are total stocks at the last year of the period

[b] India includes the whole subcontinent at all periods

[c] Includes Ireland after 1935

[d] Bracketed figures are for 1927–29

[e] Direct company investment only

Sources: Barratt Brown (1970a, tables 5, 6, 17 and 19); Department of Trade and Industry (1972)

government bonds and another third railway securities and public utilities with government backing (Rippy, 1959, table 7). The increased investment in mining in the first decade of the twentieth century only slightly reduced these proportions. There were still defaults, including the Latin American crisis involving Baring Brothers in 1891. But the investments appeared, like those in India and in the Dominions, to have a measure of government guarantee and the British Government could be relied upon to use its influence to maintain the conditions which would encourage the safety of investments. As even Ferns concedes in comparing the concentrations upon agricultural and pastoral enterprise in Argentina with the industrialization of the USA and Canada: 'Political power and/or decisive influence upon policy in Argentina has belonged until recent times to the interests with most to gain by such a concentration' (1960, p. 488).[3]

The rentier, however, along with the borrowing country, often got the least out of the deal. One historian of British foreign investment records that Latin American governments frequently 'found themselves . . . with cash in hand equivalent to about 60 per cent of the contracted debt . . . English bankers, brokers, shipping companies and agents, exporters and manufacturers and grafting Latin American bureaucrats had profited at the expense of British investors' (Rippy, 1959, pp. 22, 32).

Capital export may have maintained the rate of accumulation in the lending countries through many channels, and not only through the rentier's dividends, but evidently capitalists in the developed countries could not, by investing in underdeveloped countries, avoid Marx's predicted contradictions. These consist in a generation of surplus value which, by that very fact, made it difficult to realize more surplus value. Some capitalists could 'mop up' less efficient capitalists' markets and could benefit from real increases in productivity where this occurred. It did not occur, however, in the underdeveloping colonial countries but rather in the developing self-governing countries

3. We may well recall at this point Robinson Crusoe's Spaniards, see chapters 3 and 10.

overseas. Hence the switch of investment in the 1880s in the very opposite direction to that which Lenin's concept of super profits from the colonies suggested; but the Marxists will remind us that the source of the funds that were switched was colonial. Such switching can be seen as part of a continuing centralization of capital which is the essence of the Marxist model of capital accumulation.

The question of political pressures

The final argument of the critics of the Marxist view of late nineteenth-century imperialism as a function of capital exports is that there were other perfectly good political explanations for the expansion of European and American colonial possessions at that time. The first emphasizes political pressures arising from the balance of power in Europe between the most developed powers: in the 'strategic relevance of Egypt to the security of India', 'in the need to prevent the absorption of the Cape by an unfriendly Boer republic', in the determination of France 'to forestall an Italian take-over' of Algeria, in United States' interest in the defence of the Western Hemisphere and so on (Fieldhouse, 1967, p. 190). One is bound to ask what was the object of Indian security, of French control over Algeria, of the United States' 'manifest destiny' in the Western Hemisphere, if they did not provide markets for goods, sources of raw materials and opportunities for investment under privileged conditions? The question of the timing of capital export and the seizure of colonial possessions only becomes important *if* a sharp change of policies is assumed after 1870. There was no period of the mid-nineteenth century when Britain was not extending her Empire and the apparent speeding up of the process after 1880 involved large areas of land but relatively small populations. Existing positions were consolidated as rival capitalist groups looked for equivalent opportunities (see tables 11 and 15). Such pressures forced Britain also to move further into Africa and South East Asia to make sure of positions that the British navy had previously assured without colonial rule. There was not really a new stage of capitalism after 1870 or after 1900, but an essential continuity of spheres

T–EGI–G

of influence, as we saw in table 10, running right up to our own times.

The second political critique of the Marxist view is that the main pressures for spheres of influence came not from the centre but from the periphery. Three sorts of pressure are suggested; from local collaborators with European rule, from the army and governors in the field and from the European colonial settlers. The 'collaborative system' in European colonies, and even more in semi-dependent territories like Egypt, Sudan, Turkey and China, is regarded by Ronald Robinson as the key to an understanding of imperialism (1972), that is, of the local ruling classes and elites who collaborated with the European power. In this view, the 'white colonist [is] the ideal prefabricated collaborator' (p. 124). But what they were collaborating about, was about commerce, 'keeping export markets open and capital flowing'. The more resources involved, the more patronage available and the easier the relationship. 'Direct colonial rule represented a reconstruction of collaboration' (p. 133) made necessary by the collapse of local collaborative systems, the aim of which was to provide a local extension of the European capitalist economic system with its laws, banking and commercial practices and government safeguards. But this could have been part of wider strategic economic interests.

In his book on Africa, written with Gallagher, Robinson places great emphasis on the rise of nationalism in Egypt which, it is said, forced Britain to occupy Egypt and thereafter so much more of Africa:

From start to finish the partition of tropical Africa was driven by the persistent crisis in Egypt. When the British entered Egypt on their own, the scramble began; and as long as they stayed in Cairo, it continued until there was no more of Africa left to divide (1963, p. 465).

The main interest of the French government in Egypt may have been to collect the interest on Egyptian bonds; but Gladstone cannot be accused of this, and John Bright resigned from his cabinet at the bombing of Alexandria in 1882 (Owen, 1972, p. 208).

We are thrown back via the security of Egypt to the security of India as the determinant of British territorial expansion. Was the Indian Empire, however, itself the result of peripheral pressures? India provided just that field of enterprise for a pre-capitalist decaying military aristocracy in Britain and just that aura of national greatness for the British citizen which Schumpeter insisted on as the origin of imperialist expansion after 1870 (1955, pp. 10–11). There were similar decaying feudal aristocracies in Prussia, in France, in Russia and in Japan. But where was the feudal aristocracy in the United States? Not surely in Teddy Roosevelt? And why did other nations with decaying feudal aristocracies – Brazil or China for example – not expand their empires at this time? All the countries which did expand had in common a highly developed system of industrial capitalism and, therefore, on the Marxist view, they were all subject to competitive pressures to invest capital, expand markets and control raw materials.

Imperialism and India may have been, for Disraeli, vote-catching phrases, as Schumpeter argued, but India was still in the 1880s taking 12 per cent of British exports of goods and 11 per cent of capital exports with full government guarantees. In certain particular products, and particularly those where markets elsewhere were declining, as in textiles and iron and steel products, and in other capital goods, the proportions were higher (see table 18).

Britain ran a persistent surplus on trade with India; and this, together with £8m 'home charges' and with invisible earnings, provided Britain with annual credits of £25m in the 1880s. 'The fact was,' writes Saul, 'that Britain settled more than one-third of her deficits with Europe and the United States through India' (1960, p. 56). This happy arrangement for British capital continued right into the twentieth century. 'Had not British exports, and particularly British cottons, found a wide open market in India during the last few years before the outbreak of war, it would have been impossible for her to have indulged so heavily in investment on the American continent and elsewhere' (p. 88).

The working people of Britain, whom Disraeli enfranchised,

Table 18 UK merchandise exports by area, 1854–1913, distinguishing all exports and capital-goods exports[a]

	1854		1876		1900		1913	
	All	Capital	All	Capital	All	Capital	All	Capital
all countries total (£m)	98	22	200	36	291	61	525	109
Distribution by area (%)								
Empire[b]	35	23	32	30	32	31	37	42
Dominions	19	18	14	18	16	19	18	24
India	10	4	12	10	11·5	11	12	17·5
other Empire	6	1	6	2	4·5	1	7	0·5
Non-Empire	65	(77)	68	(70)	68	(69)	63	(58)
USA	21	—	9	—	7	—	5·5	—
N and W Europe	11	—	23	—	23	—	19	—
C and S Europe[c]	16	—	19	—	18	—	15	—
Latin America	8	—	8	—	8	—	10	—
others	9	—	9	—	12	—	13·5	—

[a] Capital goods exports (*Capital*) include iron and steel, hardware and cutlery, other metals, machinery, locomotives and carriages, arms and munitions and electrical engineering, but not ships

[b] Empire includes under capital-goods exports only those going to the Dominions, India and the British West Indies, and these are, therefore, bracketed

[c] Central and Southern Europe includes Morocco, Algeria and Tunis, but not Turkey

Sources: Schloete (1952, Appendix, tables, 20, 22, 23 and 24); Mitchell and Deane (1962, table 12)

had other reasons for their interest in the Empire, though less in the Colonial Empire than in the Dominions – reasons closely connected with the development of capitalism. Periods of high capital export seem not to have been associated with high unemployment at home, but they saw high rates of emigration (Brown, 1965, p. 53; see also table 8). Many emigrants took capital with them; others could use powerful arguments of kinship to attract capital to follow them. But the pressure for emigration cannot in the first place have been primarily from the periphery.

If income from earlier investments in Europe, India, Central America and the US was switched after 1880 into investment in the Dominions and South America, this could still have been the result of pulls from the European settlers in those countries and might have had relatively little to do with outward pressures from Britain;[4] for, they included, as Rippy suggested, the manipulations of many sorts of Europeans on the spot – export–import agents, agents of shipping and other companies and government officials, all involved in capital movements. The table on immigration, table 8, reminded us of the massive flow of Europeans into the Americas and Oceania in the second half of the nineteenth century and the first quarter of the twentieth; and these figures did not include the English settlement of Northern Ireland and subsequent import of Catholic labour from the south, nor the most recent settlement of two million European Jews in Israel. Moreover, the table did not distinguish the million and a half French in the Maghreb who returned to France after independence, the 100 000 Europeans in Egypt as early as 1882 (Owen, 1972), the Dutch in South Africa and the East Indies, the British in South Africa and Rhodesia or the Belgians in the Congo. Just to name some of these colonists shows the importance of

4. This is the view of Emmanuel (1972b). Although he does not recognize that it is the switch of direction of capital investment that matters, and dismisses capital exports altogether as an explanation of imperialism, he does recognize the importance of capital exports within his general picture of imperialism as the result of colonial settler pressure, often, he says, *against* the interests of the home government and of large financial and industrial interests at home.

peripheral explanations of imperialism. But Robinson's 'ideal prefabricated collaborator' and Emmanuel's 'poor white settlers' are rather different animals, although both share the tensions of a half-dependent, half-independent relationship to the home country; and Emmanuel surely exaggerates the inability of the colonials to come to terms with the large metropolitan company, once a measure of political independence has been won (Emmanuel, 1972b, p. 39).

All that is said about peripheral pressures may be true, but what cannot be denied is that the switch of British capital corresponded with some switch in exports of goods and particularly in capital goods from concentration on Europe and the USA to the Empire. Capital exports may have given opportunities for local agents, settlers and collaborators; but it would be a case of the tail wagging the dog to suggest that the main initiative came from overseas. The politics of holding on to India and the route to India does seem to have had a firm economic base in the centralization of capital and the search for outlets for its employment.

It is time to return then from the periphery to the question of the central causes of late nineteenth-century capital export from Europe. The thesis of Cairncross, of a correlation between good export prices in overseas countries and high levels of capital export from Britain, has been demolished, but its place has been taken by a view which relates export capacity compared with demand in both lending and borrowing countries at any period to investment in capacity in the *previous* period (Thomas, 1967). This explains, it is said, alternating cycles of British home and foreign investment and the surprising correlation of periods of high capital export by Britain *and* unfavourable terms of trade for overseas primary producers. But on this view the 'excessive' overseas investment is not explained nor is the low level of overall investment – home and foreign – in the 1890s.

We come back to the main question of the determinants of the accumulation of capital. The whole trend of the Keynesian argument is that the incentive to invest is not guaranteed by the working of the free market economy at a level necessary for full employment. The Keynesians emphasize the dependence of investment upon effective demand, checked in each boom by the rising marginal propensity to save (Robinson, 1942, p. 50). The Marxists emphasize the competitive pressures of production for production's sake, of capitalist accumulation leading to concentration of capital on labour-saving technology, reduced employment opportunities and chronic lack of balance between the capital goods industries and consumer goods industries. What is clear so far, is that foreign investment with state guarantees provided for the British rentier a seemingly secure and regular income, and for British capital-goods manufacturers a sure outlet for their surplus. The banks with state support did the same for French and German rentiers and for French and German capital goods (Landes, 1965, p. 516).

This need for state guarantees could have arisen either from lack of effective private demand to act as an incentive to investment (the Keynesian view) or from excessive investment in productive capacity which could not be realized at a profit to maintain a given rate of accumulation (the Marxist view). The importance of capital goods exports strengthens the Marxist view. The steadily rising real wages in the 1880s and 1890s, thanks to increased trade-union strength, appears to reduce the plausibility of the Keynesian view. Was there real evidence of excess capacity in the capital goods industries during this period to sustain the Marxist view? The general opinion held in Germany in the mid 1880s was that colonies were needed to solve the problem of overproduction. The Royal Commission on the Depression of Trade and Industry in Britain, in the conclusion of its Final Report of 1884, certainly believed that such evidence existed for the falling rate of profit:

We think that ... overproduction has been one of the most prominent features of the course of trade during recent years ... the remarkable feature of the present situation, and that which in our opinion distinguishes it from all previous periods of depression, is the length of time during which this overproduction has continued ... (1884, p. viii).

In the Marxist work from which this quotation is taken, much evidence is supplied for the increase of productive capacity in Britain beyond what was profitable to employ (Dobb, 1946, pp. 305–7). On this view, the competition of capitalists on an increasingly world-wide scale drove them to spread their investments and to establish privileged positions for themselves, wherever they could. We have been forced much closer to Lenin's view of a monopoly stage of capitalism in which, even as some branches of industry and some nations advance, others, and especially those like Britain which are richest in capital, become parasitic and decay (Lenin, 1933, ch. 8). In particular Lenin's picture of the First World War as a 'war for the partition of the world, for the distribution and redistribution of colonies, of spheres of influence of capital'[5] and his expectation of this struggle continuing into the future so long as capitalism survived, did receive its vindication in the Second World War. Lenin's estimation, moreover, of the monopolistic tendencies of industrial and banking capital and their proneness to merger has received new confirmation in each generation, in the 1920s, the 1940s and again in the 1960s.

5. Preface to French and German editions, 1920.

9 The Large Firm

Marxists see capitalism as an expansionary force and the capitalist as an aggressive accumulator – using money to make more money (see Marx, 1946, ch. 23, section 3). Keynesians see the 'new feature of the capitalist system', translating man's natural passion for power into the accumulation of wealth (Robinson, 1970a, p. 67). Yet in the last chapter we were explaining the export of capital at the end of the nineteenth century in terms of rentiers' desire for security of income, and the annexation of territorial possessions in terms of protected markets for producers of capital goods. This does not sound like the world of aggressive captains of industry, however much in Professor Robinson's view they 'had to present themselves as benefactors of society'. The historian of Unilever, indeed, makes a special point of the fact that, contrary to the Marxist view of the motivation for capital exports, the shareholders of Lever Bros Ltd were never anxious in the 1890s 'to put too much money in these associated companies' [i.e. overseas], as Lever himself frequently complained (Wilson, 1954, p. 110).

Men like Lever or Cecil Rhodes looked and behaved like imperialists, 'roughing out plan after plan for possible partitions of the world', as the German Ambassador described Rhodes and Joseph Chamberlain in the 1890s (Von Eckardstein, 1919, p. 234). The contrast between them and the rentiers gives evident plausibility to the classical view of imperialism as a hangover from the past, although the resemblance of Rhodes to Clive was closer than to earlier merchant adventurers. Marx, writing in the mid 1860s, had already foreseen the emergence of three very different types – the coupon-clipping rentiers, the business managers and the financial promoters and speculators – emerging from the original capitalist entrepreneur with the expanded scale of production and centralization of capital in stock companies (Marx, 1909, ch. 27); and this centralization of capital goes on until it is 'united in the hands of a single capitalist company' (1946, ch. 25, section 2).

Marx's predictions of the divorce of management from ownership in the large firm have certainly been fulfilled, but they have been variously interpreted. Those who followed Marx, like Hilferding and Lenin, thought of the financiers, who linked capital and state power, as providing the new dynamic of the system. Thus we may see that the City of London defeated Chamberlain's campaign for imperial preference, returned Britain to the Gold Standard at a higher sterling rate in 1926, re-established sterling convertibility in the 1950s and carried through the mergers and take-overs of the 1960s (Barratt Brown, 1968, pp. 36–74). The rise of 'empires of high finance' in the USA in the 1920s – the houses of Morgan, Rockefeller, First National City, Dupont, Mellon, Bank of America, Cleveland, Chicago (Perlo, 1957, p. 125) – tell the same story. The operations of the finance houses with the aid of the state were seen by Marxists following Lenin as the continuing cause of inter-imperialist rivalries in the crisis years of the 1930s, leading to the outbreak of war in 1939 (Varga and Mendelsohn, 1940, p. 153). The outflow of capital in the 1920s, especially from the United States, despite its massive internal resources and markets, the adoption of imperial preference by Britain at Ottawa in 1930, the struggle for the oil of the Middle East between Royal Dutch Shell, Standard Oil and Italian, German and French companies (Sutton, 1955, pp. 36–52), above all the challenge of Japanese, German and Italian 'state monopoly finance-capital' to the older capitalist states for markets, sources of raw material and spheres of investment, finding its very epitome in Hitler's banker, Hjalmar Schacht – all seemed to give to Lenin's prophecies the most powerful posthumous justification.

For a few years after the end of the Second World War the financial groups in the USA survived. For rather more years in Britain the merchant bankers could claim the leadership of British capital while the sterling area was revamped and the ex-colonies held within its financial embrace so that in Paish's words: 'So far from Britain providing finance for the colonial territories, the colonial territories have been providing finance for Britain and the rest of the Sterling Area' (see Barratt Brown, 1970a, ch. 7).

After decolonization and the run-down of the sterling balances, income still flowed into Britain from the ex-colonies, but financial power was shifting in Britain as in the United States to conglomerate companies, with the erosion by taxation of family fortunes, the increased supply of state funds for industry and the enlarged corporate profits of the Second World War supplemented by those of the rearmament boom that followed in the 1950s. These combined with the growth of scientific management to give to individual companies both funds for self finance and organizational strength. The large industrial and commercial firms took the place of the financial groups as the accumulators of capital, through 'maximizing retained funds net of dividends and taxes' (Penrose, 1968, p. 29).

The process of concentration of production in large firms has accelerated at certain periods – at the turn of the century, in the 1920s, 1940s and 1960s[1] – but there has been little evidence of deconcentration in between. The one hundred largest manufacturing corporations in the USA controlled 58 per cent of the land, buildings and equipment used in manufacturing in 1962 compared with 44 per cent in 1929 (Baran and Sweezy, 1966, p. 266). There is similar evidence of concentration in British industry after the mid 1950s (Hart and Prais, 1956, pp. 173–5; Evely and Little, 1960). From 1957 to 1968, while the net assets of quoted British companies operating mainly in the UK with a capital of over half a million pounds doubled, the number of such companies was reduced by merger and take-over from 2024 to 771; and the ten largest companies trebled their assets (Department of Trade and Industry, 1970). In the USA, during the latest period of concentration in the 1960s, there was a check to the rate of growth of the individual largest United

1. See Levy (1909); Plummer (1934); Evely and Little (1960); and Department of Trade and Industry (1970).

States firms (Hymer and Rowthorn, 1970), but the *number* of large firms increased and the share of these large firms in total US company assets and sales increased. Moreover, in all developed countries firms that began by increasing the share of their national markets, and then of their exports to other markets, became in the 1960s, increasingly, trans-national in their operation (Dunning, 1971).

The Marxists now argued that the modern giant corporation was the new agent of imperialism (Baran and Sweezy, 1966, p. 15; Barratt Brown, 1970a, ch. 8), and not a 'soulful corporation', as some would have it, which aimed less at maximizing profit than at a long term balancing of the claims of stockholders, employees, customers and the general public (Kaysern, 1957, pp. 313–14). For this was how it had been described in a study of the *Modern Corporation and Private Property* by Berle and Means in 1932, and popularized in 1941 in Burnham's *Managerial Revolution*. Such a concept not only challenged the Marxist analysis but undermined the whole of neo-classical theory of factor remuneration and price determination by the self-regarding actions of all economic agents (see Mason, 1958, p. 7). Its validity was in any case denied in a careful study of management literature and attitudes by Earley, who found that the 'major goals of modern, large-scale business are high managerial incomes, good profits, a strong competitive position and growth' (1956). These were to be obtained by 'cost reduction, superior methods, choosing the most profitable alternatives, uncovering new profit alternatives' and 'avoiding outside finance'; in effect, in Earley's view, long-term rather than short-term profit maximization. Yet the concept of the 'soulful corporation' continued to be propagated and even made the basis of party policies by politicians,[2] not only in the United States but in Britain also.

The connection between the modern corporation and imperialism is seen by neo-Marxists in terms of the 'need by monopolistic-type firms to control raw-material sources and markets

2. See for example Crosland (1962, p. 89), and Barratt Brown (1963), replying to Crosland's strictures on an earlier study by Barratt Brown (1959).

in order to protect their dominant position and to secure their investment ... even ... on a relatively longer-run profit perspective' (Magdoff, 1970, p. 19). Hence, the new wave of capital export, this time direct investment by mainly British and American large firms, but with others increasingly joining in, that has marked the international economy in recent years. This direct investment now comprises two-thirds of private U K foreign assets and five-sixths of private U S foreign assets, the remainder being portfolio investment. The positions were the reverse in 1929 in the case of the U K, 50/50 in the case of the U S A (Barratt Brown, 1973).

We can see from table 19 that direct investment abroad by the major industrialized countries was equal in 1967–1968 to about 9 per cent of comparable home investment, 16 per cent in the case of Britain. This is a much smaller figure than for Britain before 1913, although the overseas investment proportion in Britain's case was then, too, higher than elsewhere. After 1968, however, the outflow of capital from Britain was stepped up, so that in 1971, gross direct (non-oil) company investment, plus 300 to 400 million dollars oil investment overseas, amounted to the equivalent of 27 per cent of gross domestic investment in mining, manufacturing and construction (Central Statistical Office, 1972a; 1972b, table 15). This capital export is nearly all accounted for by a few very large firms. Eighty U S firms accounted in 1957 for 69 per cent of total U S overseas investment (U S Dept. of Commerce, 1960). Forty-nine U K firms accounted in 1962 for 83 per cent of all British overseas investments in manufacturing and the oil industry combined (Reddaway, 1967).

Much emphasis is placed by the neo-Marxists upon the 'reliance of the giant corporation for its monopolistic position, including the size of its profits, on foreign sources of raw materials. What is new in today's imperialism,' Magdoff writes, 'is that the United States has become a "have not" nation for a wide range of both common and rare minerals' (1970, p. 45). Much evidence is supplied for this last statement; but as an explanation for the new wave of overseas investment by the United States it is inadequate. The main flows of new

Table 19 Capital formation in industry at home and direct capital flows abroad for certain industrial countries 1957–1968 (annual averages, gross figures)

Country	Capital formation at home ($ billion)			Direct investment abroad ($ million)		
	1957–1960	1961–1964	1967–1968	1957–1960	1961–1964	1967–1968
EEC total (excl. UK)	9·5	18	22·5	360	610	1005
Belgium	0·5	0·9	1·2	n.a.	n.a.	40
West Germany	4	7	7·5	120	220	320
Italy	2	3·5	3·5	60	170	230
France	2·5	5·5	8·3	10	100	200
Netherlands	0·5	1	2	170	120	215
Canada	1·5	2	3·5	60	100	120
Japan	3	6	13	50	90	170
USA	13	16	28	2830	3210	3090
UK	3	3·5	5	510	670	820
total	30	45·5	72	3810	4680	5205
US percentage of total	43	35	39	74	68	59

Capital formation in industry at home comprises mining, manufacturing and construction (excluding dwellings). Direct investment abroad by the UK excludes the oil companies
Sources: OECD (1970b); Hymer and Rowthorn (1970, p. 78); Rowthorn (1971a, table 3, p. 42)

overseas investment are into manufacturing industry. Mining takes a declining proportion of US investment; even the share of oil declined in the 1960s.

This declining of overseas investment in raw-materials production need not mean that it is not still very important for the large corporations. As reserves of minerals run down (Meadows, 1972, pp. 56–60), the control of these reserves becomes in fact increasingly important for the corporations, and exercise of this control is believed by some Marxists to be the cause of the United States' involvement in Indo-China (Caldwell, 1971). Table 20 shows, however, that the direction of US investment is not now so much to ex-colonial or under-developed lands as to other industrially developed states. This is true for all the main capital-exporting countries (Hymer and Rowthorn, 1970). About a half of all their capital exports went to each other in the 1960s. At the same time, a high proportion of investment income still arises from underdeveloped lands and particularly from oil investments. There is once again a switch of investment taking place in the establishment by manufacturing firms of subsidiaries in the more, and not the less, industrially developed countries.

For Marxists the large firm, and not the nation state or the market, is the institution through which the dynamic of capitalist accumulation is expressed. On the classical liberal view, as Schumpeter stated it, albeit regretfully, the modern corporation means that:

With the decline of the driving power supplied by the family motive, the businessman's time horizon shrinks, roughly, to his life expectation . . . . He drifts into an anti-saving frame of mind . . . the decreasing importance of the functions of the entrepreneurs and capitalists . . . also decomposes the motor forces of capitalism from within. Nothing else shows so clearly that the capitalist order not only rests on props made of extra capitalist material but also derives its energy from extra capitalist patterns of behaviour which at the same time it is bound to destroy (1943, pp. 161–2).

'Marx's *vision* was right,' says Schumpeter, but adds that 'there are no purely economic reasons why capitalism should not have another successful run' (p. 163). In a new essay on

Table 20 Direct company foreign investment, USA and UK, 1929–1968

Area	USA capital						UK capital			
	Investment stake				Annual average investment flow	Annual average investment income	Investment stake		Annual average investment flow	Annual average investment income
	1929	1949	1959	1968	1960–1964	1967–1968	1960	1968	1964–1969	1967–1969
total ($ billion)	8	11	30	65	3·5	5·0	12·6	19·7	1·2	2·3
by regions (%)[a]										
Europe	19	14·5	16	30	38	22	10	13·7	18·5	13
Canada/USA	25	31	33	33	30	18	24·5	23	19·5	23
Latin America	33	39	35	17	12	27	36·5[c]	30·3[c]	22·5[c]	30[c]
other undeveloped } sterling developed[b]	23	15·5	16	20	20	33	29	33	39·5	34

by sectors (%)

manufacturing	24	33	32	41	50	26	32	36	41·5	28·5
oil	15	29	33	29	20	46	28	25	21	44
mining	16	10	10	8	10	13				
utilities	21	11	9	4	10}	15	40[d]	39[d]	37·5[d]	27·5[d]
other	24	17	16	18	10}					

[a] Regional distribution for UK investment excludes oil and finance
[b] UK investment in sterling developed areas includes Rhodesia
[c] UK capital figures are combined for Latin America and other undeveloped
[d] UK capital figures are combined for mining, utilities and other
Source: US Department of Commerce (1968, 1970, 1971b); Department of Trade and Industry (1972); Central Statistical Office (1970)

'The March into Socialism', added in 1949, Schumpeter argued that, while post-war recovery had shown 'the vast productive possibilities of the capitalist engine,' what 'Marx failed to realize', was 'the indefinitely higher mass standards of life, supplemented by *gratis* services *without* complete "expropriation of the expropriators". Yet ... it [capitalism] could be "regulated" beyond its powers of endurance' and lead to the imposition of 'an outright socialistic solution' (1943; 1949 edn, p. 419).

Schumpeter's view was that, while the manner in which Marx expected capitalist society to break down was wrong, the prediction was right. The springs of enterprise in the family firm were being destroyed and the cause was perennial inflation, itself resulting from the combined power of trade unions, in conditions of full employment, to pull up wages and of oligopolistic firms to pass these on in higher prices. But all this is on the assumption of full utilization of resources. We now know that it is possible to have high unemployment and a high rate of inflation, but we also know that mild inflation for many years encouraged investment, since the historic cost of plant was constantly being reduced in relation to the value of current output from it. Schumpeter believed, however, that any nation like Britain, which had a rate of inflation above the world average, and found the competitive position of its firms reduced, would take action to control inflation; and this would mean the 'conquest of the private enterprise system by the bureaucracy' (p. 424). What Schumpeter did not allow for was the growing power of the large firms to manage their own sales and prices on a world scale, even side-stepping the action of governments.

One of the main causes of the rising rate of inflation has been the shifting of short-term funds of large companies between financial centres. This has led to a bidding up of interest rates and to other government measures to control the balance of payments, which have tended to raise unit costs (Barratt Brown, 1972b, p. 199). In a country where above average inflation occurs, all firms will suffer in world competition, but the large firms will suffer least. If interest rates are higher than the annual rate of inflation, as they were in Britain prior to 1967 and again in 1973, large firms can find their own funds internally and either lend them out or use them for their own investment. If interest rates fall below the rate of inflation, as they did for Britain between 1967 and 1972, the large firms have the power to borrow and repay with depreciated currency. Inflation may be a killer for rentiers and small firms, but large firms will survive and grow larger. This can be seen in the merger boom in Britain in the late 1960s and in the great increase in company borrowing from the banks after 1967 (Department of Trade and Industry, 1971), when the rate of inflation rose from an average of 3 per cent a year to 7 per cent a year and in 1971 as high as 10 per cent.

The high rate of inflation, which is not confined to Britain, has been hailed by some Marxists as the response of capitalists, and particularly of those with monopolistic positions who can therefore administer prices, to the effects of trade-union militancy cutting into the return to capital (Glyn and Sutcliffe, 1972, p. 133). This is to assume, with the neo-classical theorists, the full utilization of capacity and a constant capital–output ratio. But Marx's analysis of the declining rate of profit allowed for the possibility that capitalists' profits do not rise in relation to wages but that invested capital does increase in relation to output. This certainly describes the situation in Britain in the last few years.[3] Inflation would be the result of a rising ratio of capital invested to planned output. In fact, individual capitalists can avoid raising the ratio of capital to output, and lowering their rate of profit, by cheapening capital, or by cheapening imports and distribution, and by establishing monopolistic

3. Glyn and Sutcliffe (1972, p. 231) argue that there has been no increase in the organic composition of capital during the period of declining profit rates in Britain. This is, however, only because output has failed to rise very fast and unused capacity has increased. The capital–output ratio has definitely been rising, especially if dwellings and public authorities are excluded. On this count the ratio of net capital stock to given output rose from $1 \cdot 55 : 1 \cdot 0$ to $2 \cdot 3 : 1 \cdot 0$ between 1957 and 1971; of net capital stock to net output, i.e. less capital consumption, from $1 \cdot 7 : 1 \cdot 0$ to $2 \cdot 55 : 1 \cdot 0$. See *National Income and Expenditure* Blue Books, 1967 and 1972, tables 11 and 63.

positions throughout the world. This is what the large firms do and this is how they survive. What happens to the rest of the economy is that the government has increasingly to step in, to manage prices and incomes, to finance the firms that fail to keep up and to replace the lost investment in order to maintain employment. This intervention is what Schumpeter feared would lead the 'march to socialism'. It is not quite what Marx imagined as the breakdown of capitalism through the polarization of wealth and poverty; but it does follow Marx's general line of thought that the conflict would intensify between private accumulation in larger and larger units of capital and the increasing, consciously felt, social needs of the people.

What the neo-classical writers suggest today is the use of monetary policy, both to vindicate Say's Law and to control inflation (Patinkin, 1965, pp. 350–65). It is assumed that inflation follows from the pressure of trade unions using 'wage leadership' to generalize the wages available in large firms where high profits and high productivity go together (Turner and Jackson, 1970, tables 7.4, 7.5, 7.6). But for this to follow it would be necessary to find evidence of wages in the large firms and in the small firms converging, and all the evidence is to the contrary (Barratt Brown, 1972b). Governments are, nonetheless, encouraged by neo-classical economists to reduce state support for the low-paid worker and the unprofitable firm; but the neo-classicals do not have the courage of their convictions. They retain an almost Keynesian faith either in the management of the state or in the management of the large company to help them out. Hicks calls to his aid what he calls 'the Administrative Revolution in government', which, as well as 'bringing economic nationalism and communism so much nearer', also allows so much 'in the economist's accounts' to be accommodated 'very much in many ways, to the general advantage' (Hicks, 1969, p. 151). Johnson puts his faith in the internationalism (1968, p. 130) (therefore absence of support for mercantilism) and also the immortality (therefore long time horizon) of the international corporation and its preoccupation with adaptation to the market 'through marketing, research and selling activities rather than with physical production *per se*' (Johnson, 1962,

p. 175). All this is quite at odds with Schumpeter, and the sentence that follows comes very near to the concept of the 'soulful corporation':

Effective organization, satisfactory growth, and profitable change, rather than minimization of cost for a given production function and maximization of profit for a given demand, are the key problems of the productive unit in the opulent society (Johnson, 1962, p. 175).

Whence then would come the incentive to invest?

Schumpeter's last words were as critical of the stagnationists, as he called the Keynesians, as they were of the Marxists; and once again he argued that, while their diagnosis of the reasons for stagnation was wrong, their predictions were right.

Unless people see investment opportunities they will not normally save and a situation of vanishing investment opportunity is likely to be also one of vanishing saving. [But] though there is nothing to fear from people's propensity to save, there is plenty to fear from other factors. Labour unrest, price regulation, vexatious administration and irrational taxation are quite adequate to produce the verification of the stagnationist theory (Schumpeter, 1943, 1949 edn, pp. 397–8).

The divorce between savings and investment, which Keynes identified as the cause of unemployment and source of mercantilist state policies should, then, have been largely resolved by the concentration of capital accumulation and realization *inside* the large companies. Indeed, it is the view of Keynesians like Robinson and Galbraith that they have been so resolved, but with the help of state support, as for Britain's capital exports in the nineteenth century. As Robinson writes, in part summarizing Galbraith:

The great corporations ... once launched, do not depend for finance upon individual saving. Each consists in a self-perpetuating fund controlled by a self-perpetuating cadre of managers and technicians. ... The managers are continually striving to increase profits by investments which reduce costs so as to improve their selling power. This makes it possible for real wages to rise without reducing the rate of profit. The major part of this investment is financed out of profits. . . . This system ensures for the management a high degree of independence from bankers and governments. . . . State expenditure has provided a balancing element in demand to preserve near-stability and continuous growth in the market for goods. The easier line of expenditure for the state to undertake is for so-called defence (Robinson, 1970a, pp. 83–4).

It is in the area of state expenditure on armaments that Galbraith's concept of the 'technostructure' comes into its own (Galbraith, 1967). This is made up of the specialized managers who cross and interlock the sectors of government, finance and industry and provide the element of planning against the anarchy of the market that the large-scale and long gestation periods of modern investment demand. But he does not accept that state spending need be on armaments; it could be on any other goods or services that do not compete in the private sector market (Galbraith, 1967, p. 338). He seems to be right here; unemployment in the USA has not risen and fallen with the defence budget but only with state expenditure as a whole (see Barratt Brown, 1972a, table 1, p. 122 and table 21 below). The important point is that the state should 'underwrite costs including the costs of research and development and . . . ensure a market for the resulting product' (Galbraith, 1967, p. 164). Since military expenditure provides continuous profitability, continuous growth of industry and employment and, 'so to speak as a by-product' (Robinson, 1970a, p. 86), the continuous expansion of output and consumption of marketable goods, it is necessary continuously to justify this expenditure. There could hardly be a better prescription for imperialism.

Moreover, it is Robinson's view, that the modern welfare states are the new mercantilists. Each aims to accumulate reserves by expanding exports, but the world market does not grow fast enough for the output of the productive capacity of all the industrial states:

Exports yield profits and imports (apart from raw materials) mean a loss of sales to competitors. Moreover, internal investment is easier to foster, inflation easier to fend off and the foreign exchange easier to manage in a situation of a *favourable* balance of trade – that is an excess of exports over imports. Thus every nation competes to achieve 'export-led growth', while each tries to defend itself from the exports of others (1970a, p. 92).

Quoting Myrdal, she concludes that the 'welfare state in the rich countries of the Western World is by its very nature protectionist and nationalistic'.

Unlike Galbraith, whose book is innocent of any references to the export of capital or to imperialism except as an 'ancient Marxist contention' (Galbraith, 1967, p. 338), Robinson is quite prepared to draw the conclusion from nationalism to 'neo-colonialism' by one-time imperial countries. In doing so, she identifies the international corporations as transmitting the surplus in the form of profits out of the third world countries, and using state power to keep these countries open to capitalist enterprise.

The international companies, perfectly correctly from their own point of view, arrange their investments around the world and manipulate the flow of production from one centre to another to suit the requirements of their own profitability, not to promote the viability or growth of particular national economies (Robinson, 1970a, p. 109).

There is one weakness in the analysis of both Robinson and Galbraith that a Marxist must point out, and that is the absence of any reference to competition. Both see the large corporations as agreeing together through the 'technostructure' or through the nation state to manage the market so that it can absorb their products and use resources at near full employment. There are, of course, many ways in which big corporations can come together and agree a common solution – nationally, inside national planning and other governmental bodies; internationally, inside cartels and other trade associations. The fact remains that they are in competition with each other, and not only across national borders between national firms, but increasingly inside national borders between international firms.

Some neo-Marxists[4] have also been led to underestimate the continuing importance of capitalist competition, perhaps

4. What follows is very largely a criticism of Baran and Sweezy (1966).

Table 21 Public expenditure and unemployment,
UK and USA, 1913–1969

Year	Military expenditure as percentage of GNP		All state expenditure as a percentage of GNP		Unemployment rates as a percentage of labour force	
	UK	USA	UK	USA	UK	USA
1913	3·0	—	13·5	10·5	2·1	4·4
1923	4·7	—	27·5	11	11·7	3·2
1933	3·8	—	30	16·5	19·9	24·9
1938	4·9	1·5	31·2	19·5	13·5	19·0
1948	7·4	8·0	37	24	1·8	3·4
1953	8·9	13·2	35	27·5	1·8	2·9
1958	6·4	10·1	31·5	29	2·2	6·8
1960	6·2	9·0	32·5	28	1·7	5·6
1965	5·8	7·5	34	28·5	1·5	4·5
1969	5·3	9·0	39	32	2·5	3·5

Capital formation of public corporations and government loans and
grants to industry add another 8 per cent to the UK figure of state
expenditure in 1969 (6 per cent in 1967)
Sources: London and Cambridge Economic Service (1967); OECD
(1970b); CSO (1970)

because they have accepted an underconsumptionist interpretation of Marx and therefore see the increase of surplus
value and the search for its disposal as the main source of the
continuing expansionism. Surplus value increases, they say,
because of reduced competition between capitalists. It is not
that the share of profit increases but that the gap between sales
prices and production costs increases. Advertising and other
'waste' are included in the surplus.

In fact, Baran and Sweezy failed to show in their own tables
for the United States between 1929 and 1963 that there was
a marked tendency for the surplus to rise as a proportion of
GNP (1966, p. 389); it was high in the war years and low in
the thirties and fifties, rising in the sixties. What *has* steadily
risen as a proportion of GNP has been government expenditure (see table 21). The surplus not taken by the government
remained remarkably stable as a proportion of GNP. Nor had
there been, in the USA up to 1963, a steady decrease in capacity
utilization nor an increase in unemployment (Baran and
Sweezy, 1966, pp. 242, 247). Utilization of capacity and em-

ployment were high in the war years, low in the 1930s and in the 1950s and rising in the 1960s. Underused capacity reduced the surplus but there was no long-term trend. If increasing oligopoly were reducing competition, there should be. Yet oligopoly was certainly increasing with the share of large firms in the total market, even if the largest firms did not necessarily grow fastest (Hymer and Rowthorn, 1970, p. 69).

This process is analagous to the expansion of capitalism into pre-capitalist areas in the nineteenth century. Small-scale producers are destroyed and this leaves behind unemployment in underdeveloped regions. Only state spending serves to re-employ the displaced workers. If this were a once-for-all intervention by the state to balance aggregate demand and the capacity to supply, when oligopolists set prices too high for full utilization of resources, as Keynesian theory would suggest, then it would not be necessary for the proportion of government expenditure to rise in order to maintain full employment. But this does seem to be necessary, as table 21 shows and as was proved by the attempts in Britain of both Labour and Conservative Governments to cut back the share of state spending between 1968 and 1971, with a sharp resultant increase in unemployment, so that state spending had to be raised again in 1972–3.

Oligopolistic competition between giant firms consists of a struggle for take-overs, for monopoly positions in markets, for privileged access to sources of materials, accompanied by rationalization and other forms of cost-cutting, if not by direct price-cutting. Neo-Marxists may have underemphasized the competitiveness of the oligopolies because they wanted to explain a rising surplus. Perhaps they accepted too readily the Leninist concept of 'state monopoly capitalism' and the phrases in the Communist manifesto about the 'executive power of the state [being] simply a committee for managing the common affairs of the entire bourgeois class'. They saw managers of giant firms not just as part of a neutral 'techno-structure' but as wealthy property owners themselves, trying to control the state's activities in their own interest. In this they were almost certainly right, but it led them to neglect the conformative role of the state and to exaggerate the common interest of the oligopolies. Studies of government contracts in the USA, and especially of military contracts, suggest a bitter battle between the giant firms, with each exploiting the hold it may have on a particular department of the Pentagon – Army, Airforce, Navy, Marines, Atomic Energy Commission, Space Agency – or on civilian departments, to encourage the development of those new weapons and equipment in which each firm is specially interested (Kidron, 1969, pp. 24–5, 38). Such competition could explain not only the persistently large military budget but the whole orientation of United States foreign policy.

For the very large United States companies in the early 1960s, about 20 per cent of profits came from military contracts, rising with the escalation of the Vietnam war. This proportion is, however, greatly exceeded by that obtained from overseas investment, reckoned at over 30 per cent already in 1962 (Perlo, 1963, pp. 71–81). By 1966 the sales of overseas subsidiaries of United States' firms in Europe had reached a level two and a half times that of United States total exports of goods to Europe (compared with one and a half times in 1957) (Hymer and Rowthorn, 1970, p. 76). The large firms are responsible for nearly all the foreign investment, so that 50 per cent of their profits in the mid 1960s came from military contracts and foreign investment together, although military and foreign sales for all US companies equalled respectively only 10 per cent and 5 per cent of United States GNP.

According to the figures in table 22, the manufactured output of the local subsidiaries of companies in the capitalist world has been growing somewhat faster than the trade in manufactures; but the growth of output from subsidiaries has been specially concentrated in two areas – Europe and to a much lesser extent, the underdeveloped lands. By 1966 something near one-third of all manufactured output in the underdeveloped lands, and nearly half the growth in the previous decade, came from foreign firms, whereas in the case of developed countries the share was nearer one sixth. These are total figures for all manufacturing firms, but foreign operations have, in fact, been established by quite a small number of firms, a few hundred in each country with the top 200 world companies providing about three-quarters of the investment (Hymer and Rowthorn, 1970, pp. 75–6).

Although the wide spread of trans-national operations by large firms is a recent phenomenon, one might look back to the East India companies; and certainly examples can be found in the last quarter of the nineteenth century. Some companies, like Royal Dutch Shell and Unilever, developed into multinational control as well as trans-national operation.[5] Others, like Standard Oil, General Motors, ICI or Imperial Tobacco, were owned by one group of nationals, but established subsidiaries in many countries: some wholly owned, some with only a majority shareholding by the parent company. These trans-national companies took advantage of the economics of vertical integration or exploited a monopoly in some product, patent or know-how.

The Marxist view distinguishes the process of concentration of production in larger and larger units, as technical change creates greater opportunities for economies of scale, and of centralization of capital, as smaller firms fail to stand up to the financial resources that the large firm can draw on, both in times of rapid technical change and of depressed markets. The pressure behind the expansion of large firms into trans-national operations in recent years seems to be of the second sort. Unit costs of research and development and of some other overheads can be reduced as scale increases; but the size of production units is not what is at issue in large-scale trans-national operation. Indeed, local production by overseas subsidiaries rather than exports from home production may actually in-

5. I have adopted the usage of 'trans-national' rather than 'international' or 'multinational' because 'international' or 'multinational' implies ownership shared between different nationals and there are not many cases of this type of company but many cases of large firms predominantly owned by nationals of one country but with operations in other countries. Dunning (1971) calls these MPEs (multinational producing enterprises) and the first group MOEs (multinationally owned) or MCEs (multinationally controlled enterprises).

Table 22 Output, trade and local production of manufactures originating in the developed capitalist world, 1957 and 1966 (all figures in $ billion)

Country of origin or destination	GNP (market prices)		Manufactured goods output Total		Manufactured goods output By foreign firms		Manufactured goods trade Imports		Manufactured goods trade Exports	
	1957	1966	1957	1966	1957	1966	1957	1966	1957	1966
USA	448	703	131	218	6	9·5	5·0	12	11	19
from UK, N and S[a]	—	—	—	—	4·7	7·4	1·2	2	—	—
from other Europe	—	—	—	—	0·6	1·3	2·2	4	—	—
from Japan	—	—	—	—	0·03	0·05	1	3	—	—
Japan	40	119	8	28	1	2·5	0·5	1·5	2·5	9
from US	—	—	—	—	0·6	2	0·4	1	—	—
Canada	32	58	8	13	4	7	3·5	6·5	2	5·0
from US	—	—	—	—	3·5	6	2·5	5·3	—	—
UK	65	107	20	32	4	7	1·5	4	7·5	12
from US	—	—	—	—	3·5	5·5	0·3	1·2	—	—
other Europe	260	380	86	150	10	38	14	38	20	48
from US	—	—	—	—	7	29	2	5·5	—	—
from UK	—	—	—	—	1	2·5	2	5	—	—
from other Europe	—	—	—	—	2	6	9·5	32	—	—
Oceania	19	30	6	9	4	6	1	2·5	—	—
from US	—	—	—	—	2·5	4·5	0·3	1	—	—

developed countries	865	1400	245	450	29	70	25·5	64·5	43	93
from US	—	—	—	—	17	47	4·8	11·5	—	—
from UK	—	—	—	—	7	10	3·7	7	—	—
underdeveloped countries	180	280	30	50	6	15	17·5	28·5	—	—
from US	—	—	—	—	3	8	4·7	7·2	—	—
from UK	—	—	—	—	1·5	3·5	4	5·3	—	—
capitalist world	1045	1680	275	500	35	85	43	93	—	—
communist world	350	625	110	220	—	—	1·2	3	—	—

[a] United Kingdom, Netherlands and Sweden. Many figures are rough approximations only. Developed countries' exports of manufactures comprise those of USA, Japan, Canada, EEC, UK, Sweden and Switzerland. Output by foreign firms in underdeveloped countries are estimates based on investments in manufactured industry in these areas.

Sources: UN (1969a); OECD (1970b); Rowthorn (1971a, 1971b); Department of Trade and Industry (1972); Dunning (1971, pp. 20–21); Board of Trade (1970)

volve reduction of plant size and failure to maximize scale economies. Tariffs were certainly a major reason for the establishment by large firms of local production in foreign markets. Lever Bros and the American motor car firms provide obvious examples (Wilson, 1954, p. 89; Sundelson, 1970, pp. 243–72). Tariffs can also be overcome by sale of patents; in any case tariffs have been reduced in the last two decades, while the export of capital has grown.

To some writers it is the strength of the currencies in which equities are quoted that explains the trans-national operations of companies (Aliber, 1971; 1972). Thus British firms before 1913, United States firms thereafter, and Swiss, Dutch and German firms most recently, could export capital because of the currency premium of their countries of origin. British and Japanese firms and those of other national origins export capital to the USA today because of the dollar premiums which they then attach to their income streams. The argument is unsatisfactory; the currency might be strong because of the large companies using it rather than the reverse. The argument can, however, be generalized to suggest an advantage in access to finance of the largest companies, whatever their country of origin, and going with this an advantage in hedging risks by movement of funds earned in different currencies. This has been greatly facilitated by the growth of the Eurodollar and Eurobond markets (Dunning, 1971, p. 57).

Another explanation for the expansion of the large firm is based upon the sociology of the firm itself. The growth of the firm as a dynamic process internal to the firm, rather than as an adjustment to optimum or most profitable economic size in given conditions, was first proposed by Penrose (1959). She argued that each new expansion created new inducements for the organization of the firm as a whole to expand further, for reasons akin to the Keynesian view of power and prestige as central elements in the quest for wealth. Assuming that 'in general the financial and investment decisions of firms are controlled by a desire to increase total long-run profits . . .' she argues that 'firms will want to expand as fast as they can take advantage of opportunities for expansion that they consider profitable' (p. 29). Thus, on her argument, 'growth and profits become equivalent for the selection of investment programmes' (p. 30).

Penrose distinguishes those entrepreneurial ambitions which she calls 'product minded or goodwill builders' from those of the 'empire builders' who 'collect firms' (pp. 39–40). 'The internal inducements to expansion arise largely from the existence of a pool of unused production services, resources and specialized knowledge' (p. 66). . . .'Just as the division of labour in the economy as a whole is limited by the demand for goods and services, so within a firm the division of labour, or the specialization of resources, is limited by the total output of the firm, for the firm's output controls its "demand" for productive services' (pp. 71–2).

Increases of scale are demanded not only for full utilization of resources but also for exploiting new technology and for monopolistic advantage and to preclude the entry of new competitors, by diversification, backward integration and control over sources of supply (p. 65). But diversification of the firm's resources is largely an internal dynamic for Penrose, and she illustrates this from General Motors' entry into refrigerator, aeroplane, radio and diesel manufacture and into military activities (pp. 120–23). A completely non-specialized firm is as vulnerable to competition as a completely specialized firm, in conditions of rapid innovation (p. 132):

In the long run, profitability, survival and growth [of a firm depends on] its ability to establish one or more wide and relatively impregnable bases from which it can adapt and extend its operations in an uncertain, changing and competitive world (p. 137).

Competition sets limits to the internal dynamic of the expansion of companies so that it 'induces and even forces the extensive research and innovation in which they engage and provides the justification for the whole system' (p. 164).

The process of company acquisitions and mergers inside a national economy can be equally applied to competition in the international economy. Concentration, according to Penrose, would be discouraged in periods of rapid economic growth and encouraged during stagnation or slump. This was because of the opportunities in periods of growth for smaller companies to expand, as she calls it, 'in the interstices', unless the large firms can set barriers to this expansion (pp. 258–60).

The export of capital in the period after the mid 1870s could, on this view, be related in a period of stagnation to unused resources in the firm – that is of skills and knowledge as well as of capital equipment and finance. In the Western World in the late 1950s and 1960s, the growth rate in Britain and in the United States was well below the average; and it was largely British and United States firms that were most involved in direct overseas investment. These are suggestive examples, but the increase of foreign investment by Japanese, German and other European manufacturers in the 1960s, when their own economies were booming, does not fit the theory.

One explanation might be that the boom in the German and Japanese economies has been export-oriented, the growth of home consumption being deliberately held back. Wartime destruction of plant in these countries and the restriction on their arms expenditure in the early 1950s gave their reconstructed industries a competitive edge in the world market, especially for capital goods, which provided for them a large export surplus. By not up-valuing their currencies in line with their higher rate of growth of productivity, relative to that of other countries, and especially of the USA and UK, they were enabled to permit a distribution of income at home that maintained a high share of profits for reinvestment, even at the expense of a slower growth in the home market, and to expand their export sales at a rapid rate. In this way surpluses available for overseas investment were built up which the large firms could use when trans-national production was indicated as a necessary successor to direct export. That home markets were deliberately held down in favour of exporting was possible just so long as other countries, and especially the US and UK, ran deficits. This indeed they did throughout the 1960s, the deficits being financed respectively by gold sales and foreign borrowing. When action was taken to end these deficits in the late 1960s, the struggle between the rival industrial centres became more acute (Barratt Brown, 1972b, pp. 190–97). But was the struggle between firms or states?

The competitive strength of trans-national companies has been described here in terms of the national origins of these companies and their integration with nation-state policies. The larger the firms are, however, and the more they operate transnationally, the more the nation states, apart from the superstates – USA, EEC, Japan and the USSR – are forced into a client relationship with the giant companies. This is the meaning of the long struggle over the incorporation of Britain into the EEC, for which the British-based trans-national companies have taken the initiative all along. The competition of the corporations has become the driving force in international relations, not the rivalry of nation states. The identity between 'finance capital' and 'capitalist powers' was not complete even when Lenin was writing. The state was called in to protect the interests of national capitalist groups as can be seen in General Smedley D. Butler's *Memoirs* on ' How I helped to make Mexico . . . safe for American oil interests' (see Huberman, 1940, pp. 259–60), but each had to fight for its own state's support.

The Keynesian view is clearly of a number of large, developed nation states pursuing mercantilist policies in the interests of national economic and political power, with their giant companies adapting to these policies as best they may;[6] while the Marxist view presented here is of a number of giant transnational firms pursuing the going rate of capital accumulation in strong competition with each other and manipulating nation state policies as far as they can (see Murray, 1972). For the Marxists the state also has a conformative role in reconciling sectional and even class interests. Large firms compete for state orders and democratic governments have to win majority support for their policies. The giant company is the inheritor

6. In a paper delivered to a Chatham House Conference in July 1972 (Knapp, 1972) which was a variant of his *Lloyds Bank Review* article (1973), adapted for delivery to an audience of non-economist scholars interested in the study of international relations, Knapp stated that he took 'special pride in the fact that he had not mentioned the international company'.

and beneficiary of the whole range of state activities, which we have seen supporting capitalist development even during periods of ostensible free trade and *laissez-faire*.

One crucial role of the state in developed countries today is in providing economic aid to the underdeveloped countries including tied credits for exports. This aid is concentrated in those areas where private investments have been made, as repayment of earlier loans might otherwise be in jeopardy (Barratt Brown, 1972a, p. 142). It is, of course, a coincidence that public aid and direct investment income almost exactly balance each other in the US and UK accounts given in table 23, but it is nonetheless a remarkable coincidence. Figures for French aid and debt repayments to and from the Franc Zone correspond in the same way (Barratt Brown, 1973).

These operations are only a part, however, of the whole 'multinational synergy', as it is now called, available to a large trans-national firm – movement of funds to minimize exchange losses, transfer pricing to minimize taxation, switching location to avert the effects of labour disputes, production of components in countries at different levels of technology according to whether labour is cheap where labour-intensive operations are indicated, capital cheap where capital-intensive operations are advantageous. Orchestration of all these instruments justifies trans-national operations. Production can be distributed between countries having different cost structures and also different 'risk lives'.[7] Countries can be sequenced as markets for different products according to their standards of consumption, so that monopoly positions in a new product or technique can be maintained. Transport costs and the optimal size of plant can be balanced according to anticipated demand in each area (Vernon, 1960; 1970). This implies the inclusion of the less developed lands in the total 'synergy'. But trans-national expansion might be a once-for-all process, resulting from the widened span of control, made

7. ICI's overseas coordination director is quoted as saying 'Your investment plan would be to have a *minimum* of 80 per cent of your investment in countries you regarded as really safe and 20 per cent or less in three groups (out of four) with varying "risk lives" ' (Turner 1969, p. 26).

Table 23 US and UK direct foreign investment income of companies and movements of public capital, by regions, 1967–1969

Region	USA ($m)		UK (£m)	
	Direct investment income	Provision of public funds	Direct investment income	Provision of public funds
all developed	2000	—	390	—
North America	900	—	130	—
Europe	900	—	90	—
sterling area	200	—	160	—
all underdeveloped	3000	3200	170	165
Latin America	500	650	33	12
SW Asia and Korea	1500	1800	3	20
sterling area	200	500	130	133
other	800	250	4	—
total	5000	3200	560	165

Sources: US Department of Commerce (1971a); Department of Trade and Industry (1972); OECD (1970a)

possible by the computer, and from the monopolistic opportunities for exploiting the gap between new and old at the current rapidly changing state of technology. The Marxists might still not be right in assuming that the process of centralization will continue until, in the words of a non-Marxist, 'on current projections some 200 companies will own most of the world's assets by the turn of the century' (Dunning, 1970).

If that happened the relative power of the nation state would be weakened. Conflicts between the interests of large firms and the nation state seem already to be serious (Penrose, 1971; Murray, 1971a; Hymer and Rowthorn, 1970). Long-term and short-term movements of capital, transfer pricing policies, subsidiary production instead of exports – all these actions by trans-national companies tend to undermine the economic management of even large nation states like Britain. Such companies may become quite opportunistic about the state to which they look for protection and turn increasingly from small states to super states like the EEC to provide the all-round economic climate that suits them. Smaller and less developed nation states may find that they are negotiating with companies rather than with governments and may have to adapt their taxation, fiscal and social policies to the requirements of large investing firms if their investment is to be attracted and retained (Streeten, 1971).

These new developments provide support for a Marxist analysis of the dynamic of capital accumulation in the firm as the origin of empire building (but see Warren, 1971, for an alternative Marxist view). Hilferding's and Lenin's emphasis on finance capital and its links with the state as the central elements in their model of imperialism reflected a passing and particular stage of development of German industry. What lay behind was the expansion of the private capitalist firm, whose aim, even in the era of free trade, was to achieve and hold a monopolistic position first in the home market and then elsewhere, in colonies and in other foreign markets where control over raw materials and investment opportunities could be asserted. The world-wide 'synergy' of the trans-national company is, on this view, the logical conclusion of a long historical process of capital accumulation and territorial assimilation.

10 The Terms of Trade and the Dual Economy

One of the forms of inequality that appears in the relations between nations, is the unequal exchange contained in the terms of trade. With abundant resources or mechanical aids a rich country can obtain more direct labour and provide less in the goods exchanged than a poor country, so that wealth and poverty become cumulatively polarized; and this widening gap is compounded by steadily deteriorating terms of trade for the poor countries, i.e. the prices of their products rise more slowly or fall faster than those of the rich countries' products. The concept of 'unequal exchange' as the essence of the 'imperialism of trade' has been the subject of extensive recent debate among French Marxists and particularly between Denis, Emmanuel, Bettelheim and Palloix.

It is the view of some of those neo-Marxists, who emphasize the importance of unequal exchange, that the prices of different products entering world trade depend upon the level of wages in the countries that produce them. Wages have been established historically at high levels in certain countries because of successful trade-union struggle, which has been at the expense of both the capitalists in the high wage countries and the peoples of the low wage countries (Emmanuel, 1972a, pp. 61, 120, 170, 189). The existing terms of trade and the movements in the terms of trade, therefore, reflect these wage levels and relative changes in them. Differences in productivity are regarded as the result, not the cause, of differences in wages (p. 164),[1] but these differences are perpetuated by the non-mobility of labour between countries (pp. 258–9). It is emphasized that the wide and widening inequality in the terms of

1. Exception is made in the case of the same goods being produced in different countries (see p. 136).

trade is between rich and poor countries as a whole, and only between the products exported in so far as these are specific to rich or to poor countries (pp. 176–7). Emmanuel sums up the object of his study as being 'to prove that under capitalist production relations one earns as much as one spends and that prices depend on wages' (p. 172), and 'the fundamental assumption made in *Unequal Exchange* is the tendency to equalization of rates of profit on the world scale' (p. 381).

This theory of unequal exchange is quite contrary both to the neo-classical view of comparative costs and to Marx's argument that the rate of capital accumulation and the socially necessary labour time involved in production are the determinants of prices. It has, however, much in common with the Keynesian view; and, indeed, in defending himself against Bettelheim, Emmanuel has recourse to arguments that are frankly of a Keynesian type.

We begin with the end, with consumption [on] the classical model of the capitalist road [on which North America and Australia were developed], by creating a market actual or potential which is sufficiently large. In this way capital is attracted, and the corresponding consumer goods are produced. When these industries become extensive enough, and their need for mechanization (owing to higher wages) is great enough, a second market is created for capital goods, and this in turn attracts further capital, which establishes heavy industry. We keep on going upstream all the time (pp. 378–80).

Emmanuel concedes that this is not a way that others could necessarily follow who do not enjoy wages that are high to start with, and 'the market a promising one'; there were 'exceptional historical circumstances' in North America (p. 379). 'Wealth begets wealth', he says, and 'poverty begets poverty', working through the process of 'unequal exchange' (pp. 130–31). This is, in effect, similar to Myrdal's view that the polarization process between rich and poor countries is one of 'cumulative causation' from a strong or weak starting point (1954, p. 11). It does not tell us why wages were high or low in the first place; nor how some countries broke out of the process, while others did not.

The terms of trade may be defined:

1 As the relative quantities of goods imported and exported by any country (gross barter terms of trade) (Taussig, 1925, pp. 1–10).

2 As the relative prices of exports and imports, net barter terms of trade or commodity terms of trade (Viner, 1955, pp. 562–3). 1 and 2 can be multiplied together to show:

3 The movements of relative current market values (market or trade balance) (Imlah, 1958, pp. 92–3).

It is also possible to compare the quantities of labour and capital contained in the exports and imports of any country (factoral terms of trade) (Pigou, 1920, p. 150).

Movements over time of 1, 2 and 3 can be measured. Price movements can be measured for one country's total imports and exports in relation to those of other countries, or for particular aggregates within the total from all countries entering world trade, for example, the terms of trade of manufactures and primary products. Prices at any time can be stated in terms of a common currency at current exchange rates. But what lies behind these prices, the factoral terms of trade, present serious problems for measurement. The whole concept of unequal exchange between developed and underdeveloped lands is based on measuring hours of labour going into the production of goods that enter world trade, profit rates being assumed to be equalized.

This, however, leaves out of account the productivity of labour under different technical conditions. Emmanuel assumes that techniques are secondary to intensity of labour utilization and to the historic level of wages in the two sets of countries. 'Output of labour, given the same equipment for the average worker in the underdeveloped areas' he estimates at 50 to 60 per cent of [that of] the average worker in the industrialized areas' (1972a, p. 48). This halves the 30:1 ratio apparent for wages in developed and underdeveloped lands. But differences in productivity can be shown to be even greater than 30:1 (see table 24).

Table 24 Wages and productivity in manufacturing industry
for certain countries, 1950–1955

Country	Wages per hour		Net output per head per year	
	(in $)	(as percentage of USA)	(in $)	(as percentage) of USA)
USA	1·70	100	5730	100
UK	0·454	27	2260	40
Belgium	0·378	22	2320	41
France	0·335	20	1860	32
W Germany	0·331	19	1610	28
Italy	0·265	16	1030	18
Japan	0·25	15	1340	23
Latin America	0·25 – 0·35	15–20	800–900	12–14
'Black Africa'	0·2 – 0·25	12–15	600–800	10–12
Philippines	0·3	17	400	7
India	0·1	6	220	4
Pakistan	0·075	4	90	1·5

Wages are averages for 1950–1955; net output is for 1950 at 1955 prices;
wages in India and Africa include salaried employees' earnings
Sources: Emmanuel (1972a, p. 47); UN (1960, table 169); Maizels
(1963, table 1.4, p. 31)

Emmanuel argues that the differences in productivity are
the result of different wage levels, not the other way round.
Wages in underdeveloped lands are based on subsistence
levels; those in the developed lands include a 'socio-historical
element' (1972a, p. 49), resulting from trade union struggles
and won precisely out of the unequal exchange between the
two. But how was the difference established?

In neo-classical thinking each factor of production is
'rewarded' according to its relative scarcity and marginal contribution to production. Goods will enter foreign trade
according to the comparative cost advantages of production
in each country and the strength of world demand for them.
But these cost advantages have themselves to be explained, and
some of them we have seen to be historical. The theory of
comparative costs, moreover, assumes not only perfect competition and full employment with trade balanced, but a static
condition of population, resources and technology, with no
movements of capital or labour. These are quite unrealistic

assumptions and the gains from trade in any case need not be equally distributed between the parties to trade exchanges. The level of taxes and tariffs is, on this view, just a matter for value judgements, so long as economic incentives are not destroyed in the process. The harmonious relationship in a single national economy reproduces itself through free trade in the world economy. Attempts of governments to benefit their peoples by turning the terms of trade in their favour are as self-defeating as measures of protection.

The Keynesians reject all this for a quite hard-headed approach to the terms of trade, seeing them as the outcome of bargaining by nation states, each following mercantilist policies (Robinson, 1962, p. 64). There are no determinants of the level of wages or the rate of profit except the bargaining power of the parties concerned. Such bargaining between nations, as between producers, will depend in the short run, on current conditions of supply and demand and on the income and price elasticities of demand for different commodities. This would be acceptable also to neo-classical economists, but the Keynesians like Robinson would add that, where there are monopoly positions, prices will be raised above the normal equilibrium level, and this may be most typical where demand is least elastic (Robinson, 1962). A few manufacturers in developed countries may join together in cartels more easily than the many scattered primary producers in poor countries (Singer, 1950). Above all, the governments of large nation states can restrict imports and force exports and benefit their capitalists by opening up investment opportunities abroad. Political power will be as important here as economic power; and there were special geo-political circumstances involved in the emergence of European and especially British power in the nineteenth century.

Marx was not content to leave the distribution of income between different producers in a national market, or in different countries in the world market, to an explanation based on the bargaining power of the parties concerned. There was a lower limit to wages in the subsistence level, which would vary from country to country; and there was an upper limit in the needs of competitive capital accumulation. Somewhere in between wages settled down at a level that included what Marx called a 'historical and moral element'. This allowed not only for the reproduction and training and education of workers, but for something more – which trade unions had won and could fight to hold on to in the long run, and which the pressure of the unemployed reserve army of labour at home and abroad could reduce in the short run (Marx, 1946, ch. 6). For Marx, however, the wage was not the invariable as it is for Emmanuel. The rate of accumulation was the one invariable. Real wages could rise with rising productivity, even in relation to 'any particular level of unemployment, provided that they did not interfere with the process of accumulation. If they did, the result would be higher unemployment and pressure to reduce them.

In her *Essay on Marxian Economics*, Robinson argued that 'as soon as the rigid subsistence level theory is abandoned, it [Marx's theory of wages] provides no definite answer to the central question – what determines the division of the total produce between capital and labour?' (1942, p. 33).[2] However, Steindl showed that Marx's long-run rate of accumulation, established between competing capitalists, really does provide a theory of the determination of real wages and therefore of the distribution of income. It is only in the short run that real wages determine the rate of accumulation; in the long run it is the other way round.

What Marx did not allow for was that the state should step in to maintain full employment. In that event, which has of course been *the* event, if the rate of accumulation is regarded as the invariable, there would be three alternatives for a Marxian view; (a) real wages would be kept in check by

2. In the article referred to above, Robinson does suggest a very Marxian alternative to that of 'the balance of power in bargaining between employer and worker [to] determine the share of wages in net proceeds' when she adds as a question: 'Or is it rather the requirements of profits that determine what is left over for wages for a given level of physical output?'

oligopolistic pricing policies; (b) incomes would be made subject to state control; or (c) a dual economy would emerge: one sector maintaining the going rate of accumulation with high wages and high profits from above average productivity while the other sector, with or without state support, suffered low wages and low profits from below average productivity.

The relevance of Marx's theory of wages for the determination of the terms of trade is not only that the classical view is rejected, i.e. that differences in prices in different countries and in prices of the particular products of different countries can be said to be due to international factor and commodity substitution working through supply and demand in the world as a whole to maximize the benefit from given resources; but also that the neo-Marxist view, apparently accepted by Robinson (1962, p. 64), is rejected, i.e. that differences in prices are due to differences in bargaining power to raise wage levels. Rather, the differences, according to Marx, result from different subsistence levels and different capital–labour ratios and productivity levels, in producing the same or different commodities in the same or different countries. This last point challenges the whole of Emmanuel's argument that in international trade 'the inequality of wages, as such, all other things being equal, is alone the cause of the inequality of exchange' (Emmanuel, 1972a, p. 61).[3] And Emmanuel makes clear in the context that productivity is not one of the 'other things' that are equal.

Marx abstracted from the many different concrete costs of production with different capital–labour ratios the concept of socially necessary labour time (1946, vol. 1, ch. 1). If rates of profit are assumed to be equalized by competition between capitalists, then the price of any commodity will reflect the cost of production using the average degree of skill and intensity of work with the normal technical conditions of that time and place, that is to say that they will reflect that proportion of a society's total labour time, necessary for the production of the amount of the commodity that is demanded.

3. See Bettelheim's reply (1972, pp. 294–9).

Capitalists using techniques that reduce labour time will be able to cut their costs and capture the market, or if they are operating internationally, may enjoy a higher rate of profit (Marx, 1909, ch. 14, section 5). In fact, although rates of profit are equalized by competition over the short to medium term, technical conditions (implying different capital–labour ratios) vary greatly and are not at all quickly equalized. Capital–labour ratios are largely a matter of technical conditions, but the same technique may have different capital–labour ratios at different rates of profit, since the value of capital can only be measured in terms of the rate of profit actually earned from it. This is one of the implications of the neo-Ricardian critique of neo-classical capital theory. Between countries, and particularly between developed and underdeveloped economies, the differences in capital–labour ratios are likely to be greater than they will be inside any one country. Marx, more than 100 years ago, suggested as an example of different capital–labour ratios in a European and an Asiatic country the following comparative make-up of national products (Marx, 1909, ch. 8).

'European country: 84 to capital + 16 to labour + 16 to profit = 116,

i.e. rate of profit 16 per cent and rate of exploitation (surplus/labour) 100 per cent.

Asiatic country: 16 to capital + 84 to labour + 21 to profit = 121,

i.e. rate of profit 21 per cent and rate of exploitation 25 per cent.'

These are purely imaginary figures but they serve to show that similar rates of profit can be based on very dissimilar rates of surplus, and that the rate of surplus may be higher when the rate of profit is lower. This means that the rate of profit per unit of capital laid out on wages and on capital equipment consumed, i.e. depreciation, may be higher where the ratio of labour to capital equipment is higher, but capitalists will not as a result necessarily invest where labour is cheapest because the rate of surplus per worker is lower, and accumulation depends on reproducing surplus.[4] In order to compete, capitalists must keep reducing their costs, mainly by investing to increase labour productivity. Where they locate their investment will depend in part on the extent of the market, in part on the availability of skills, on the adequacy of the infrastructure and on the security for capital.

Marx expected that the rate of profit would fall as capital–labour value ratios rose, which led him to see foreign trade as a counteracting force. But in the long run each capitalist must compete with others operating at the same technical level, although each may try to avoid this by nation-state protection and similar means. If capitalists invested where they saw opportunities for maximizing the rate of profit, and not the rate of surplus, because there was no cost advantage from more productive techniques, then we should have seen throughout the history of capitalism, investment going to the countries with a labour surplus. The rate of accumulation would then have been very low because of the small increase in capital generated per unit of labour. In fact, investment has been in countries with a labour shortage, even to the extent that slave and indentured labour have been imported to provide the surplus.

There can then be unequal exchange in foreign trade. As Marx put it (1909, ch. 14, section 5), 'The favoured country recovers more labour for less labour', but he went on to add, 'although this difference, this surplus, is pocketed by a certain class, as it is in any exchange between labour and capital.'

4. In Marx's notation

$$\text{rate of profit} = \frac{\text{surplus } (S)}{\text{constant capital } (C) \text{ plus variable capital } (V)}$$

and rate of surplus $= \dfrac{\text{surplus}}{\text{variable capital,}}$

where constant capital = materials and capital consumption, and variable capital = wages paid.

This, therefore, describes the rate of profit in relation to turnover, and not to the total of capital invested by each capitalist.

In the economy as a whole $S/(C+V)$ can stand for the *average rate of profit*.

Marx considered Ricardo's objection that this may be 'at best but a temporary advantage of the favoured spheres of production over others', and concluded that he saw 'no reason why these higher rates of profit realized by capitals invested in certain lines and sent home by them should not enter as elements into the average rate of profit and tend to keep it up to that extent'. Hence his view of foreign trade as a counter*acting* tendency to the falling rate of profit. But he makes it clear that he did not expect it to be a counter-*balancing* tendency. For the fact that unequal labour time is exchanged on the world market cannot be taken to imply that the value of output being exchanged is unequal. Capitalists will pick up surplus wherever they can find it, but they must sell their output at costs that are competitive.

It was Luxemburg's argument that capitalists' profits from outside the closed capitalist system are necessary to continued accumulation (1951, pp. 419–28), but Marx was quite clear that they must come from inside, where the going rate of accumulation determines the distribution of wages and profits. The low wages of slaves and indentured labour provided a boost to capital accumulation at the birth of capitalism and on many subsequent occasions, but the dynamic of capitalism in the Marxian view comes from increasing the surplus from the higher productivity of labour. Slaves were not as productive as wage labourers and slavery was abolished. Marx was absolutely clear, that 'the more the productive forces are developed, the more the proletarians are exploited, that is, the higher the proportion of surplus labour to necessary labour', and Bettleheim adds, 'Reciprocally of course this means that, despite their low wages, the workers of the underdeveloped countries are less exploited than those of the advanced, and so dominant, countries' (see Emmanuel, 1972a, p. 302).

Suppose, however, we imagine a dual economy within the capitalist system with a high wage/high profit sector, insulated in part from the low wage/low profit sector by labour immobility; and this is not at all unrealistic. The location of capitalist accumulation remains the main feature of development and underdevelopment. But the way in which the market allocates profits between capitalists does not necessarily guarantee to each capitalist the surplus created by his workers, only that part which the price on the market for commodities and the price of capital allows him out of the total social profit. Marx insisted that: 'The whole difficulty arises from the fact that commodities are not exchanged simply as commodities, but as products of capitals, which claim equal shares of the amount of surplus value, if they are of equal magnitude, or shares proportionate to their different magnitudes' (1909, ch. 10).

Different rates of accumulation occur in different branches of production, and even more different rates in different countries. The Marxist view is that the rate of profit between branches and countries will tend to be equalized throughout the capitalist world to sustain a going rate of competitive accumulation; but prices are made up not only of a rate of profit but also of direct labour costs per unit of output sold in a competitive market. The cost of labour per unit, like all other costs, is determined in the Marxian system by the socially necessary labour time required to produce it and reproduce it. If this can be reduced by cheapening the cost of the necessities of life, by greater intensification of the work process, by resisting trade union demands for an increase in the moral element in the wage, then, any and all of these means will be adopted by capitalists. But the cost reductions that can be made in this way may be quite small compared with those made possible by applying more machinery. For this reason Marx's abstraction of 'average profit' was based on production with average productivity (socially necessary labour time). Unless relative wages are as low as relative productivity – and anything like this can only happen in different countries or in a dualistic economy – then capitalists will invest in higher productivity.

It is possible in any single country to talk about socially necessary labour-time because there is a norm for technical conditions of production from which deviations are not very great, but between countries the idea of an average world-wide socially necessary labour-time in production has very little meaning, as the wide range of wages and productivity in table 24 indicates. As Palloix has pointed out, rates of surplus value would have to be subject to some measure independent of international prices (1972). Exchange rates depend upon the bargaining position of different countries in the world market.[5] The weakness of the underdeveloped countries lies in their relatively low levels of productivity in the particular commodities to the production of which the historical development of capitalism has assigned them.

Wages and productivity are closely related; in table 24 the ranking is almost identical. The low level of wages in the underdeveloped lands is evident, but the point is that this is associated with *even lower* levels of productivity. The table only includes wages in the manufacturing sector, which can be assumed to be well above the general urban average, let alone rural earnings. Emmanuel quotes figures of 'wages of unskilled urban workers in Black Africa of 3 to 6 cents per hour (and rural workers coming to nearly half as much as this)' (1972a, p. 47). But it is not unreasonable to assume that their productivity is even lower.

In the case of manufactured goods, those produced with low wages and low productivity must compete with those produced with higher wages and still higher productivity. It is only in the case of goods that cannot be produced or substituted for in developed countries that low wages in underdeveloped countries would carry an advantage. This is, in effect, acknowledged by Emmanuel (1972a, p. 177); but examples of such products are hard to find, especially today when synthetic materials replace so many natural materials. Where they are found, as in the case of coffee, cocoa, bananas or tea, and were found in the past, in the case of coir, rubber, jute or sugar, low wages and low productivity could be profitable. Hence the use of slave and indentured labour on plantations. The list is extremely small today (see table 2), and this, in fact, is one of the problems facing the underdeveloped countries.

This is quite disastrous for Emmanuel's argument, because he admits that when 'there are differences in wages between

5. And this almost certainly accounts for the relatively low wages in the developed countries outside the USA, compared with their relative productivity levels, in table 24.

countries that regularly export the same articles, these differences correspond, under conditions of perfect freedom of trade and competition as well as of equalization of the rate of profit, to a proportionate difference in productivity' (1972a, p. 136). It could still be argued by Emmanuel that the list was once much longer, but his main argument is that certain countries pushed up their wages, whatever the commodities they produced in the first place; other countries failed to do so. It is not in his view the product, not even the concentration on primary production, that earned the low wages but the low wages that lowered the price of the product. Timber prices are high because timber comes from rich countries – Sweden, Finland and Canada – and despite the many substitutes for timber and the falling demand for it. Oil prices are low, despite its lack of substitutes and growing demand, because oil comes from poor countries in the Middle East and Latin America. His references to relative prices in fact consist of relative price *movements*. 'Oil prices fell from index 100 in 1913 and index 43 in 1952 and index 27 in 1962, while those of timber rose from index 100 in 1913 to index 559 in 1952' (pp. 172–3). He has, moreover, chosen two commodities which fit his argument or did so before 1973. Others do not, as can be seen in table 25.

Emmanuel's main argument is based on the respectively low and high wages established in the first place in the currently developed and underdeveloped countries. His explanation of development in North America and Oceania is that they were peopled from countries with high wages already, while Latin America was not. The 'moral element' in the wage, for which trade unionists struggle, becomes for him, the determinant of development – 'what society regards, in a certain place and at a certain moment, as the standard of wages. It depends on a certain level of attainment, which is itself the result of past struggles and evolutions' (1972a, p. 119). A few pages later, he goes on:

Once a country has got ahead, through some historical accident, even if this be merely that a harsher climate has given men additional needs, this country starts to make other countries pay for its high wage level through unequal exchange (p. 130).

This is Toynbee's principle of χαλεπὰ τὰ καλά (1931,vol. 2, p.1) (pleasures are man's burden), but it falls far short in explanatory

Table 25 Measures of price movements of certain primary products, by rich and poor countries, 1913–1970 (1913 = 100)

Commodity	Source of measure	1929	1937	1953	1970
mainly rich countries					
wheat and wheat flour	A[a]	123	120	214	157
	B[b]	103	99	183	134
meat	B	130	108	290	400
dairy produce	B	152	111	247	175
sawn soft wood	A	153	152	472	490
lumber	B	110	106	281	—
wool	A	169	140	367	210
	B	110	115	287	163
mainly poor countries					
rice	A	143	85	458	328
	B	141	118	474	340
tea	B	150	134	275	286
coffee	B	137	74	422	304
cocoa	B	68	51	210	268
edible oil	B	95	69	177	165
sugar	A	100	102	230	250
	B	84	62	157	175
cotton	B	149	96	276	198
rubber	A	28	28	33	28
	B	85	87	84	73
crude petroleum		157	119	250	265
refined petroleum		157	118	248	264
all countries					
all manufactures		140	124	275	340
all primary products		119	102	236	236

[a] A = FAO estimates
[b] B = trade censuses
Sources: Yates (1959, table A.15); International Monetary Fund (1972)

power of other explanations – the deliberate creation of an artificial world division of labour by industrial capitalists, the opening up of new lands overseas by Europeans.

Wages in North America and Oceania were high, we argued earlier, because of the existence of abundant land for settlement. Emmanuel does not regard land as being part of the development of productive forces and cites Marx's support for this view (Emmanuel, 1972a, p. 337). But Marx's constant capital is made up of machinery *and materials* used up in production (Marx, 1946, ch. 8). The labour productivity in North America or Australia is high because of the large areas of land employed in agricultural production per unit of labour. Emmanuel argues that feudal institutions in Latin America, *plus* workers from low-wage countries, slavery in the Southern States of the USA, convicts and the land tax in Australia, the Bantu invasions in South Africa, all in their way served to hold back economic development in these countries compared with that in the north of North America (pp. 370–71).

This argument is offered in relation to countries, apart from Latin America, which are among those with the highest level of development in the world. Emmanuel says that it was 'free access to land' which raised wages and was so important for development. But was this not a function of abundance of land? Latin America's failure of development and Japanese success in development are not so easily explained on this thesis. They do support the view that it was the establishment of the capitalist mode of production and of the process of capital accumulation that mattered (Emmanuel, 1972a, p. 336).[6] Abundant land could have made up for higher labour productivity from mechanized aids, but we have seen that it was not enough on its own to generate development where pre-capitalist formations survived and were sustained by European capitalists, with the aim not so much to increase the rate of exploitation as to prevent competition from rival capitalists. Japan immunized herself from European restrictions, as did the USA and the British Dominions. Latin

6. Emmanuel admits this in the case of Japan, despite the country's low wage-level.

American countries failed to do so. If the origins of the division between developed and underdeveloped lands are not to be found in respective wage levels, can the subsequent widening gap, nevertheless, be explained in this way?

The answer to this question should decide the argument between Bettelheim, defending the traditional Marxist view, and Emmanuel (1972a, p. 288).[7] On the Marxist view it is the relation between workers and employers in the process of production, together with the rate of accumulation throughout the capitalist world, that determines wages. The transfer of wealth through relations of exchange in the terms of trade between developed and underdeveloped countries is of less importance than the artificial division of labour between manufacturing and primary production.

On the theory of comparative costs the gap between productivity in manufacturing and in agriculture would be expected to be greater in a country exporting manufactures, such as Britain, than in countries exporting agricultural products, such as the USA or Canada in the nineteenth century. The evidence, however, does not support this expectation (Maizels, 1963, p. 28). It was summed up by E. A. G. Robinson some years ago:

The gain that we secured by specialization derived from the terms of trade subsisting everywhere between manufactures and primary products. Over the greater part of the last eighty years there has been an advantage to any economy anywhere (with exceptions in Australasia and South America) which moved out of agriculture into industry and which exported manufactures and imported primary products. We in Britain could benefit through the fact that our technical lead, our financial resources and our geographical setting put us in the position to move more quickly than others (1954, p. 451).

There were, and are, other reasons besides the lower productivity of agriculture to explain why the artificial world division of labour is disadvantageous to those countries which remain solely producers of primary products for the international market. Dependence on demand for one or two crops or minerals, low income elasticity of demand for many

7. See Bettelheim (1972) for his reply to Emmanuel.

primary products, absence of alternative employment opportunities in an undiversified economy, lack of storage for perishable commodities, difficulties of organizing thousands of agricultural producers to control output in comparison with the ease of organization into cartels of a few industrial producers, the reliance on imports of machinery for increasing agricultural productivity, the development of substitutes for minerals and natural materials – all these tend to weaken the bargaining power of primary producers compared with that of manufacturers. Only the availability of abundant land plus the determination to diversify behind protective walls enabled countries like the USA and Australia and Sweden to break out of the strait-jacket of primary production.

The historical record of the movements in the terms of trade provides the proof that Emmanuel's emphasis is wrong. Throughout the nineteenth century the prices of primary products fell, with occasional periods of recovery in the 1870s and 1890s, but the prices of manufactures fell even faster (see table 26).

Up to the 1850s the volume of manufactures exported (at least by Britain) rose faster than the volume of primary products imported (by Britain), but from then to the 1930s the volume of primary products in world trade rose faster. Over the whole period up to the 1950s there is a strong inverse association between the gross barter terms of trade of manufactures for primary products and their net barter terms. As relative volumes rose, relative prices fell and *vice versa*. The rate of change is different in different periods: relative volumes changing more than relative prices between the 1850s and 1920s, thereafter relative prices changing more than relative volumes. After the 1950s relative volumes *and* relative prices moved together and in favour of manufactures. It is only in that recent period that the reinforcing effect of all the disadvantages of primary producers in relation to manufacturers was felt; and there is evidence of a most recent recovery in the relative volumes and prices of primary products after 1969. The market balance moved steadily to the disadvantage of manufactures up to the 1880s; thereafter some-

Table 26 Terms of trade: manufactures and primary products, world or UK, 1796–1973 (annual averages for years)

| Years | Volumes | | Unit values | | Market balance |
	Manufactures	Primary products	Gross barter terms	Manufactures	Primary products	Net barter terms	
UK only (1880 = 100)							
1796–1798	4	5	80	350	175	200	160
1802–1803	4·5	7	65	400	180	220	143
1820–1821	7	8	87	230	145	160	139
1854–1855	40	31	130	107	116	92	119
1872–1873	87	76	115	133	115	115	132
1880	100	100	100	100	100	100	100

World (1913 = 100)

1876–1880	32	31	103	98	105	93	96
1896–1900	48	60	80	91	78	117	94
1913	100	100	100	100	100	100	100
1921–1925	87	100	87	153	134	124	108
1926–1930	120	130	93	135	125	108	101
1931–1933	85	130	93	96	59	163	106
1936–1938	110	133	83	119	87	136	113
1948–1950	125	125	100	225	250	90	90
1951–1953	140	145	97	246	274	90	87
1954–1955	220	155	140	237	255	93	130
1960–1963	400	220	180	254	237	106	191
1967–1968	650	310	210	273	240	114	240
1971–1972	800	560	143	330	300	110	158
1973 (est.) 1000	600	165	345	450	77	127

For UK only, 1796–1880, manufactures = UK exports; primary products = UK imports;
for world, 1876/80–1967/8, primary products = all non-manufactures.
Dates are chosen to mark major turning points; market balance = gross barter × net barter terms of trade;
1973 (est.) excludes petroleum

Sources: Imlah (1958, table 8); Yates (1959, table 11); UN (1969a, table 13; 1973)

what to their advantage up to 1913 and again in the 1930s and finally most strikingly so in the 1960s with remissions between times.

The inverse association of relative volumes and relative prices would seem to support a neo-classical view of the self-defeating results of forced exports. The Keynesians would, however, point to the advantages to home employment (since Say's Law does not operate) in the more rapid increase in manufactured exports and of rapidly cheapening imports right up to 1913. The Marxists would emphasize the contradictions involved for capitalists in expanding competitive investment in manufacturing, while relying on cheap labour in primary production. What cannot be demonstrated is that low wages amongst the primary producers led through unequal exchange to lower and lower relative wages. However they are defined, the terms of trade, up to the 1960s, did not steadily deteriorate for the primary producers. There were ups and downs, and indeed in the crucial take-off period for British industry a steady favourable movement for primary producers carrying right through the first half of the nineteenth century.

Emmanuel, however, argues that it is not the terms of trade between manufactures and primary products that we must look at, but those between the developed and underdeveloped countries. A rough division of products along these lines for the period since 1913 was made in table 25, and overall figures for developed and underdeveloped countries' terms of trade and market balance for the period since 1876 are shown in table 27.

The movements in these terms of trade were favourable for the developed countries up to 1900, then most unfavourable to 1913, with thereafter little apparent improvement until the most favourable movement for them after the 1950s. The sources for this table do not, unfortunately, enable us to see the results for different countries of the gains for the manufacturers in the early 1930s or their losses in the late 1930s and 1940s, although a hint of this is given in the fall in the market balance of developed countries in 1937. The important point is that the underdeveloped lands gained in volume terms *and* in unit values from 1900 right up to 1928.

Table 27 Terms of trade: developed and underdeveloped countries, 1876/80–1973 (1913 = 100)

Year	Export volumes			Export unit values			Market balance[a]		
	Developed	Under-developed	Gross barter terms dev./under.	Developed	Under-developed	Net barter terms dev./under.	Developed	Under-developed	Balance gross/net
1876–1880	30	50	60	94	67	140	29	34	85
1896–1900	62	83	75	84	54	155	52	43	121
1913	100	100	100	100	100	100	100	100	100
1928	127	150	84	134	130	103	170	195	87
1937	107	175	61	118	100	118	126	175	72
1953	176	284	62	250	163	154	440	462	95
1962–1963	315	450	70	255	143	177	800	640	125
1967–1968	470	600	78	270	155	173	1270	930	136
1973 (est.)	830	970	86	385	186	205	3200	1800	176

[a]Market balance = export volume indices × export unit values and gross barter × net barter terms of trade. Reference to table 26 will show that prior to 1880 the balance of gross barter terms and net barter terms for Britain fell steadily; 1973 (est.) excludes petroleum

Sources: Yates (1959, tables A.18, A.19, A.20); United Nations (1969a, tables 10, 11, 12, 13; 1973)

A further analysis can be made of the movement in the terms of trade of the developed countries' manufactures with the underdeveloped countries' primary products (see table 28). This analysis can then be compared both with the terms of trade movements of developed and underdeveloped lands and with those of manufactures and primary products. What this table shows is that the losses of the developed countries up to 1913, and equally their gains after the 1950s, were caused more by *other* reasons than by the relative fall in the first period of manufactured goods prices and their rise in the second period. The terms of trade between manufactured and primary products, however, accounted for most of the changes in the developed and underdeveloped countries' terms of trade between the two World Wars.

It is hardly a strong argument for Emmanuel that the gains of the underdeveloped lands between 1880 and 1913 (and on into the 1920s) were due to their exporting those primary products which evidently fared better in price than the primary products exported by developed lands in this period. For this means that the more developed primary producers, whose wages were presumably higher, were faring worse than the less developed primary producers whose wages were presumably lower. This goes against Emmanuel's view that it is to relative wage levels, and not to market demand or to relative productivity levels, that we have to look for the explanation of the terms of trade.

There can, of course, be no doubt about the disastrous results for the underdeveloped lands of the movements in the terms of trade after the 1950s, although they have enjoyed some improvement since 1969.

We have followed a traditional Marxist criticism of Emmanuel's theory of unequal exchange as being in the last resort a bargaining theory, similar to that of a Keynesian like Robinson. We have, however, not felt able to accept entirely a Marxist view of the matter, since this would involve the working of the law of value on an international scale to impose a world-wide socially necessary labour-time. Marx expected this because he expected the colonies to be developed, albeit within

Table 28 Terms of trade: manufactures (*mfg*) and primary products (*pps*), by developed and underdeveloped countries, 1876/80–1973 (1913=100)

Years	All goods exports: developed/underdeveloped unit values			All countries exports: manufactures/primary products unit values			Developed countries mfg/underdeveloped primary products unit values		
	dev.	underdev.	t of t[a]	mfg	pps	t of t	dev. mfg	underdev. pps	t of t
1876–1880	94	67	140	98	105	93	98	69	142
1896–1900	84	54	155	91	78	117	94	52	180
1913	100	100	100	100	100	100	100	100	100
1928	134	130	103	135	125	108	135	130	104
1937	118	100	118	119	87	136	122	100	122
1953	250	163	154	235	260	90	275	163	170
1962–1963	255	143	177	260	240	107	275	148	185
1967–1968	270	155	173	273	240	114	285	153	187
1973 (est.)	385	186	205	364	430	85	380	260	146

[a] t of t = net barter terms of trade; 1973 (est.) excludes petroleum

Sources: Yates (1959, tables A18, A19, A20); UN (1969a, tables 10, 11, 12, 13; 1973)

the capitalist framework; in the long run, levels of productivity would be evened up through the pressure for equalizing profit rates. The fact that this has not happened has undermined the traditional Marxist view as presented by Bettelheim (1972, p. 293).

What has happened is that a dualism has emerged within the capitalist mode of production divided between developed and underdeveloped economies. This is the result of the artificial world division of labour that was first created by Britain's industrialization and then exploited by Britain and other successfully industrializing nations to retain their monopolistic advantage in manufacturing and particularly in capital goods' manufacture. Intercapitalist competition drove them to do this; but the mechanism was, in part, free trade, in part, deliberate restrictions on the development of competing industrial centres and, in part, restrictions on the movement of labour.

This last reason is the one theoretical argument of Emmanuel's that Bettelheim finds most valuable (1972, pp. 310, 351), but he rejects the conclusions which Emmanuel draws from it. The cause of the widening gap between wages in different parts of the world, according to Emmanuel, is the non-mobility of labour or 'merely marginal mobility' (1972a, p. 52). This provides his main refutation of Ricardo's Law of Comparative Advantage because, while capital and technology are mobile, labour is non-mobile. This is not, in fact, wholly true; firstly, there have been major movements of labour from Europe to the lands of European settlement in North and South America and in Africa; *and* there have been movements of forced labour from Asia and Africa to North America, the West Indies, Malaysia and Australia, as well as voluntary migration to the Americas and Oceania. Recently there have been quite large movements of labour from India and Pakistan and the West Indies to Britain, from Central Europe to Australia and from North Africa and Southern Europe to the Common Market. But these last movements have been held within a framework that is similar to that of a dual economy. Migrants have been admitted but mainly young men, and often on a temporary basis and without their wives and families (Castles and Losack, 1972).[8]

Secondly, in a dual economy on a world scale, capital does not necessarily flow where labour is cheapest, because local markets and external economies are more important than wage levels in determining profit rates and industrial location. At the same time, labour is very largely prevented by lack of education and by artificial restrictions from moving to where capital investment is taking place and wages are higher. As a result, such a dual economy encourages the artificial division of labour: capital-intensive manufacturing industry developing in the richer countries, labour-intensive production in the poorer countries. And even this division is distorted by the measures of protection of agriculture and of labour intensive industry in the rich countries. Thus economic diversification occurs in the rich countries paralleled by specialization in the poor countries on a few products which cannot be produced in the rich countries.

Iida (1965)[9] has offered several models of a dual national economy with technically advanced and backward sectors, the first having higher wage rates and profit rates than the latter. These models may be applied with even more realism internationally, where the assumption of one of Iida's models is that labour cannot move from the backward to the advanced sector, while capital can move either way. Factor prices in the backward sector are thus determined by those in the advanced. Wage earners in the backward sector must choose a low wage offered or unemployment, since the marginal product of labour is zero (see Meade, 1964, ch. 1); but – and here we go beyond Iida's model – if wage earners in the advanced sector attempt to raise their wages without incurring unemployment, they can do this but only if they prevent capital flowing to the backward

8. See also Westlake (1973), who concludes that 'the developed countries are having by far the better part of the bargain'.
9. I am much indebted to Jan Otto Anderson of Abo Academy, Finland, for some most stimulating reflections on Iida's model, submitted to the Elsinore Symposium on Imperialism in May 1971. I do not, however, accept his conclusions which tend to support Emmanuel's position.

sector. This they can do in advanced countries by measures of protection – through tariffs and subsidies – and by capital export controls against the backward countries. What is more, they may be able to prevent the flow of labour from the backward country to the advanced. This dual structure is self-perpetuating and self-reinforcing, since wealth attracts and poverty repels investment on the Myrdal model of cumulative causation (Myrdal, 1954). Owners of capital in capital-intensive industries of the advanced countries *could* import labour from the backward countries and reject the protectionism of workers and employers in labour-intensive industries in the advanced countries; but they do not do so, because of the political strength of these interest groups (see Travis, 1964). There is thus a dualism inside the economy of the advanced countries as well as between them and the underdeveloped countries.

This bears on the political implications of Emmanuel's concept of unequal exchange, which Bettelheim most sharply rejects, namely that: 'this formulation leads to making the proletarians of the rich countries "appear" to be the "exploiters" of the poor ones' (see Emmanuel, 1972a, p. 301). Bettelheim regards unequal exchange as 'a transfer of surplus value from the capitalists (or other exploiters) of the poor countries to the capitalists of the rich ones', and, we must add, of the backward industries to the advanced industries. 'It is not possible,' he says, 'to give a strict meaning to the notion of exploitation of one *country* by another *country*'. And yet there cannot be any doubt that the support of trade unions for policies of protection, however short sighted this may be, just like the support of trade unions for differential wages inside one country, does have the effect of establishing an advantage for those whose position is protected through the imperfections of competition. It is, as Marx clearly saw in relation to differences in soil fertility, a kind of differential rent which creates what he calls a 'false social value', and, in the example he is discussing, 'if it were abolished, society would not buy this product of the soil at two and a half times the labour contained in it' (1909, ch. 39).

There is, then, some clash of interest between workers in developed and underdeveloped countries in a dual world economy, just as there is between the better paid and worse paid in any one country, but in a Marxian view this is a minor clash compared with the major common interest of all workers who suffer exploitation by the capitalists. There is a fresh instance of the clash in the recent subjection of even developed capitalist nations to the dominant capitalist power, through the movements of capital. Bettelheim suggests that there is today 'an increasingly *hierarchical* structure of capitalist world economy' (1972, p. 301). Others have gone further to propose a 'chain of exploitative relationships' (Frank, 1969a, pp. 146–7), but this is the subject of the next chapter.

What Bettelheim is insisting on in the Marxist view is that the study of imperialism should go beyond the question of relations of exchange in the terms of trade, to the production relations inside capitalism, the whole economic structure, that is to say, of a world division of labour between developed and underdeveloped countries (see Emmanuel, 1972a, p. 288). For he sees the weakness of Emmanuel's theory just in this, that Emmanuel regards the level of wages and the terms of trade as prior to the division of labour in the process of capitalist production. The same criticism has been applied by Marxists to both Keynesian and neo-classical views. Imperialism in a Marxian sense is not an aggregation of unequal flows of goods or of capital, but the extension of capitalism on a world scale, dating back to the middle of the eighteenth century. In its most recent guise it appears outside the developed industrial capitalist lands in the form of neo-colonialism, but this is one feature only of a total capitalist world economy.

11 Neo-Colonialism

The concept of neo-colonialism was invented by French Marxists in the late 1950s, taken up by the leaders of the 'non-aligned' Asian and African ex-colonies in the early 1960s and incorporated thereafter into Marxist writings (Mandel, 1964, p. 17). The new leaders of ex-colonial African states described neo-colonialism as 'the survival of the colonial system in spite of formal recognition of political independence in emerging countries, which became the victims of an indirect and subtle form of domination by political, economic, social, military or technical (forces) . . .' (see O'Connor, 1970, p. 117).

The economic forces they listed were: continuing economic dependence on the colonial power; integration into colonial economic blocs; economic infiltration through capital investments, loans, aid, unequal concessions and finances directly controlled by colonial powers (Balogh, 1962). The main aim of neo-colonialism, according to Marxists, was the use of the state apparatus of the colonial powers to transfer political rule to a domestic ruling class, so as to keep the ex-colonial territories 'securely in the world capitalist system' (O'Connor, 1970, p. 118).

Most of the mechanisms of neo-colonialism, like earlier forms of imperialism, work automatically. They do not require to be positively set in motion by the colonial power for the day after the grant of independence, but they would have to be positively stopped by the successor government if the ties of economic as well as political dependence were to be loosened. Hence the importance attached by the colonial powers to the succession. We have seen the automatic working of free trade to maintain an artificial world division of labour and the subsequent institution of measures of protection by every state that has successfully industrialized. We have also seen the cumulative effects of wealth and poverty in respectively attracting and repelling capital investment. We have recognized the persistent shift of capital earnings out of the underdeveloped and into the developed lands. We have just looked at the terms of trade resulting from concentration of any economy on one or two crops or minerals for export, and the consequent necessity for developing countries to diversify their output.

To this list of the mechanisms of imperialism we may now add several new variants. First, there is the holding in the metropoles of currency reserves of ex-French and ex-British colonies. Although political independence allowed that these might be run down below the one-for-one sterling or franc standard against local currency issues, the 'credit-worthiness' of an ex-colony continued to depend, in the eyes of financial institutions, both international and metropolitan, on the level of its foreign currency reserves. Such reserves held in the metropoles remain short-term, if not long-term, loans from the ex-colony to the metropolis (Balogh, 1962). Secondly, the continuing presence of metropolitan-based companies on the soil of the ex-colonies has tended not only to extract profit for repatriation to the metropolis but also to determine the growth path and even the taxation and wider economic policies of the successor governments. A third feature is the role of the branches of metropolitan banks in attracting local savings both for their own international operations and increasingly also for financing the local operations of transnational companies. Any ex-colonial state which extracts itself from such a strait-jacket must have a government with great determination and commitment to the needs of its people and with material resources adequate to support such a commitment.

It may appear almost miraculous that any states have ever escaped from a condition of dependence in the world capitalist system once they had been incorporated into it. Indeed it is only the largest states that can be said to be economically independent, but others have achieved economic development.

The longer the period of incorporation at a particular level of development the more difficult escape must be, as political and economic, internal and external restrictions reinforce each other. The Latin American states have the longest history of political independence and economic dependence, and it is, perhaps, not surprising that it is from economic historians of Latin America that the main theses of neo-colonialism have come. For the first examples of neo-colonialism were to be found in the Latin American states after their independence from Spain and Portugal was established in the first quarter of the nineteenth century. Indeed, the historical precedence of neo-colonialism in Latin America has led Andre Frank, and others like Keith Griffin who have followed him, to interpret neo-colonialism in Africa and Asia, as well as in Latin America today, in the light of that experience (Frank, 1969a, pp. 1–120; 1969b, pp. 3–17, 222–230; Griffin, 1969).

Frank's thesis is that the Spanish and Portuguese colonies were so completely integrated into the world capitalist system in the sixteenth century that their chances of achieving their own economic development were slight. There was a moment in the 1830s, just as there had been at the beginning of the seventeenth century, when this seemed possible, but the ties of metropolis–satellite relations in the world market, reproduced inside the Latin American nations themselves, proved too strong (Frank, 1969a, pp. 57–66).

The fundamental metropolis–satellite structure has remained the same throughout, but the basis of metropolitan monopoly has changed over the centuries. During the mercantilist period the basis ... was military force ... the satellites were denied freedom of trade. During the nineteenth century ... 'liberalism' permitted or even enforced the satellite's freedom of trade, but denied them freedom of industrial production. By the first half of the twentieth century, the basis ... shifted to capital and intermediate goods ... (p. 177).

He believes that the same process of underdevelopment was at work everywhere and in every age:

To extract the fruits of their labour through pillage, slavery, forced labour, free labour, raw materials, or through monopoly trade – no

less today than in the times of Cortez and Pizarro in Mexico and
Peru, Clive in India, Rhodes in Africa, the 'Open Door' in China –
the metropolis destroyed and/or totally transformed the earlier
viable social and economic systems of these societies, incorporated
them into the metropolitan-dominated, world-wide capitalist system
and converted them into sources for its own capital accumulation
and development (1969b, p. 225).

In his earlier book Frank draws the lesson:

... neither Chile nor any other country in the world which had
already previously been firmly incorporated into the world capitalist
system has, since the nineteenth century, managed to escape from
this status to achieve economic development by relying on national
capitalism. The new countries which have developed since then had,
like the United States, Canada and Australia, already achieved substantial internal and external economic independence, or like
Germany and, most significantly, Japan, had never been satellites,
or like the Soviet Union have broken out of the world capitalist
system by revolution. Notably, these now more or less developed
countries were not richer when they began their development than
was Chile when it made its attempt to do the same. But ... they
were not already underdeveloped (1969a, p. 56).

If this means that these countries were not firmly incorporated in the world capitalist market, it is just not true. North
America was most decidedly caught up, so was Russia and
Oceania almost equally; and their internal and external
economic independence, prior to political independence, was
not at all 'substantial'. Their ties with the European metropolis were in no way less strong than those of the now underdeveloped countries of Latin America, Asia and Africa (1969a,
p. 12). Dependence for them did not necessarily mean non-
development.

A more valid distinction was one we drew earlier, between
economic settlement from Britain that was capitalist-based
and the feudal-based settlement of Spaniards and Portuguese.[1]
This has been given support by a Latin American scholar,
Ernesto Laclau, who has criticized Frank's thesis on the

1. I have emphasized this point in *After Imperialism* (Barratt Brown,
1970a, preface, p. xii).

grounds that, in a quite un-Marxist way, it emphasizes exchange relations in the world market rather than production relations (Laclau, 1971, p. 19).[2] It is the capitalist mode of production that was established in North America and Oceania by British settlers, despite the use of slaves and convicts; it was a feudal mode of production that was established by Spain and Portugal in Latin America. Frank's insistence that capitalist and not feudal *market relations* existed from the sixteenth century onwards in Latin America glosses over the fact that a feudal *mode of production* was established. This was even intensified later by the demands of the European market in the nineteenth century (Laclau, pp. 30–31).

Frank seems anxious to wish away both feudalism and a national capitalist class from the Latin American political scene and with them the conflict between national capitalism and feudalism, so that, in his view, no possibility of a bourgeois democratic revolution can be said to exist for Latin American countries. This possibility may or may not exist, but Laclau's argument has shown that Frank's thesis does not establish the case either way: British and American capitalism have always had a powerful stake in Latin America; capitalist forms of agriculture have been established where the indigenous population was sparse or could be wiped out, as in North America, Argentina and Oceania; some centres of capitalist economic development have been built up, as Frank rightly argues, in the periods of European wars when the ties of dependence were weakened; *but* the feudal mode of production survived and even the 'refeudalization of peripheral areas' occured – as in Eastern Europe in the nineteenth century (Laclau, p. 31).

Politically, the retention of feudal economic relations on the land was, moreover, of great importance to colonial powers wherever indigenous societies survived in their colonies. Apart from the role of the *latifundia* in Spanish America and planta-

2. The point has been made even more strongly in an essay by Arrighi contributed to a seminar in Elsinore, Denmark in May 1971 on *Imperialism: Its Place in the Social Sciences Today* and entitled 'The relationship between the colonial and the class structures: A critique of A. G. Frank's theory of the development of underdevelopment'.

tions in other British colonies, some of which began as capitalist institutions and became feudalized, the colonial powers relied increasingly on a landlord class, in India a princely class, as indirect rulers on their behalf. In India the *Zamindars* had indeed been created as landowners from among the Moghul tax collectors at the permanent settlement of Bengal. It may well be (Barratt Brown, 1970a, pp. 54, 177), that the crucial distinction between lands that were underdeveloped and lands that were developed by capitalism was whether they had a large indigenous settled people with their own institutions that could not be wiped out but must be indirectly ruled; or whether capitalism could start with a *tabula rasa*. On this argument, Argentina, which was very sparsely settled prior to Spanish settlement, and Mexico, where the population was almost wiped out by Spanish arms, should have been developed as North America and Oceania were. The fact is that they very nearly were; and they are still today more developed than the rest of Latin America, as Rhodesia and South Africa are among the African states, and for the same reason. Hence the heavy British investments in Argentina in the nineteenth century; but the origin of Argentine settlers, in feudal Spain rather than in capitalist Britain, would then explain the failure of development there.

In the concept of neo-colonialism a key role is played by local capitalists after political decolonization. As the direct result of Mao Tse-tung's text book of *The Chinese Revolution and the Chinese Communist Party*, which became widely available in the West after the Chinese Revolution was achieved by the Chinese Communist Party in 1949 (ten years after the publication of the book), a distinction began to be drawn by Marxists between 'comprador' and national capitalists. According to Mao: 'The big bourgeoisie of a comprador character is a class that directly serves the capitalists of the imperialist countries and is fed by them; countless ties connect it closely with the feudal forces in the countryside' (1954, pp. 88–9).

In the 1950s Marxist writers on imperialism associated this distinction with Marx's and Engels's insistence on the differences between merchant and industrial capital. The one may grow out of the other, but it is only with the emergence of an industrial capitalist class that capitalism as a new mode of production, and with it continuous technological change, become possible. Comprador capital is merchant capital and engaged in buying or selling on behalf of a foreign industrial capitalist. This dependence has been maintained by the imperialist powers 'from Omichund the millionaire merchant in Clive's day to the Sheikh of Kuwait in our own time'.[3] Potential industrial capitalists in the colonies were destroyed in competition with the more advanced manufactures of the colonial power, and emerged only slowly in the interstices of the colonial economy. But emerge they did; especially, as Frank rightly insists, when the ties of the capitalist world market were broken in the two World Wars and industrialization in Latin America leapt ahead (Frank, 1969a, p. 170). The same can be said of India (Anstey, 1929, pp. 505–8).

With the straight-jacket removed, national industrial capitalists proliferated. Six thousand new industrial firms were established in Brazil between 1915 and 1919, almost as many as in the previous twenty-five years (Frank, 1969a). A similar scale of development took place in India in both world wars (Kidron, 1965, pp. 20–21). Between the wars, however, the mushroom growth everywhere collapsed, as free trade was reestablished. Something remained, but the tendency between the wars was for metropolitan-based companies to move in and to supply the market with the products of superior technology, first through metropolitan exports and then through local subsidiary production, as soon as any market appeared, drawing on local supplies on a scale that made much more technically advanced production profitable (Cardoso, 1972, pp. 89–91; Alavi, 1964). Capital-goods industries remained behind in the metropolitan countries (Kidron, 1965, p. 21; Griffin, 1969, pp. 271–2).

3. This theme of the role of the comprador in imperialist relations runs right through my earlier book *After Imperialism*; and perhaps I may here be allowed to claim that this theme was at the centre of lectures I gave in the early 1950s before the publication of Baran's *Political Economy of Growth* (1957), from which some American Marxists have rather unkindly suggested that I plagiarized.

There has been, until recently, an evident failure of sustained indigenous capitalist development outside of Europe, North America, Oceania and Japan, a relative if not absolute under-development. Marxists have insisted on this against the more optimistic 'dualist' thesis of economic development. This is a different sort of dualism from that discussed in the last chapter. It has been widely accepted among neo-classical economists in recent years (see Lewis, 1954, pp. 139–91; 1955), and is based on the supposed dualism in underdeveloped economies between a backward feudal agricultural sector and a progressive capitalist industrial sector that would ultimately overtake and overrule the former. It was in order to challenge this thesis of dualism in underdeveloped economies that Frank set out to expose what he called the myth of feudalism in Brazilian agriculture.

In the concept of dual economy discussed in the last chapter immobility of labour was assumed between and even within capitalist economies. In the neo-classical concept of dual economy it is assumed that the only connection between the two sectors of the economy is precisely the movement of un-limited supplies of unemployed or underemployed labour from the agrarian to the industrial sector. We have seen reason to doubt this. As we saw it, dualism was not necessarily a con-cept of two coeval modes of production, but this was not ruled out. Within the capitalist world market, and even within the world division of labour, systems of slavery were encouraged and a feudal mode of production was retained, or even estab-lished and intensified in settled colonial territories, in the in-terests of metropolitan capitalists on political as well as economic grounds. The capitalist mode was still the dominant one. Marx, and Lenin too, certainly expected the capitalist industrial sector to establish the law of value internationally, by completing the process of penetration of the whole economy including the countryside. It is because the Communist Parties of Latin America have held on to Marx's expectation, that Frank regards this question as being of such importance (1969b, p. 225). If feudal modes of production cannot be wished away, and labour does not move easily into industry even when it moves out of the countryside, what form of dualism corresponds to the actual facts of economic underdevelopment today?

Laclau has argued that in Latin America 'even the most backward peasant regions are bound by fine threads (which have not yet been adequately studied) to the "dynamic" sector of the national economy and through it to the world market' (1971, p. 23). The picture of 'enclaves of development' amidst an undisturbed subsistence economy does not stand up. Frank has certainly established this point.[4] The concept of dualism within a predominantly capitalist economy must allow for capital and goods to move between sectors even though capital moves mainly to the high-profit sector. Dualism is an inadequate concept if it implies that no connections exist between the industrial and the agrarian sector or that there is only the movement of labour, and if its advocates insist on labelling the first sector as 'progressive' and the second as 'backward' (Furtado, 1964).

Griffin (1969, pp. 19–31) has shown how unhelpful the assumption of such a dualistic economic model may be in designing growth strategies. Rural unemployment or underemployment cannot be assumed if there are village handicraft activities outside the season of agricultural activities; rural labour does not necessarily receive more than its marginal product if there are commercial activities in the countryside in addition to subsistence farming; there is no evidence for backward-sloping supply curves in the offer of rural labour on the market; nor for the absence of peasant savings and non-mobility of these savings. As a result there is no reason on this dualistic model why agricultural output and population should rise in line and why *per capita* incomes overall should rise with rising output in the industrial sector and with constant real incomes in the rural sector.

There has, however, been a major change in the last two decades. The fact is that industrial output and employment do

4. After reading Frank's works I felt bound in the Preface to *After Imperialism* (1970a, p. x), to abandon the concept of 'enclaves of development' which I had taken from Nurkse (1960).

seem to have risen faster than population in the underdeveloped regions since the 1950s.

Griffin provided statistical evidence to suggest that in some countries in Latin America and in Africa *per capita* incomes had fallen in the years up to 1960; for output had failed to keep up with population growth, and the percentage of the labour force in industry had not risen or had even declined (1969, p. 58). Over the whole period of colonial rule we have seen these things happening. The process of underdevelopment in the colonies began precisely at the time of the development of Europe and of the lands of European settlement. Griffin's more recent statistics, covering the period since political decoloniza-tion, are less convincing (pp. 29, 55). There is no doubt that unemployment has risen in the cities of all underdeveloped countries as the rural population has flocked into them, but has found industrial employment hard to obtain. In Latin America the unemployed may amount to one third of the city population (Griffin, 1969, pp. 185–91; Quijano, 1971); but industrial output and employment have nonetheless been increasing. It takes a great difference in growth rates to begin to close a gap in industrial development, when 44 per cent of the world's population are responsible for only 8 per cent of the world's industry. Their share was probably raised in the 1960s as a result of the fact that the rate of growth, both in industrial output and employment, in relation to population growth, in all of the underdeveloped regions taken together, was faster than in the developed regions. Agriculture fared less well, even disastrously. *Per capita* food and agricultural output declined in Africa after 1963 and were barely stabilized in Asia and South America (see table 30); while both rose sharply in the developed world outside North America.

The facts of the rise in industrial production per head alongside agricultural stagnation do seriously challenge the model of underdevelopment employed by Frank and by Griffin. Such industrial development, albeit from a low base in Asia, Africa and Latin America, does suggest that the model of a continuous process of 'sucking out' of the wealth of the poor countries to develop the rich proves too much. If

Table 29 World changes in population, industrial output and employment by regions, 1950–1968/71 (1963 = 100)

Region	Population				Industrial output					Industrial employment		
	1950	1955	1968	1963	1950	1955	1968	1971	1963	1950[c]	1955	1968
world	79	87	110	100	46	63	140	166	100	(84)	81	112
communist[a]	80	87	106	33	26	47	151	192	29	(80)	76	119
capitalist	78	87	113	67	54	69	135	156	71	(86)	82	111
all developed	—	—	—	23	55	70	135	154	63	—	87	106
N America	77	86	109	9	63	77	133	141	33	(82)	99	115
Europe	90	93	104	10	49	66	128	152	25·5	(92)	88	100
Japan	83	93	105	3	10	40	193	250	3·5	—	60	110
Oceania	75	84	110	0·5	58	65	133	163	1	(83)	88	114
all underdeveloped	—	—	—	44	42	57	141	178	7	—	74	119
Latin America	71	82	115	5	45	65	134	170	4	(74)	89	123
Asia excl. Japan[b] and Israel	78	86	111	30	40	54	145	182	2·5	(84)	70	117
Africa	75	84	113	9	—	—	—	—	1	(83)	—	(111)[c]

[a] USSR only for population index
[b] All Asia for population index
[c] All economically active and therefore placed in brackets
Sources: UN (1969a; 1972a)

Table 30 World output of food and agriculture, by regions, 1952–1970 (*per capita* per cent of 1963)

Regions (excl. China)	Agriculture		Food	
	1952	1970	1952	1970
world	91	105	90	108
developed				
N America	101	101	99	104
Europe	80	116	80	116
Oceania	90	112	91	118
USSR	79	134	78	136
underdeveloped				
Far East Asia (incl. Japan)	89	101	88	102
Near East Asia	88	102	88	102
South America	96	101	96	101
Africa	92	97	94	99

Source: UN (1969a)

neo-colonialism is a new stage in Frank's analysis, how does it relate to earlier stages of colonialism which seem, in his view, to merge into one another as successive forms of under-development from the sixteenth to the twentieth century (Frank, 1969a, pp. 282–9)? In this book we have seen different stages of capitalism finding their reflection in different colonial relationships, i.e. of capitalist production relations as well as of exchange relations (as Laclau (1971) emphasizes most strongly). If industrial development is occurring today in the under-developed countries, this is a new stage reflecting both a change in capitalism in the developed countries and a change to a new mode of production in the underdeveloped countries.[5] This is

5. In a preface to the Spanish edition of *After Imperialism*, I suggested a number of stages of imperialism in contradistinction to Frank's stages and arrived at the concept of a 'latest stage of protected capitalist development', see *Essays on Imperialism* (1972a). See also Arrighi (1971).

what is new about *neo*-colonialism. Completing the first quotation above from *Capitalism and Underdevelopment in Latin America*, we find Frank writing of the period after 1900:

The satellites were now increasingly free to produce textiles and other light industry consumer goods – indeed, they were even forced to do so by imperialism's metropolitan factories set up on their soil – but they were denied the freedom to establish their own capital and intermediate equipment industry. . . . Then, in the second half of the twentieth century, the basis of metropolitan monopoly was to shift again, now increasingly to technology, combined with still greater penetration of metropolitan international monopoly corporations into the satellite economies (1969a, pp. 177–8).

Evidence from Latin America for these propositions is provided by Frank and others, particularly, the movement of United States capital abroad out of mining and plantations and into manufacturing investment (34 per cent of the total in 1968 compared with 13 per cent in 1946) (Cardoso, 1972; Quijano, 1971). But such a combination of increased dependency *and* development is not quite the expected end-result of 400 years of continuous *under*development on Frank's thesis. It seems more likely to be a response by United States capital to the pressures inside Latin America for diversification from the old mineral and plantation economy.

The most forthright criticism of the thesis has come from Cardoso (1972, p. 94) who bases his analysis on a pioneering paper by O'Connor on the new forms of economic imperialism today (1970, p. 162). The original element in this paper was the delineation of the new role of the giant trans-national corporations in associating themselves in joint ventures with local capital in underdeveloped countries, and particularly with state capital, both from the developed and the under-developed states. Cardoso quotes a study by the United Nations Commission for Latin America to show the high and increasing proportion of local funds involved in the sum of direct investment between 1957 and 1965 of United States companies in Latin America and also in other areas outside the developed areas of Canada and Europe (1972, p. 92). By the end of this period the proportion was around 40 per cent, and another 40 per cent was being found from internal funds by local plough-back of profits. Only about 20 per cent was being supplied from the United States, which was receiving much more back from repayment of past debts than was going out in new investment. This is indeed a new kind of local comprador capitalism to be found in many underdeveloped countries, one which has moved away from mining and plantations into manufacturing industry.

It may seem, after glancing at table 31 and starting from the bottom, where the countries are found with the highest rates of industrial development in the 1960s, that, apart from the three Communist countries, industrial development is a function of United States military involvement. That might itself be an important facet of modern imperialism. The foreign exchange costs of the Vietnam war for the United States between 1963 and 1968 alone were estimated at $1900 millions (UN, 1968b, p. 118). Most of this went to South Vietnam,

Table 31 Indices of output of manufactures and agriculture, and of population and industrial employment by countries, 1948–1970 (1963 = 100 except where indicated)

Countries grouped by manufactured output index	Manufactured output		Industrial employment	Agricultural output	Population
	1948	1970	1970	1970	1970
100–149					
Senegal	—	116	—	—	119
Chile	47	121	99	109	118
UK	60	127	100	110	104
Tunisia	—	120[a]	—	100	122
Egypt	16	124[b]	—	—	119
Guatemala	57	132	110	—	122
Luxemburg	67	132	108	—	105
India	41	135	121	114	115
USA	55	139	114	107	108
Australia	—	140	119	130	115
Switzerland	—	142	95	126	108
Norway	45	143	110	115	105
Philippines	—	144	110	125	127
Belgium	52	144	97	120	104
Canada	49	149	116	112	113
Venezuela	—	149	116	135	128

Table 31 – *continued*

Countries grouped by manufactured output index	Manufactured output		Industrial employment	Agricultural output	Population
	1948	1970	1970	1970	1970
150–199					
Italy	25	151	107	121	105
Sweden	52	151	99	122	105
Eire	48	152	116	122	103
Greece	26	152	117	117	104
Hungary	22	152	120	—	101
France	41	154	100	125	106
New Zealand	40	154	126	128	111
Austria	26	154	104	110	103
Ghana	—	156	—	—	120
W Germany	17	156	107	119	107
Denmark	48	157	108	110	105
Czechoslovakia	30	158	—	—	104
South Africa	—	159	152	120	117
Finland	40	161	116	111	103
E Germany	18	162	—	—	100
S Rhodesia	—	163	—	—	125
Netherlands	37	166	100	130	108
Argentina	—	172	—	100	111
Portugal	—	173	—	101	106
Yugoslavia	25	174	119	120	107
USSR	17	178	—	146	108
Poland	17	180	126	—	107
Pakistan	—	185	—	127	114
Mexico	36	189	—	131	127
Singapore	—	183[a]	—	—	116
Mozambique	—	177[b]	—	—	109
200–299					
Israel	40	202	133	153	122
Spain	—	210	125	114	107
S Vietnam	—	210	—	—	119
Iran	—	218	—	142	123
Bulgaria	11	230	136	—	105
Rumania	10	230	135	—	107
Zambia	—	235	128	—	122
Japan	8	264	120	137	108
300–399					
N Korea	12	300	—	—	118
Taiwan	12	342	—	141	120
S Korea	—	390	216	130	118

[a] 1966 = 100
[b] Figure given is for 1968
Sources: UN (1969a; 1972a)

Japan, Korea and also to Thailand (which would certainly appear at the end of table 31 if the United Nations statistical office felt able to provide statistics). Singapore, as an entrepot port, certainly stood to benefit also from the war. Israel we have regarded as a special case of settlement by capitalist 'kith and kin'. But Spain and Portugal are only in small part being developed as United States war bases. Zambia is nobody's base. Iran, Pakistan, Mexico and Argentina are certainly spheres of direct United States interest. Bolivia, Peru, Equador and El Salvador would also appear in the higher brackets, if recent figures were available, as of course would Hong Kong.

Only Mexico, Pakistan and Argentina of these countries are at all important as markets for developed countries' manufactures. The rest suggest a quite different reason for development. This is the potentiality, shared by some of the bases for Unites States off-shore military purchases, of providing cheap labour for certain parts of the multi national 'synergy' of the giant corporations. Several of the countries with developing industrial sectors became, in the 1960s, major exporters of manufactured goods. Hong Kong is the example *par excellence*, but South Korea, Israel, Malta and Pakistan had all raised the proportion of manufactured goods in their exports to a figure of over 60 per cent by 1968; India to 50 per cent, Singapore and Spain to over 33 per cent and Guatemala and El Salvador to 25 per cent (OECD, 1968). In some cases (India, Malta and El Salvador) these manufactures consisted mainly of textiles; but elsewhere the total was made up of electronics, transport equipment etc. and machinery. In the smaller countries exports amount to one-third of the national product, and two-thirds in the case of oil exporters. Much of this was from subsidiaries and subcontractors of large companies based in developed countries.

These might be called mere 'enclaves of development' but for two further facts shown in table 31. First, the countries having most rapid industrial development, with the exception of Argentina and Portugal, have not suffered the decline or stagnation in agricultural output per head typical of some other underdeveloped countries. Secondly, the two most politically independent of the underdeveloped countries, Egypt and India, have not fared so well in industrial development as the obviously less independent countries. These two important facts neither fit a picture of enclave development nor Frank's thesis of dependent *under*development. What they do fit is a pattern of dependent economic development by large trans-national companies with local capital and with the involvement of the state of the underdeveloped countries in a division of labour that assigns certain processes to areas of cheap labour, just like the earlier slave plantations.[6]

O'Connor has argued against the view of some Marxist writers that governments of ex-colonial, underdeveloped countries were likely to reject or at least obstruct the penetration of foreign capital (1970, p. 127). This might well have been assumed from the declarations of the conferences of non-aligned states in the late 1950s, such as that of the African Conference, with which we opened this chapter.[7] The so-called 'Bandoeng Powers' certainly announced their determination to avoid foreign capital exploitation of their resources by encouraging instead mutual trading arrangements. The death in 1961 of Prime Minister Nehru of India, however, and the collapse of non-aligned governments in Algeria, Brazil, Ghana, Guiana, Indonesia and Iraq soon after, opened the way for a new 'Partnership in Development' the aims of which may be summarized from a World Bank Commission report with that title: 'We have received the definite impression that most low-income countries would welcome a larger flow of foreign in-

6. Since this was written, Warren (1973) has argued that this development is not so dependent according to his criteria, but he cannot show that these countries are, as yet, independent centres of capital accumulation – the crucial test.

7. I certainly assumed this and built it into the argument for a framework to international economic development of positive neutralism in the concluding section of my book *After Imperialism* (1970a). I was proved wrong in my estimate of the strength of populist regimes in the underdeveloped countries and recognized in the Preface that movements for social change in underdeveloped countries will have to come from below, and not from above, through the elites of successor governments, but that economic development could still occur with state support.

vestment, sharing our belief that such flows would contribute to faster growth' (Pearson *et al.*, 1969, p. 105). So runs the opening sentence of the chapter on Private Foreign Investment, and it goes on to recommend to the governments of under-developed countries that they provide tax concessions and other investment incentives and remove balance of payments restrictions and other barriers to the free entry of private capital.

The relationship of the state with the process of private capital accumulation has evidently again become of central importance for capitalist economic development. It appears in underdeveloped countries to be a largely dependent relation-ship of individual states upon foreign capital, represented through trans-national firms or international institutions like the World Bank. But the weakness of small states in the face of such bodies cannot be greater than their historic weakness in relation to the colonial powers. While we have emphasized the increasing power of the firm relative to the state, we argued that popular pressure would provide a *raison d'être* for nation states – large and small – to survive even within a superstate like the EEC. The need for the power of the state in under-developed countries is likely to be that much greater in holding together the different classes within one nation and in resisting outside pressures. As Penrose has put it:

... for as long as we can conveniently foresee, governments must insist on a high degree of sovereignty over their economic affairs in order to provide a national economic framework for the activities of their people on the one hand, and on the other to ensure that their economic needs are represented as identifiable claimants for international consideration (1971, pp. 238–9).

It is an ironical fact that Marxists who espouse the cause of *national* liberation movements in colonial lands tend to dismiss the nation state in the metropolis as a decaying and dis-integrating organism and nationalism as mere cultural chauvin-ism (Nairn, 1972). It must be accepted, on the other hand, that, when national liberation movements come out of the woods and mountains or out of the gaols, the forces that have come together in a struggle for national liberation tend not only to disintegrate but to move towards accommodation with the powers from which they have just liberated themselves. This is the essence of neo-colonialism. In the governments that have succeeded the colonial powers, three elements tend to appear in the successor ruling classes – native capitalists, feudal landlords and the comprador agents of capital left over from the days of colonial power.

Alavi has drawn attention to the role of the post-colonial state, using what he designates as an 'overdeveloped' bureaucratic–military apparatus in 'mediating between the competing interests of the three propertied classes . . . while at the same time acting on behalf of them all to preserve . . . the institution of private property and the capitalist mode as the dominant mode of production' (1972, p. 62).

Neo-colonialism as a continuation of economic imperialism is, in Alavi's view, 'the greatest beneficiary of the relative autonomy of the bureaucratic–military oligarchy' (p. 70). 'The concept of national bourgeoisie which is presumed to become increasingly anti-imperialist as it grows bigger . . . is one which is derived from an analysis of colonial and not post-colonial experience' (p. 75).[8] But this need not imply such a weakening of neo-colonial bargaining power as he suggests.

A rather different view is taken by some Marxists who see the matter the other way round. The local bourgeoisie in underdeveloped countries, unlike its predecessors in Europe, does not feel itself strong enough to challenge both its own growing proletariat and the landed classes. Then, 'compromising with feudalism, it is forced to compromise with imperialism', as Patnaik has put it (1972, p. 229). This does not seem to be logically necessary, nor is it obvious that the Indian bourgeoisie is collaborating with feudal elements rather than with capitalist elements in the countryside. The facts of their links with the trans-national corporations are not in doubt,

8. This bureaucratic–military apparatus may also have been overdeveloped by the conditions of national liberation struggle, as in most of the communist countries today; just as much as by the type of colonial rule that preceded liberation. But it is only the latter situation that Alavi is thinking about, naturally enough in relation to Pakistan.

but by use of the state sector a considerable degree of economic independence has been retained, and the result has been a certain measure of industrial development, albeit held back within the structure of the world capitalist economy (Chandra, 1973).

Populist forms of government in the ex-colonial under-developed lands were overthrown mainly because they failed to develop their economies. Such development has only been successful in the past where settlers came from a capitalist background. Recent economic development of Taiwan, Hong Kong and Singapore could be explained as the work of Chinese capitalists who fled there from mainland China; and capitalists from the North who fled to the South of both Korea and Vietnam could account also for these apparently rapidly developing economies. There has been a similar immigration into Israel; but industrial development is occurring without such immigration in Spain, Mexico, Brazil, Argentina and even in India. We know that all this is dependent development. Over two-thirds of the United States investment stock in Argentina, Brazil and Mexico is now in manufacturing industry compared with about one-third at the end of the Second World War (Cardoso, 1972, p. 89). A half of UK investment stock in India is now in manufacturing industry and, indeed, over a third of all UK investment stock in developing countries is in manufacturing industry, concentrated as to almost a half of the total in India, Nigeria and Guiana (Board of Trade, 1970).

This means that *new* US and new UK investments in these 'developing lands' show much higher proportions involved in manufacturing. In 1969–70 nearly half of UK investment that went into developing lands was in manufacturing industry, almost the whole of new investment in India was so (see table 20). The involvement of local and particularly of state capital in joint ventures implies a rising local capitalist class, both antagonistic to metropolitan capital and dependent on it. But it is developing. There is a growing home as well as export market; the range of industries is widening even to include capital goods, steel and heavy engineering; local finance is being raised; an independent technology is being established.

Perhaps Marxists have been so anxious to insist on the lack of independence that they have missed the fact of development. The Australian capitalist class was dependent on British capital, and is today, to some extent, dependent on British and United States capital; the Canadian capitalist class is still more dependent on United States capital. But these countries' economies became developed.

What is emerging in the underdeveloped countries is a form of dualism, not between a subsistence sector of agriculture within a feudal framework and a market industrial capitalist sector, but between a high profit/high wage international oligopolistic capitalist sector and a low profit/low wage competitive local capitalist sector. Dualism need not mean that there are no ties between the two, nor only the flow of labour from agriculture into industry. Capital may move easily from the local to the international sector but *not* labour. Analyses of dual economy in Italy (Lutz, 1962, pp. 3–4) and in Japan (Broadbridge, 1966, p. 6) have found dualism in both industry *and* agriculture. In both these countries the characteristics of large-scale operation, modern capital-using methods, wage labour and high income per head are to be found in one sector; minutely small-scale operations, minimum provision of capital, artisan or family labour and low income per head in the other (Lutz, 1962).[9] The persistence of this dualism, at least in Japan, has led many Japanese economists to attempt explanations, such as we saw earlier in Iida's several models (1965).

This is not a situation confined to developing economies. A large-scale survey of employment in Birmingham, Glasgow and two other Scottish industrial centres in the 1960s revealed inside each centre that wage differentials for doing the same job in large- and small-scale enterprises ranged from 2:1 and the fringe benefits in the large-scale enterprises made the difference nearer 3:1 (Mackay, 1971, pp. 71–2). In chapter 9 it was suggested that such differentials were widening, not narrowing, in developed countries, and there is evidence that

9. This does not exclude the possibility of large firms using cheap labour, even in quite large plants, for some labour-intensive processes.

differentials that are still greater exist in underdeveloped economies (Gannagé, 1968, p. 346). If labour cannot easily move from one sector to the other, it must be supposed that the subsequent disparities of income will lead, on a Marxist view, to surpluses that cannot be absorbed, or on a Keynesian view, to ineffective demand. In both cases an export-oriented economy (Japan and Italy are examples) may save the situation, but this is a zero-sum game. Some economy has to be import-oriented to balance the excess exports.

There is no necessary reason, then, why a dual economy should achieve sustained development, unless the state taxes the high profit/high wage sector to finance growth in the low profit/low wage sector. In a dependent economy, by definition, the state's power to tax is limited. Where international capital acts to prevent such redistributive taxation, with the support of local comprador capitalist elements, growth of the home market will be slow and general economic growth held back even if export prices are raised. The relative strength of different groups inside the underdeveloped nation states will become crucial for sustaining economic development.

Different interests will ally themselves differently with the foreign-owned firm. Among those who will side with it are bribed officials, the small employed aristocracy of workers who enjoy high wages and security, the satellite bourgeoisie to whom world-wide mobility and prospects are opened, and the domestic industries producing complementary goods who benefit from the concession which the MPE [multi-product enterprise] has achieved for itself. On the other side of the fence are the masses of unemployed, non-employed and underemployed, those who suffer from the higher costs, the competitors, actual and potential, and those who dislike foreigners (Streeten, 1971, p. 157).

This is what Singer has called the dualism of the employed and the unemployed (1970).

Streeten, in the paragraphs that follow the above quotation, suggests two reasons why even ruling elites in underdeveloped nation states may be forced to stand up to the trans-national corporations: firstly, the obvious dangers of competitive concessions to the corporations may encourage cooperation between the several underdeveloped states – such as we have seen among the oil producing countries in OPEC; secondly, the competition between trans-national corporations may provide a determined government of an underdeveloped country with the chance to attempt a policy of dividing and conquering, such as President Nasser for some time successfully pursued (Streeten, 1971). On this last point, the competition of the communist world has to be taken into account. Indeed, the weakening of this competition after about 1962, with the reduced rate of growth of the national product, and consequently of the imports and the overseas aid, of the Communist Bloc was as important in the fading potential of the Third World in the early 1960s as the collapse of populist regimes under United States pressure (Barratt Brown, 1970a, p. xxiv).

An improvement in the terms of trade through increased competition for the products of underdeveloped countries implies evident benefits. If the view of Emmanuel of 'unequal exchange' and the view of Frank of 'development of underdevelopment' were correct, such an improvement would reduce the extraction of surplus by the metropoles, and therefore permit development. A rise in the consuming power of underdeveloped countries through the terms of trade or through locally induced growth could also improve the relative position of the underdeveloped countries on the view of Sweezy, who sees them as absorbing rather than creating surplus.[10] But all this is to see the terms of trade as distinct from the whole capitalist world division of labour.

The importance of the underdeveloped countries seemed always to be to provide a surplus from a lower organic composition of capital to make up for the tendency to declining rates of profit at home. Sectors of the economy with reserves of cheap labour were retained for this purpose,[11] but this

10. O'Connor raises the question of absorption or creation of surplus at the end of his statement but does not answer it (1970, p. 141).

11. An extraordinary example of this came to my attention near Aligarh in India (Uttar Pradesh) where a Glaxo milk-processing factory had an almost total annual turnover of labour so that trades unions were discouraged and wage rates kept to the minimum.

relationship could not be maintained. Capitalist accumulation, quickened by continuing competition, drives capitalists to raise productivity wherever they can. In a phrase taken from Luxemburg, the process of metropolis–satellite development is one of 'assimilation and transformation'. Thus Lee (1971) describes how Luxemburg goes beyond her own view of a surplus, of goods from the metropolis being absorbed by the periphery, to postulate the industrialization of the periphery as supplier of its own internal market but under the predominance of metropolitan capital. Assimilation implies transformation. Slowly and painfully industrialization has spread, held back by the extraction of surplus to the metropolitan countries, by the concentration on primary production and by the slow growth of internal markets. The terms of trade are but a small part of the whole dependent relationship.

The concentration on primary production was, it is true, disastrous for the underdeveloped lands in the decades of the 1950s and 1960s because of the falling terms of trade, and because of the relative decline of primary produce entering world trade compared with manufactured goods. Moreover, the industrialized countries have once more been raising their share of world exports in primary products through measures of agricultural protection. All these trends are shown in table 32, and the position would look much worse for the underdeveloped lands if a table was prepared showing them separately from the USSR, Eastern Europe and Australia which are all included in this table as non-industrial lands.

The importance of the underdeveloped lands for the developed might seem then to be much reduced; but despite the great increases in labour productivity, where machines can replace manpower, the advantages of cheap direct labour inputs remain (see Gillman, 1958); the developed capitalist centres still need to assimilate the less developed periphery within their total production process. Continuing competition between giant trans-national firms leads them to tie all new industrial development everywhere into their synergy, and not only to pre-empt resources and 'mop up' markets at the expense of rivals, as British and later United States, German and Japanese

Table 32 Chief flows and terms of world trade, 1876–1970 (at current prices).

Flows as a percentage of world trade	1876–1880	1913	1928	1938	1953	1960	1970
industrial lands	71	67	60	59	55	63	68
to industrial	45	43	38	35	33	42	52
to non-industrial	26	24	22	24	22	21	16
non-industrial lands	29	33	40	41	45	37	32
to industrial	25	28	26	29	24	20	18
to non-industrial	4	5	14	12	21	17	14
primary products as a percentage of total trade	64	64	61	63	52	45	34
industrial lands' percentage of primary products exports	42	55	40	36	40	47	44
primary products/ manufactures: terms of trade	107	100	93	73	111	93	86

Industrial lands comprise USA, Canada, Japan, EEC and EFTA.
Non-industrial lands include the USSR and E Europe, Australia and New Zealand
Sources: Yates (1959, ch. 3); GATT (1958; 1970)

capitalists did in the nineteenth and early twentieth century.

Today the large firms themselves have a degree of independence of their national base; but they are increasingly aware of the conflict between their aims and the resulting tendencies. They have three alternatives: to fight it out between them in the whole world market, to carve out their own protected areas of development or to agree together on measures of world-wide development similar to Keynesian measures applied at home. To abandon the underdeveloped world as 'marginal' and to fight it out in the developed lands alone (see Cardoso, 1972, p. 93), they do not seem willingly to do. It is true that most investment by the developed capitalist centres is now being concentrated in cross-investment between themselves, but the interest of capitalists everywhere is to resist any part of the world dropping out of their demesne and above all, on Marxist theory, to retain potential labour for exploitation within their control.

For these reasons the emphasis that has been put in this book upon continuing oligopolistic competition has been challenged by Arrighi, who sees the interest of oligopolies in the under-developed countries as essentially collusive (1970, p. 257). An opposite view is presented by Mandel, who sees the competition still as one between national capitals – United States, European and Japanese (1970a). If competition today is between the transnational companies themselves, with quite opportunistic attitudes to nation-state interests, then the possibility exists of a new division of the world between the giant companies less on national lines than through agreement between them on an international framework of institutions, to replace those established at Bretton Woods. Such a framework will only contain the rivalry between the trans-national companies as a cartel contains the conflicting interests of its members. The superstates – the USA, the EEC and Japan – will still be required by the giant firms based in them to take action to protect the development of the main areas within their power to assimilate.

The EEC is showing the way in the conventions with its associated states; some real economic development in Southern Europe and North Africa is being encouraged, limited always by a kind of international dual economy between advanced and backward sectors (Barratt Brown, 1972a, p. 137). Those who argue that this kind of 'protected development' will not develop must look at the dual economies of Italy and Japan. Some development does take place; and in the process not only is there born an industrial working class with ambitions beyond what can be provided for a few elite in the trans-national companies, but also a frustrated rural peasantry excluded from the benefits of those who have land enough and capital enough to afford the 'Green Revolution'. These two provide revolutionary tinder.

All this will be regarded by neo-classical economists as mere political speculation built around a conclusion that simply confirms their view that capitalism *does* develop. Dual economies are, then, the result of the most perverse political interference with the beneficent working of economic forces, and 'where the big company shares the growing belief that small companies exist, not to be exploited, but to be reorganized and re-equipped to increase productivity on a broad front, substantial progress can be made' (Broadbridge, 1966, p. 93; Allen, 1965). This is the conclusion of a study of industrial dualism in Japan, which is notably more cautious about dualism in agriculture. The fact is that massive government intervention has been required to break down the dual structure of the Japanese economy, just as massive government intervention has been needed to maintain development in the declining regions of advanced industrial countries (Macrone, 1969, p. 149).

Governments have in effect taxed the high profit/high wage and developing sector to transfer capital to the low profit/low wage, underdeveloped sector. The ending of dualism has not occurred as a result of the free working of market forces; and economic aid has barely succeeded in narrowing the gap between advanced and backward even inside the developed nations, let alone between them and the underdeveloped. Yet some narrowing of the gap has occurred and the reason is clearly because it is in the interests of the high profit/high wage sector to pay taxes and to lend funds to state authorities for transfer to the low profit/low wage sector. This is both because in this way underutilized resources are brought into use and because, insofar as the state takes over production in the low profit/low wage sector, the surplus from the state sector can be made to flow back to the high profit/high wage sector through cheaper (because non-profit making) inputs to the production processes of the latter. This is the exact situation of Britain's nationalized industries, as even neo-classical economists admit (Meade, 1964, pp. 68–9); and, although it may be very discouraging, except in terms of the heightened consciousness of workers, for those who saw these industries as a step towards socialism, nationalization has certainly sustained economic growth.

The role of the state-owned industries in underdeveloped capitalist countries is even more ambiguous than it is in developed countries. If industries that are state owned provide cheap inputs for giant trans-national companies operating in the high profit/high wage sector, then local growth will be slow because the transfer of surplus will be to the metropolis. It may be said that this is all the more difficult for governments of underdeveloped countries to manage, because the supply of capital is of direct investment by giant corporations in local subsidiaries, and no longer of indirect investment in local government stocks by rentiers from the advanced capitalist countries (Sutcliffe, 1972, p. 175). Since this is 'risk' capital, however, and not state guaranteed stock, the possibility of repudiation is greater. The trans-national companies themselves can be nationalized, or at least that part of them operating in that country.

Nationalization will contribute to local economic development, the more the company is concerned with production for a local market in one or more underdeveloped countries, and the more stages of production of the company concerned take place inside the underdeveloped country (or countries), including the key stage of production of the capital equipment itself. The more nearly the underdeveloped country, or group of such countries acting together, can exercise a monopoly position over the major stages of production of the company, the stronger their position will be – and the more strongly such nationalization will be resisted. The resistance to the nationalization of copper mining in Zambia, Zaire and Chile provide good examples, but it is an important fact also that the governments of these three countries have failed so far to work together effectively through their joint organization, CIPEC. The oil producing countries have done better, although they lacked control not only over marketing, as is the case with CIPEC, but also over refining (Penrose, 1968, p. 208).

Short of nationalization of the assets of foreign companies, attempts by governments to regulate profits or terms of trade, or even the balance of trade, can fairly easily be aborted by the pricing policies of the companies, but taxes and physical controls can be enforced. Economic aid may be seen as a form of transfer of surplus from high profit/high wage regions to low profit/low wage regions in such a way that it flows back again to expand accumulation in the metropoles, but it does cover a part of the cost of debt redemption. The threat lies in the strings attached. The most detailed study of the working of international economic aid in Latin America reveals not only that policies based on neo-classical monetary theory were quite disastrously attached to aid programmes (Hayter, 1971, p. 136), but also that Keynesian-type policies were not much more successful. In any case, this same study reveals that an internal policy memorandum of the World Bank rules that aid is not available 'to countries which nationalize foreign owned assets without compensation, which fail to repay debts or in which there are claims on behalf of foreign investors which the Bank considers should be settled' (Hayter, 1971, p. 15).[12]

We may conclude that the continuing interest of metropolitan capitalists in the underdeveloped countries, where today this involves investment in manufacturing more than in primary production, implies *some* economic development, but *dependent* development; at the same time, their lack of interest in more rapid development shows that it is not expanding markets but retention of the productive process within a capitalist framework that is the chief objective of the metropolitan capitalist groups. This is the meaning of neo-colonialism; and within this the 'symbiosis', as it has been called (Penrose, 1968, pp. 251–2), of the large trans-national company and the state in underdeveloped countries is the central reality.

12. The major problem of the Chilean Government led by the late Dr Allende had been its running battle with the United States owned copper companies over the terms of compensation to be paid. See the *Financial Times*, 7 December 1972.

12 Soviet Economic Imperialism ?

The concept of a Soviet form of imperialism may appear at once to imply a non-economic explanation for imperialism. Soviet imperialism in the neo-classical view, is essentially a political phenomenon.

The trouble with Russia is not that she is Socialist but that she is Russia. As a matter of fact the Stalinist regime is essentially a militarist autocracy ... the work of one man who was strong enough to keep that population in abject poverty and submission and to concentrate all the forces of an undeveloped and defective industrial apparatus on the one military purpose (Schumpeter, 1943; 1947 edn, pp. 398–9).

Post-Stalinist regimes in Russia have not been so militaristic or so autocratic. Yet the invasions by Russian troops of Poland (twice), Hungary, Czechoslovakia and China have occurred since Stalin's death. The excuse that they were designed to put down capitalist, imperialist, counter-revolutionary forces cannot be taken seriously. The sight of two self-avowedly socialist states on the brink of full-scale war – as the Soviet Union and China have been – must seem incredible to a Marxist. It will be no surprise to Keynesians any more than to neo-classical liberals, to find nationalism 'dominant in the Soviet sphere' (Robinson, 1970a, pp. 98–9) and not at all confined to capitalist states.

To diagnose Soviet foreign policy as imperialist in a Marxist sense it would be necessary to suppose some similar features of Soviet economic structure corresponding to those of capitalist economic structures. One might look for failures in effective demand at home because of inequalities of income, or for under-used capacity and surplus goods arising from irrational planning. There have been Soviet surpluses; but there is no reason to suppose that Soviet planning cannot in general avoid such surpluses and ensure a balance of savings and investment and of supply and demand for goods. Yet there have been accusations of economic exploitation made against the USSR.

The argument that led to Che Guevara's dismissal from Dr Castro's government in Cuba was that:

Socialism cannot exist without a change in conscience provoking a new fraternal attitude toward humanity.... We believe the responsibility of aiding dependent countries should be approached with such a spirit and there should not be any more talk about developing trade for mutual benefit based on prices rigged against underdeveloped countries by the law of value and international relations of unequal exchange brought about by that law of value (Guevara, 1965).

It must, however, be said that Cuba is not a satellite of the USSR in the same sense that other Latin American States are satellites of the USA. The elimination of unemployment in Cuba and the steady improvement in the living standards of Cubans are authoritatively vouched for (Seers, 1964; Fagen, 1972). Economic development in the East European communist states is equally evident (see table 26). The Roumanians' claim may be accepted that this development could have been faster on the basis of local socialist efforts without Soviet economic hegemony (Newens, 1972); but the rate of development is impressively faster than that in almost all the capitalist underdeveloped countries. Soviet aid to non-communist underdeveloped lands has been extremely small, especially since 1965 (see table 35 below) – the exception is military aid, to Egypt for example – but the terms of the aid granted have been regarded by the recipients as markedly generous compared with capitalist aid (see Nkrumah, 1965, p. 243).

If the main objective of Soviet policy has been keeping the communist states within the framework of the Soviet bloc, was the rationale for this wholly political? Or was there, as in the similar objectives of capitalist policy, an underlying economic reason? We may notice first that most Marxists outside the Soviet Union recognize a 'transition period' prior to the two phases of Communist Society which Marx distinguished in his *Critique of the Gotha Programme*. This is in line with Marx's description of the '*first* phases of Communist Society as it is when it has just emerged *after* prolonged birth pangs from capitalist society' (1935b, p. 565) and of the way Marx goes on to write:

Between capitalist and communist society lies the period of the revolutionary transformation of the one into the other. There corresponds to this also a political transition period in which the state can be nothing but the revolutionary dictatorship of the proletariat (p. 577).

This transitional period is likely to be prolonged where an underdeveloped country, like Russia in 1917, has first to industrialize before it can reach even the first phase of communism. The road of industrialization is a hard one. Accumulation for tomorrow has to come out of the tiny surpluses of today. Capitalist accumulation involved slave and indentured labour in mines and plantations overseas, women and child labour in mines and mills at home. 'The iron heel of primitive accumulation', as Preobrazhensky called it in 1926 (English edn, 1965), descends, so that the margin between bare subsistence and starvation can be accumulated for the future. The process has never yet been accomplished except by dictatorship and repression. The excesses of Stalin have to be related to the Combination Acts, Tolpuddle and Peterloo in Britain and slavery in the British colonies. The Russian Revolution of 1917 on this view was not so much a combination of a capitalist and socialist revolution as Deutscher believes (1967), as an industrial revolution carried out by Communists (Carr, 1968). This certainly helps to explain the unexpectedly bitter struggles inside and between self-styled 'socialist' societies.

Inside the Soviet economy industrialization was carried through by accumulation at the expense of the overwhelming mass of the population which consisted of the peasantry. There was no revolution in the Russian countryside until the peasantry was forcibly collectivized in 1929 (Shanin, 1972a, pp. 145–61). The 'revolution from above' involved what Lange described as 'the assent of the population . . . obtained *ex post facto* through the propaganda and educational activities of the Communist Party' (1944), but also through the power of Stalin's secret police. Both the Soviet military establishment and the Soviet centralized bureaucracy were required to sustain such a revolution against internal tensions as much as to defend it against external pressures. Marx would not have expected a rapid transition to socialism from such a low technological base as existed in pre-revolutionary Russia; and once the repressive apparatus was established it was hard to dismantle. Externally, Soviet power exhibited continuing strong predatory tendencies.

If, however, the Soviet economy is not a socialist economy, it is certainly not capitalist. The drives towards domination of satellite states do not seem to be explicable by the laws of capitalist accumulation. We should perhaps modify what we said about the unlikely emergence of an unplanned surplus of products created in the Soviet economy seeking markets outside it. For Stalin (1952), while denying the possibility of crises of overproduction in a planned economy, did rather surprisingly speak 'confidently' of the possibility that the 'socialist countries will themselves feel the necessity of finding an outside market for their surplus products'. Given the regulation of savings, wages and prices, surpluses can surely be avoided in a planned economy. But we have not taken an underconsumptionist interpretation of Marx to provide the central Marxist explanation of imperialism in developed capitalist economies. That we have regarded as being rather the Keynesian view of capitalist economies. Our interpretation has been based on the conflict between the aim of competitive capitalist accumulation and the tendency of increased productivity to reduce the labour force which has to provide the surplus for accumulation. Is there some similar conflict in the Soviet economy?

Those Marxists who see such a similarity base their view on the continuation of commodity production in the Soviet economy. Stalin argued that commodity production, and thus the Marxist law of value, still operated in the Soviet Union, because 'the state disposes only of the products of state enterprises ... but the collective farms are unwilling to alienate their products except in the form of commodities, in exchange for which they desire to receive the commodities they need' (1952, pp. 19–20). Bettelheim has argued that:

... this is not good enough. The process of coordination by plan reduces the area within which commodity relations manifest themselves ... But a plan can effectively coordinate only on conditions, political ('effective participation of the masses') and economic ('scientific economic and social analysis') which are not yet present. ... Surplus value under state capitalism [as he designates the Soviet economy] can be used for socialist purposes by a workers' state but it can be misappropriated by a 'ruling class' consisting of an alliance of managers and their [state] controllers (1970a, pp. 53–4, 76–7).

What he means by 'the effective participation of the masses', he characterized in a later article as 'domination by the immediate producers over their conditions of existence and, therefore, in the first instance, over their means of production and products' (1970b, p. 2). Sweezy comments that this must mean more than control by workers over their means of production, or even than their 'possession' of them, as in Yugoslavia (1972, p. 9). This distinction between possession and domination is central to Bettelheim's analysis. If 'the state apparatus is not effectively dominated by the workers', the state officials become 'the effective owners' and not only dispose of the surplus as they think best but are 'compelled to grant a dominant role to the market and to profitability criterion' (Bettelheim, 1970a, p. 81).

Some of the conditions for domination by the workers were spelled out by Sweezy at a seminar on the transition to Socialism held in Santiago, Chile, during October 1971, from which we have just quoted. They include the placing of equality before efficiency, the beginning of the abolition of the distinction between mental and physical work and between industry and agriculture, complete freedom of discussion and criticism, the treatment of work as a creative activity, an end not a means, and the continuous extension of free provision in place of the distribution of resources through earning and spending money incomes (Sweezy, 1972, pp. 10–12). Practically none of these developments is taking place in the Soviet Union or Eastern Europe, although some of them are to be found in China according to Robinson (1969) and in Cuba according to Fagen (1972).

The other requirement posed by Bettelheim for making the coordination by a state plan into an instrument of socialism, that might reduce and ultimately replace commodity exchange, is the development of scientific, economic and social analysis based on economic as opposed to monetary calculation. Stalin argued that the law of value of commodity exchange extends also to production in the state sector as well as to exchanges between industry and agriculture, not as a 'regulating function' but as an 'influence on production'. This is because, he says, 'such things as cost accounting and profitableness, production costs, prices, etc. are of actual importance in our enterprises. Consequently, our enterprises cannot, and must not, function without taking the law of value into account'; and Stalin goes on (writing, it should be remembered, in 1952 and not in 1942 or 1932):

Under present conditions this really is not a bad thing since it trains our business executives ... to count production magnitudes ... accurately ... to look for, find and utilize hidden reserves ... to lower production costs, to practise cost accounting, and to make their enterprises pay (1952, p. 23).

That this was so, is just what Bettelheim criticizes. But to replace monetary calculation by economic calculation it is necessary to establish a measure of social utility. This involves a calculation of 'different kinds of labour and products ... in order to regulate on the basis of this measure, the distribution of labours [i.e. of social labour] among different productions' (1970a). But while, under the capitalist mode of production, this can be based on a concept of socially necessary labour-time and measured by the return to capital, under a socialist mode of production the return to capital is irrelevant. Labour-time should become the relevant measure; but different industries will still be at different levels of productivity. The neo-Ricardian critique of capital theory faced the same prob-

lem. Return to capital is not a measure of capital intensity. Even
less can it be so under socialism. Some other measure is required
(see Chattophadhay, 1972, pp. 13–29). Sraffa's concept of
'dated labour' might fill the bill here, given some rate of interest generally accepted as a determinant of the rate of growth
(1960, p. 38).

It is not necessary for our purposes to go further into this
discussion,[1] but only to note that in the Soviet Union the
absence of a non-monetary measure of the social utility of
labour and the persistence of commodity production implies
not only the dominance of the bureaucratic state apparatus
and its managers over the workers inside the Soviet Union,
but also their dominance over workers in countries whose
economies are integrated with that of the Soviet Union. It
implies also, through the Soviet planners' acceptance, *faute de
mieux*, of capitalist world prices in their foreign trade relations,
that the Soviet economy is, as it were, plugged into the capitalist world economy and thereby into competitive imperialist
relations. This is the conclusion of Mattick in his study of
'state capitalism', as he also terms the economy of the Soviet
Union. 'There is only one compelling reason for retaining the
law of value in its Russian definition and that is to give the
conditions of inequality, such as prevail in the state-capitalist
economy, the semblance of an economic law' (1969, p. 317).

As Marx always made clear, the effect of commodity production is to draw a veil over the social relations involved in
the productive process and over the relative contributions and
rewards of each individual involved in the process (1946,
ch. 1, section 4). The rate of accumulation in the Soviet

1. It should perhaps be said that Nove in his critical but exceedingly
fair review of Bettelheim's work (1972), seems almost wantonly
unwilling to understand the kind of calculation Bettelheim is
indicating and seems only anxious to explore comparisons with the
writings of Trotsky and Yurovsky in the 1920s. Since that time the
development of computers has made possible the evolution of shadow
prices by linear programming models. What is needed to advance
such work is precisely the conceptual framework which Bettelheim
has begun to construct. See also, for a further exploration of the
problem, Bodington (1973).

Union could not have been achieved, if the working population, and certainly the agricultural population, had been aware of the proportion of their current labour time that was being taken from them to invest in the future through the relative prices and wages that were being centrally fixed. It is, in large part, this concealing of relative non-monetary values in commodity exchanges between the Soviet Union, members of the Soviet bloc and other underdeveloped countries that has led to the accusation of 'Soviet imperialism' (Zauberman, 1955).

This might appear to be very similar to the exploitation of underdeveloped countries by owners of capital in the developed countries of the capitalist world. Indeed there is a widely held view that the Soviet and capitalist systems are converging (see Tinbergen, 1962, pp. 34–9). This idea of converging systems could mean that the increase of state planning in capitalist economies makes them less dependent on exploitation, especially exploitation of other countries, and that the increased role of the market in the Soviet system makes it more liable to develop exploitative relations. There is little evidence, however, that in the Soviet countries the central plan could be subordinated to the working of market relations without massive resistance from the state bureaucracies; equally, the subordination of the market to a central plan in the capitalist countries could not be achieved without fierce resistance from the owners of capital. Bettelheim and Sweezy, in a debate on the question of market socialism, agreed that:

> ... to put increasing reliance on the market not as a temporary retreat [like Lenin's NEP] but as an ostensible step towards a more efficient 'socialist' economy ... rather than to weaken the bureaucracy, politicize the masses and ensure increasing initiative and responsibility to the workers themselves ... [would be] the road back to class domination and ultimately the restoration of capitalism (Sweezy, 1970, p. 21).

The only real evidence is the case of Yugoslavia (see Singleton, 1971–2; 1972). There, the principle of decentralization has not meant weakening the bureaucracy so much as decentralizing it; without a strong central plan, the devolution of political power to the states had enabled the richer states to develop at the expense of the poorer; with uncontrolled market competition between enterprises, owned by the workers but operated on the principle of profitability rather than under a social plan, again, the richer profit at the expense of the poorer; similarly with the peasantry, cooperatives which enjoy an export market in hops or wines thrive, while the mass of individual peasants is squeezed. The result is that we find in Yugoslavia 'all the contradictions characteristic of capitalist market relations, such as disproportional development, business failures, unemployment *and* inflation and the ups and downs of the business cycle' (Mattick, 1969, p. 288). There is no sign, however, of the Soviet Union or the other countries in the Soviet bloc moving in this direction; and it must be said that Ota Sik, the Economics Minister of the Dubcek government in the 'Prague Spring', who is often seen as the idealogue of market socialism, showed no intention of relaxing strong social planning of resource allocation when he encouraged maximum workers' participation in that planning and in the execution of plans throughout the economy (Sik, 1967; 1968, summarized in Barratt Brown, 1970b, ch. 8).

It seems likely that, where internal difficulties, originally caused in the case of Yugoslavia by the abrupt termination of promised Soviet deliveries, are met by successively greater reliance on market relations at the expense of a social plan, intensified exploitation of the poor by the rich will follow. Such evidence as there is suggests a decrease of inequality in the last twenty years, at least in the Soviet Union, if not in other countries in the Soviet bloc, rather than an increase (Wiles and Markowski, 1971, p. 344). So long as discussion is not free, workers are not in a position to dominate the social plan and so long as non-monetary calculation of economic contributions has not been devised and instituted, tensions can be expected to build up in the Soviet bloc such as those that exploded in Yugoslavia in 1949, in Budapest and Warsaw in 1956, in China in 1960, in Prague in 1967 and in the Baltic ports of Poland in 1970. So long, moreover, as the Soviet Union feels the pressure of imperialist competition, the response to such explosions will be tank fire and repression; but it does not seem to be justifiable to see in Soviet aggression the same strength of economic pressures as we have identified in United States aggression. That the first is largely a response to the second is accepted by some non-Marxists as well as Marxists (Robinson, 1969, p. 42).

Evidence for Soviet 'economic imperialism' is said to be found in three main fields – the mixed Soviet-satellite enterprises of the post-war years, price discrimination by the USSR against other members of the Soviet bloc and the use of Comecon, the Council of Mutual Economic Assistance, by the Soviet Union and the richer members of the bloc to exploit the poorer. In addition, a more general point is made that the whole Soviet system involves a kind of economic imperialism in which wealth is funnelled into the Communist Party hierarchy, the so-called 'New Class' (Djilas, 1957).

To take first the mixed enterprises, these were denounced by the Yugoslavs in 1950, but in fact they date back to the 1920s when they were tried out in Mongolia (Prybla, 1964, p. 471). The essence of the complaints from Eastern Europe in the 1950s was that the joint stock companies were based upon unfair valuations of the investment of the two parties, and were designed to restrict development that did not fit in with Soviet plans; but they also included the charges of monopolization of the market at the expense of independent local operators, discrimination in tariffs and pricing policies, and defaulting by the Soviet Union on supplies. Stalin is quoted by Dedijer as having agreed with Tito that such companies were 'unsuitable for Yugoslavia and should only be established in former enemy countries' (1953, pp. 285–96). They may thus perhaps be regarded as part of the Soviet policy of extracting war reparations.

Price discrimination was a bitter complaint of the Poles and the Hungarians against the Soviet Union in 1956, and should perhaps also be regarded as part of the Soviet war reparations policy. Evidence that it continued into the 1960s has since been offered by Mendershausen who:

found that there was a tendency for the Soviets to charge the bloc more for exports and pay them less for imports in those instances in which the bloc and Western Europe both bought or sold similar commodity categories from [to] the USSR. This tendency was much more clear cut in the case of exports than imports (see Holzman, 1965, p. 44).

These tendencies have, however, been shown to be due rather to Western discrimination against the bloc nations and also to some deliberate autarchic policies in the Soviet bloc, whereby all exchanges between members tend to take place at prices somewhat below world prices (Holzman, 1965).

The more serious complaint which comes from the less developed members of the Soviet bloc themselves is against the use, in their intra-bloc trade, of capitalist world prices as a basis for bargaining rather than prices based on production costs inside the bloc (Pryor, 1963, p. 156). An alternative set of shadow prices has already been worked out by Polish economists from a linear programming model of the whole bloc, but has not been adopted. It is significant that pressure for continuing use of capitalist world prices comes from the more advanced countries, East Germany and Czechoslovakia, and the opposition from the less advanced – Poland, Bulgaria and Roumania – with strong support, however, from at least one Soviet economist, Ostrovityanov (see Pryor, 1965, p. 156). The failure of the opposing group to agree on how the costs of production of several states at different levels of technological development should be measured has left capitalist world prices holding the field. The problem of determining the appropriate level of subsidy or protection for strategic industries, infant industries and countries with temporary balance of payments difficulties has so far not been resolved. Once again the reason is the absence of a non-monetary basis of calculation in a commodity exchange economy. This, as we have seen before, raises great difficulties for Marxists in comparing prices in countries with very different levels of socially necessary labour-time.

In the Roumanian dispute with Comecon, the basis of the

Roumanian argument has been one that we have met before; that capitalist world prices are set by productivity levels in the most developed countries. Thus a Roumanian economist writes:

If the criterion of economizing social labour-time were to be made the basis for the international division of labour [i.e. if specialization were determined by relative labour costs], this would tend to perpetuate the backwardness of the underdeveloped countries and to conserve the old economic structure inherited from the domination of monopolistic trusts (see Montias, 1964, p. 32).

So the Roumanians wanted protection *for* infant industries and *against* balance of payments difficulties; and were answered by a Czechoslovak economist who wanted 'to assign given lines of production, by mutual agreement, to countries in possession of the most advanced technology' (see Montias, 1964, p. 132) and another who complained that 'some underdeveloped countries [in the Soviet bloc] neglected their export commitments and thus jeopardized the fulfilment of their partners' plans' (Montias, 1964, p. 144). What worries the Roumanians and other underdeveloped countries in the Soviet bloc is precisely the results of the artificial world division of labour in which they have for so long been held. The East Germans and Czechs may have good reason for questioning the claim of each of the Soviet bloc members to set up the whole range of basic industries, including, for example, a steel industry where a state has no coal or iron ore; but the claim of underdeveloped countries to diversify and to build up some capital-goods industries is the claim to escape neo-colonial status. It is the same claim that the underdeveloped states inside Yugoslavia have been making as well as underdeveloped countries everywhere in the capitalist world. It is interesting in the light of our discussion of Emmanuel's concept of unequal exchange that it is not so much the low level of wages in the underdeveloped countries that the underdeveloped members of the Soviet bloc cite as the cause of their weak position, but the low level of productivity of their industries.

The Soviet Union, as a large country with rich natural resources for whom foreign trade is relatively unimportant, stands somewhere in the middle of this argument. A Soviet specialist in economic affairs was quoted in 1961 as saying that:

Many countries [in the Soviet bloc] are far from exploiting the possibilities of the international division of labour for the development of their socialist production. . . . On the world socialist market there is no mercenary spirit or speculation, no unequivalent exchange, characteristic of trade among capitalist countries (see Montias, 1964, p. 143).

It was Che Guevara's 'mistake' to believe that there was.

Yet the facts shown in table 33 indicate that the trade of the various members of the Soviet bloc is very unbalanced, and also compared with capitalist countries rather underdeveloped. From this it would appear that attempts to achieve economic autarchy have been quite irrationally successful. The Hungarian steel industry, for example, imports iron ore at a price that exceeds the cost of imported steel from Poland. Similarly, with pig iron and coke (from brown coal) production in East Germany, and with synthetic oil production in Czechoslovakia and East Germany, costs are much higher than the cost of natural oil imports (Pryor, 1963, pp. 28–9). Specialization among the Soviet bloc countries appears to have been actually reduced in the 1950s and only a little increased thereafter (p. 44). Most countries have increased the share of capital goods in their trade to about half of the total and consequently reduced the share in their trade of food and raw materials, while trade in consumer goods remains a very small part of the total (5 per cent to 15 per cent). But there is no evidence of the division of labour, typical of the capitalist world, between capital goods and other finished manufactured exports from the developed countries in exchange for raw materials from the underdeveloped.

By contrast, in the greatly expanded trade between east and west in Europe in the 1960s, there has been an increase of imports from the West of capital goods and also of manufactured consumer goods against a continuing high proportion of exports from the East of semi-manufactures and raw materials (UN, 1969b, ch. 2, table 32).

Table 33 Role and direction of trade – capitalist world, Soviet bloc countries and China, 1970

Place	Exports value ($ billion)	Exports as percentage of GDP	Direction of exports (percentage of total)				
			Soviet bloc (incl. USSR, excl. China)	USSR, alone	China etc.	Capitalist developed	Capitalist underdeveloped
world	311	9·6	9·2	3·5	0·9	71·4	18·5
capitalist, developed	225	10·6	3·3	1·3	0·7	77	19
capitalist, underdeveloped	54	15·7	4·6	2·4	0·8	74·8	19·8
Soviet bloc	31	5·4	64	21·5	3·0	23	10
USSR	12·8	2·4	52·8	—	5	21·7	20·5
Bulgaria	2·0	2·1	75·5	53·8	(0·8)	16·0	7·7
Czechoslovakia	3·8	8·5	64·7	32·2	(1·1)	24·4	9·8
East Germany	4·6	8·9	68·4	38	(2·2)	23·8	5·6
Hungary	23	12	61·5	34·9	(1·5)	31	6
Poland	3·5	5·1	60·4	35·3	(1·5)	30·3	7·8
Roumania	1·8	7·6	50·1	28·6	(4·9)	34·5	10·5
China etc.	2·4	—	21	10	—	33	46

China etc. includes North Korea, Mongolia and North Vietnam
Exports as a percentage of GDP are for 1963 not 1970; figures in brackets are assumed from remainders
Sources: UN (1969a, 1972a); GATT (1970, table 81)

One more indicator of some kind of 'economic imperialism' in the Soviet bloc is the suggested element of economic control exercised in their common interests by the Soviet bureaucracy through the Party bureaucracies of the Soviet satellites. Such control by its very nature would be hard to substantiate, but there is the extraordinary vehemence of Soviet responses to acts of independence in Czechoslovakia in 1968 and more recently in Poland, and there is the whole question of the Sino–Soviet dispute. In the invasion of Czechoslovakia the tanks were mainly Russian, in Poland they were Polish, but behind them stood Soviet support and after the tanks came massive economic support for the Soviet puppet government. Such large-scale economic aid cannot have been too willingly granted by Soviet rulers who were faced with great difficulties in feeding their own people (Deutscher, 1970, pp. 268–72). But of course the aid did not come from the pockets or profits of the Soviet elite. It was the most insistent argument that was put to me when I was in Prague in 1968, by Czech intellectuals and workers in the factories alike, that Czechoslovak industry was built into the Soviet economic plan. The inputs and outputs of Czech factories were geared to the giant enterprises in the Soviet Union. The Czech Party bureaucracy was there to keep it that way and to grow fat on the proceeds.

This may be an exaggerated view, and there were obviously problems for the management of Soviet internal politics in the event of successful Czechoslovak democratization. But the direct economic interest of large firms in the Soviet system, in managing their inputs and outputs as we have seen them doing in the capitalist system, cannot be gainsaid (see Rawin, 1965, pp. 1–16). Decentralization in the Soviet Union is not, however, moving as far as it has moved in Yugoslavia. There is every evidence of recentralization since Khruschev's downfall. The requirements of large-scale investment in modern technology have their own logic for the central planners in the Soviet Union as they do for the trans-national capitalist company (see Portes, 1972, p. 629). But the source of power and privilege of the Soviet bureaucracy is not primarily economic; it is political. The control by the Party and its agents over the economic

Table 34 Composition of Soviet bloc foreign trade by commodity, 1950s and 1960s (%)

Commodities	USSR		E Germany		Czechoslovakia		Hungary		Poland		Roumania		Bulgaria	
	1955	1965	1954	1965 plan	1955	1965 plan	1955	1965 plan	1955	1965 plan	1957–1959	1964–1966	1957–1959	1964–1966
all exports														
food	27	—	3	3	6	2	31	20	16	18	—	—	—	—
raw materials	36	—	30	25	39	20	24	21	63	38	—	—	—	—
manufactures	37	—	67	72	55	78	45	60	21	44	—	—	—	—
capital goods	17	—	57	55	44	63	29	46	14	39	—	—	—	—
semi-finished manufactures	10	—	—	—	—	—	—	—	—	—	—	—	—	—
consumer	10	—	10	17	11	17	16	14	7	5	—	—	—	—
exports to W Europe														
food and raw materials	77	73	15	19	39	36	57	51	78	71	81	72	80	69
manufactures	23	27	85	81	61	64	43	49	22	29	9	18	20	31
capital goods	2	3·5	23	21	13·5	14	14·5	8	3	6	1	1	1·5	2·5
semi-finished manufactures	20	21	45	43	30·5	34	19·5	31	17·5	20	7	15	17	26
consumer	1	2·5	17	17	11	16	9	10	1·5	3	1	2	1·5	2·5

Exports to W Europe: figures are for 1957–1959 and 1964–1966. All exports: semi-finished manufactures except for USSR are included in raw materials

Sources: Pryor (1963, table 1.8, p. 45); Scott (1958, table III, p. 153); UN (1968a, ch. 2, table 32, p. 75)

surplus is through the political structure of the state, not as in capitalism through private ownership of capital. The bureaucracy carried through the first stages of accumulation for industrialization in Russia and in Eastern Europe; but the old bureaucracy has come under challenge from a new industrial technocracy. As a French Marxist, Mallet has explained it:

When ... the level of production is insufficient to assure both the maintenance of the structures of production and the standard of living of the ruling classes, the weight of the bureaucracy becomes oppressive. Facing the consequences of popular discontent the bureaucracy seeks to obtain a maximum of political autonomy, and to set itself up as a ruling class ... But as Eastern European societies were transformed from agrarian into industrial societies ... the appropriation of surplus value through external control became an obstacle to the internal growth of productive forces ... The revival of the market was a means of giving economic initiative to the directors of enterprises and of taking it away from the centralized state bureaucracy ... (1970).

Mallet does not see this in Marxist terms as the restoration of capitalism nor, at the opposite extreme, as a guarantee of socialism. The technocracy, including scientists and economists as well as managers, from its interest in the qualitative development of the productive forces, is led to seek the 'participation' of the workers in the functioning of the enterprise. But to secure its power over investments, prices and product orientation, having no power over the ownership of capital, it has the tendency, just like its Western counterparts, 'to redirect the workers' demands for managerial power toward the satisfaction of their consumer needs'; and this involves the creation of a prosperous consumer market in the advanced industrial sectors and in the more developed areas at the expense of backwardness in other sectors and less developed areas.

This is the dual economy that we have met elsewhere, and the duality is somewhat underestimated by Mallet in his insistence on the 'homogenization of living conditions and style of life' (Mallet, 1970, p. 10). What has happened in Yugoslavia shows the road that the other Eastern European countries and even the Soviet Union could take. But Mallet believes that, whereas the technocrats are winning in the East European countries, and will increasingly win there, the old established bureaucracy in the Soviet Union cannot allow them to go too far lest they become dominant in the Soviet Union itself. Since the Soviet bureaucracy has neither the economic levers of capitalist power – investment capital, control over patents and know-how – nor, because of its resistance to its own technocracy, the actual technological superiority, it has no other means to impose its will on the rest of the Soviet bloc than by the naked force of arms. The growing contrast, however, between the economic development and open discussion of problems in Eastern Europe and the backwardness and repression in the Soviet Union is likely to create an alliance of the technocracy and the industrial working class to challenge the old bureaucracy (see Sakharov, 1968). This can be a long struggle because the old bureaucracy can draw strength from appealing to the underdeveloped regions, to the workers in the more backward industries and beyond them to the collective farmers. In a situation of such tension imperialist postures could once again be used to smooth over social contradictions.

This must surely be the main explanation for Soviet policy towards China, although the Sino–Soviet split and the vehemence of Soviet responses remains the most enigmatic for an economic view of imperialism. The Chinese challenge to the political leadership of the Soviet bureaucracy over the Communist world and, by extension, over the whole underdeveloped world provides the most obvious explanation. Soviet economic aid has, more obviously even than capitalist aid, been tied in to political objectives. The confluence of capitalist economic aid, investment and exports was demonstrated in the last chapter. Soviet aid is oriented in the same way, as table 34 makes clear. The overwhelming concentration is on the historic Russian spheres of influence – the Middle East, India and on the frontier states of China. My own experience in India, talking to Soviet experts, confirms that they see themselves there somewhat in the role of successors to the British Raj.

There is one particular indication of the importance attached by both the Soviet Union and China to control over the small

Table 35 Soviet bloc: aid to underdeveloped countries, 1954–1968 (annual averages $m)

	1954–1961	*1962–4*	*1965–7*	*1968 (est.)*
commitments	600	640	860	760
by donor				
USSR	400	350	500	370
East Europe	150	160	345	350
China	50	130	15	40
by region and country of recipient				
Latin America	50	—	70	20
Algeria	—	100	60	—
Egypt	100	200	85	170
other Africa	100	90	90	55
India	120	40	250	—
Indonesia	100	20	—	—
Iran	—	30	110	440
other Asia	100	150	105	45
Syria	30	10	80	30
actual net flows	—	210	180	—
donors				
USSR	—	150	130	—
East Europe	—	60	50	—
recipients				
Egypt	—	40	60	—
India	—	90	60	—
Indonesia	—	13	—	—
Iran	—	—	15	—
Pakistan	—	—	10	—
others	—	67	35	—

The large figure for other Asia in 1962–4 consisted mainly of a payment in 1962 by the USSR of $200 million to Afghanistan
Source: UN (1966; 1969a)

underdeveloped communist countries in Asia. To win the friendship of North Korea, North Vietnam and Outer Mongolia in the years leading up to the rift between the Soviet Union and China in 1963, each of these two communist powers granted aid in excess of $1000 million – the USSR $1700 million and China $1300 million. This may be compared with Soviet aid to China over the same period of some $790 million and is reported to have been overwhelmingly economic rather than purely military (Prybla, 1964, p. 464). Was the aim wholly political, wholly charitable or partly economic, designed to incorporate outlying territories in a total politico–economic system?

Whatever the answer, while we have seen that Soviet imperialism has in many ways to be analysed differently, it does seem to have something in common with economic imperialism in the capitalist world. But the struggle between a bureaucracy which carried out the first stage of industrialization and a technocracy which has inevitably emerged in the second stage of more advanced techniques of production adds a special dimension to the picture. It remains a very Marxist type of explanation to see the continuation of Russian imperialism as deriving from the persistence of commodity production in a world of potential abundance and from the conflict between developing technical forces of production and an outmoded economic structure of relations in the productive process. The Marxist conclusion would be that consciousness of the possibilities of democratic socialism will spread as the conflict becomes more and more obvious; and this changing consciousness will more easily affect the whole social formation since the means of production are nationalized and the rhetoric of national government ideology is basically socialist.

13 Practice and Prescription

The test of theory in relatively deterministic systems must be the successful predictions that have been based upon it. This test cannot be applied in the social sciences because, in contrast with the natural sciences, man stands inside the social model and the more influential the prediction the more thorough the avoiding action that he will take, so that the theory is not permitted to work itself out. The test of social theory must be successful practice, past and present.[1] 'The function of social science is quite different from that of the natural sciences – it is to provide society with an organ of self-consciousness' (Robinson, 1970a, p. 120).[2] Each of the groups of theories looked at in this book to obtain insights into the economics of imperialism can claim successful practice but each must admit to failures.

The free-trade theory of neo-classical economists led them to expect disaster from the protectionist, beggar-my-neighbour policies of the developed capitalist nations in the 1930s; and it came. The deliberate re-establishment of free trade inside the European Economic Community after 1949 certainly inaugurated an era of prosperity, although the result of the external tariff was a trade diversion as well as a trade creation effect. The Kennedy rounds of tariff reduction had some success in reducing, at least, the industrial tariff. What the free traders cannot claim is the successful industrialization by any nation through free trade and a free market. All nations that have industrialized have had to give strong protection to their

1. I have argued for the energizing effect of Marx's thought as one of its major claims to be regarded as a valuable model in political economy (see Shanin, 1972b).
2. This is very close to a Marxist view.

infant industries and state support for their development. Moreover, capitalism as it has matured has not very obviously cleansed itself of the violently expansive characteristics that seemed to neo-classical liberals to be no more than a hangover from earlier social formations.

The Keynesian record is rather better. The developed capitalist states have managed aggregate demand in their economies so as to maintain steady capital investment and near full employment for a quarter of a century. If the rentier has not been put to sleep, his role has been reduced. His (or her) place has, however, been taken by the self-governing, self-financing, self-perpetuating private corporation as well as by an enlarged public sector. In the same period the international financial institutions, which Keynes and others established at Bretton Woods, have served as a framework for a continuous and very rapid growth of world trade. But, underdeveloped lands have only in small part, and very recently, shared in this growth, and as the world entered the decade of the 1970s both national and international Keynesian policies were in disarray. The ending of the hegemony of the United States over the capitalist world and the rise of giant trans-national corporations seems to have set problems for which the new mercantilism was providing answers of an unexpected nature. A steadily increasing role for state expenditures in each national economy and a vast burden of expenditure on armaments and space exploration had, moreover, been envisaged by Kalecki for supplying the inducement to invest (1943).

Marxist theory too can claim successes but must recognize inadequacies. Of Marx's five major predictions – the centralization of capital, the polarization of wealth and poverty, the falling rate of profit, the rising proportion of unemployed and the increasing instability of the system – the first two have been fulfilled on a world-wide scale, the second two have not however, appeared (unless very recent developments prove irreversible) and the last still remains in doubt. Crises certainly became more severe up to 1929 and 1937, but Marx's counteracting tendencies of cheapening capital equipment and expanding foreign trade have perhaps continued to operate for longer than he expected. It is, however, the steady extension of active state intervention in what Marx regarded as an essentially self-regulating economy that has proved Marx to be wrong about the falling rate of profit and rising unemployment. Whether such intervention can correct the labour-saving effect of the Second Industrial Revolution and the remaining gap between developed and underdeveloped economies, has still to be seen. It would be the general view of Marxists that it cannot, but we have had cause to question this view.

Successful practice, based on the different models of imperialism reviewed in this book, will have to respond to the following questions:

1 Can the power of the giant trans-national company be limited in relation to that of the nation states, both developed and underdeveloped? (The answer to this question will affect the answers given to the questions that follow.)

2 Can the main underdeveloped countries achieve economic development within the general economic structure of the capitalist world? This is the central test of the meaning of imperialism.

3 If not, can they in some other way achieve a really substantial measure of development?

4 Can the developed countries re-establish measures of international economic cooperation to replace those established at Bretton Woods?

5 If so, what forms would these take: (a) re-establishment of US hegemony, (b) carving out of spheres of influence by the super powers, or (c) some new international institutions that recognize the changed balance of power?

6 Can the communist Governments play a role that is markedly different from that of the capitalist powers in their relations with underdeveloped countries?

7 Is there any possibility of cooperation emerging between the working class in developed countries (capitalist and communist) and the liberation movements in underdeveloped countries?

8 What effect would such cooperation or its absence have upon the prospects of world-wide socialist revolutions of a Marxist type?

The answers of neo-classical economists can be seen first in the prognoses made in 1949 by Schumpeter. Both Marx and the Keynesians were, according to him, wrong in their analysis but right in their respective predictions of the eventual breakdown of capitalism and its tendency to stagnation – 'with sufficient help from the public sector' on what Schumpeter called despairingly, 'the march to socialism' (1943; 1949 edn, p. 425). His despair arose from his distrust of increased regulation and restriction of the initiative of capitalist entrepreneurs by bureaucratic controls instituted to meet the inflationary pressure that the strength of trade unions and of other special interest groups were putting upon the economy.

Today's neo-classicists like Hicks and Johnson are more self-confident.[3] Governments need only to be convinced of the necessity of standing up to the pressure groups. The giant company may grow, but its internationalism and immortality and its interest in marketing as much as in production serve to make its influence benign (Johnson, 1968, p. 130). In the 'administrative revolution' the key posts will be captured by liberal neo-classical economists in developed and underdeveloped countries alike; and they have learnt the lessons of the 'failure of mercantilism' (Hicks, 1969, p. 164). Capitalist development should then spread *via* free trade throughout the world, restricted only by the 'strains on what the richer countries have to spare from their resources' (Hicks, 1969, p. 166). Freeing resources to move where they may be most profitably used, freeing exchange rates, ending the protection of agriculture and of other labour-intensive industries in the richer countries, all these can be made the main aim of international institutions to replace the perverse aim of encouraging investment where it is not profitable and protecting industries in developing countries where they are not viable (Johnson, 1965, pp. 10–12,

3. For a summary and critique of these confident views, see Knapp (1973).

46–8, 94–100). The Communist regimes which reject such freedoms as anathema will suffer for it, once the 'psychic satisfactions' of national prestige and military power wear off (Johnson, 1968, pp. 8–9, 133–4). Since the hostility to the large international corporations, both of workers in advanced countries and of the peoples of less developed countries, can be regarded as equally irrational (pp. 140–41), talk of revolutions becomes irrelevant.

The Keynesians are less confident than they were. They reject the *laissez-faire* 'belief that the pursuit of self-interest by each individual rebounds to the benefit of all' (Robinson, 1970a, p. 124); but 'without the anodyne of *laissez-faire* the moral problem, on a world scale, stares us in the face' (Robinson, 1962, p. 129). 'The average man . . . is in fact strongly addicted to the money-making passion' (Keynes, 1960, p. 374); but while human nature cannot be transmuted it can perhaps be managed. Interest rates may fall and the rentier suffer euthanasia, as capital is 'deprived of its scarcity value within one or two generations' (Keynes, 1960, p. 373). We are well into the second generation since those words were written and are suffering from the highest rates of interest for over 100 years (with the exception of three weeks in 1873 and four days in August of 1914).

It was Keynes's conviction 'that the power of vested interests' – and he specified the 'competitive struggle for markets' and 'the economic forces calculated to set the interest of one country against that of its neighbours' – 'is vastly exaggerated compared with the gradual encroachment of ideas' (1960, pp. 382–3). But Harrod, Phelps Brown, Kaldor and Worswick all doubt whether our ideas, at least our economic theories, are adequate (see Knapp, 1973; Kaldor, 1972, p. 1237). Robinson seems rather to doubt our capacity ever to settle the conflicts of what she calls 'the moral problem'. Yet she concludes that 'while social life will always present mankind with a choice of evils' (1962, pp. 146–7), nonetheless it is essential 'to combat, not foster, the ideology which pretends that values which can be measured in terms of money are the only ones that ought to count'.

Keynes predicted that 'it will be possible for communal saving through the agency of the state to be maintained at a level which will allow the growth of capital up to the point when it ceases to be scarce' (1960, p. 221). The economic problem might be finally solved when 'our absolute needs are satisfied', even though a sense of relative deprivation in relation to fellow human beings may continue, and we come to 'prefer to devote our further energies to non-economic purposes' (1932a, p. 365). Schumpeter's fears of stagnation and Marx's expectation of falling rates of profit are 'converted from a nightmare into an agreeable day dream' (Robinson, 1962, p. 103).

Robinson has quoted a less optimistic prediction from Kalecki. The opposition to Keynesian ideas of those who would wish to 'teach the workers a lesson', in the event of state-financed full employment, 'and in particular of big business – as a rule influential in Government departments – would most probably induce the Government to return to the orthodox policy of cutting down the budget deficit' (Robinson, 1962, p. 94, quoting Kalecki, 1943). We have seen just such pressures at work in Britain in the restrictive measures of the 1960s and early 1970s and equally their succession by further and expanded state investment, so that Kalecki's forecast of a 'political business cycle' has come true, at least in Britain.[4] But Keynes was convinced that 'coordinated acts of intelligent judgement' (1932b, p. 318) could be relied upon to regulate saving and investment, and even in the 1970s the amplitude of the post-war 'political business cycles' has not equalled that of the pre-war cycles. There seems to be little danger of the return to orthodoxy being carried in Britain beyond the point of one million unemployed.

The Keynesian view, therefore, on the future of the transnational company must be that its power, however great it is today and however far from having the benign influence

4. It is apparent that successful politicians *follow* the business cycle; this must be so because the cycle continues to be a world-wide phenomenon and election dates do not have a fixed and coincidental term in all countries.

granted to it by the neo-classicists, either in developed or underdeveloped economies (see Robinson, 1970a, pp. 83, 109), is likely to wane with the declining scarcity of capital. For this scarcity is what provides its power. But Robinson is quite clear that the results of the operations of the trans-national companies are precisely to prevent capital ceasing to be scarce in the underdeveloped countries – thus 'depriving the new national governments of the independence which was granted on paper when they were set up' (1970a, p. 109). She nevertheless sees 'development going on in the world', although this is 'largely nullified by the growth of population', encouraged by both 'Catholic and Marxist orthodoxy', and concludes by instancing Chinese experience as having 'shown what development requires':

To get the whole population engaged with good will in the economic effort and to organize employment so that all can contribute; to increase productivity in agriculture so that a surplus can be extracted without the need to use brutal methods; to check inequality so as not to waste resources on unnecessary consumption and undermine morale by generating envy; to raise the general level of health and to institute birth control; to build up the basis of heavy industry so as to be able to modernize production as fast as possible, and meanwhile to encourage handicrafts to mechanize themselves by means of 'intermediate techniques'[5]; to spread education and develop self-reliance (at every level from the paddy field to the atomic laboratory) and applying the scientific method of experiment in every activity (1970a, p. 112).

Robinson ends this passage by adding that 'it remains to be seen whether any other prescription will prove possible'. And two problems remain for most underdeveloped countries: first, how they may break out of the capitalist framework which makes such prescriptions impossible to apply, and, secondly, how they (and even the Chinese people) may be encouraged to carry through such a set of measures, given what she herself describes as the 'enormous inertia of history'. Her prescription comes rather surprisingly from a Keynesian for whom man's love of money, and of increased relative power

5. The reference given here by Robinson is to Schumacher (1967).

through increased relative wealth, are supposed to have acted as the main determinants of economic activity from a period of history that goes far beyond the limits of capitalism. Moreover, Keynesians like Robinson and Kalecki see the distribution of income not at all as a matter for value judgement, as neo-classical thought has it, but as a determinant of successful economic growth. This is not only a question of incentives but of getting growth without inflation. 'The central problem is at whose expense the country is to be developed' (Kalecki, 1971, p. 76). The consumption of non-essentials has to be restrained if the consumption of essentials is to be raised. Even in a socialist economy there is a 'problem of sacrificing present for future consumption', and the more rapid the rate of growth the greater the sacrifice.

Knapp has put forward a sketch for pilot experiments, which could, if successful, issue in policy prescriptions in a more Keynesian mould. His idea is that governments, especially, but not only, in underdeveloped countries, might come to adopt policies of a novel Keynesian type, which he calls 'vent management'. This would be designed to eliminate involuntary underemployment or 'frustrated supply', as Knapp calls it.

This would consist of an offer based on preliminary resource surveys on the one hand, and studies of potential investment and consumer demands at increased levels of productivity as the extent of the market is enlarged, on the other hand, to buy and sell a wide range of selected and specified goods and services at stated prices against money, on a cash on delivery or on a completion basis, at selected points in this economy.

[This might be effective quite on its own] even in countries like India, where the pressure of population on the land is [said to be] so great that much of the agricultural population subsists at starvation levels, [so that] it is unlikely that anything can happen by way of increased food production without deliberate Government measures to change the technique of agricultural production, the systems of tenure and of marketing, etc. This may be true so far as the poorest peasants are concerned, but I would personally be reluctant to accept this argument on *a priori* grounds even in regard to them. [But] the efficiency of food production might, in part, be held down by the inability of the poor peasants to buy such things as simple agricultural implements and fertilizers, which they would like to, but cannot afford to buy, given the prices associated with the going extent of the market. Thus, unless fertilizers and farm tools were already available to poor peasants free of charge previously, an administered offer which increased the prospective money receipts of farmers would increase their food production, if the supply of farm tools and fertilizers to them can be increased, possibly on credit terms. It has been suggested to me that supplies of these latter may not be capable of expansion. They might well, of course, themselves be included in the list of goods for which offers to buy and sell would be made by the authorities. Heavy rural indebtedness to moneylenders might be a source of complications, but does not really affect the principle of the argument. Furthermore, as the capital intensity of cultivation of poor peasants increased in the way sketched above, they might be led to *employ* more family or other labour on their holdings, since the marginal product of labour on these holdings might well rise when they are better equipped. Thus, the underutilization of labour and land may fall in response to the offer *pari passu* with the emergence of a larger stock of equipment being used in conjunction with them.

Another point seems worth making in regard to possibilities of increasing agricultural output. There is no need to confine the offers to regions in which population concentrations are actually to be found. There may exist large areas, eminently suitable for cultivation, in areas remote enough from existing markets and from the existing areas of settlement, for them to be left unused. Given the going extent of the market, the cultivation of such areas can appear to be 'uneconomic'. It might well be reasonable to locate some offers to buy and sell goods and services in such areas with a view to inducing migrations of population to them. This suggestion should appeal to believers in the New Frontier. There seems to be no reason why the offers should not include offers for new construction of transport and housing facilities, etc. It does, in general, appear likely that the offers would mostly be made some distance away from existing market centres, where frustrated supply will, in general, be likely to be relatively large, at least in relation to the existing standard of living. However it does not follow that the growth of production in these areas in response to the administered extension of the market may not be reinforced by a movement of labour, entrepreneurs, finance, and possibly, of supplies of goods flowing out to the area of the offer from the already existing centres of greater development within our underdeveloped country.

This may happen in spite of our assumption of initial Keynesian full employment, because there may well be frustrated supply in the more highly developed market centres of the country also, e.g. workshop foremen, or their assistants, in a capital town may migrate to become managers in the hinterland where the market is now enlarged and skill is scarce. Moreover, there seem to be no obvious reasons why reinforcing factor-movements of this kind, including private international movements of capital, should not take place over the frontiers of a country as well as between regions within it.

There is no necessary reason why the authority which makes the offer to buy and sell goods and services should, in fact, in the outcome, find itself making any purchases and sales at all, since the expansion of employment and incomes associated with the increased investment and consumption expenditures generated by the offer, may, in a neatly designed set of offers, absorb all the increases in production generated by it. For the same reasons, the Government's budget should benefit from the experiment, rather than facing a deficit as a result of it.

The experiment would, in a sense, be 'inflationary', since the prices offered would presumably often entail raising local prices (in some cases, it would only entail raising the elasticity of demand facing producers, at given prices) and the repercussions of the offer may often raise prices further. However, insofar as these price-developments were associated with a reduction of frustrated supply, they would be analogous to a price increase which occurs in the process of recovery from a slump.[6]

I can offer two pieces of personal experience in support of Knapp's ideas. The first was an early stage of 'buying and selling agricultural cooperatives' which I studied in Yugoslavia in 1959. Measures just such as here prescribed were effective, but severely limited by overall national taxation policies imposed in the interests of rapid industrialization (Barratt Brown, 1960). The second was more recent. The late Minister of Steel and Power in Mrs Gandhi's government of India, Dr Kumaramangalam, told me in the spring of 1972 that

6. Knapp (1969, pp. 78–9). This is the first occasion on which this article has been published in English and for this reason the argument is quoted at length. I am most grateful to Mr Knapp for granting his permission for publication.

his government proposed to introduce such a scheme of state buying and selling of basic necessities into the Indian economy. The problem was to find enough uncorrupt civil servants to carry out the scheme.

Knapp's proposal appeals to the profit motive in a mixed economy and should not be confused with the appeal of the Chinese communes, which owe most of their success to the introduction to the villages of light industries whose output provides the necessary incentive to increased agricultural production (Myrdal and Kessle, 1971, p. 75; Wheelwright and MacFarlane, 1973, p. 50).

A Marxist might well have doubts about the implications of such pilot schemes as Knapp proposes, in the light of the experience of the 'Green Revolution', where the offer of seeds and fertilizer has greatly benefited the landowner, and particularly the large landowner at the expense of the small holder and landless labourers who have been driven into the towns to join the urban unemployed. It should be noted, however, that, in contrast to Robinson and Kalecki, and in truly Keynesian fashion, Knapp's conception of vent management does not envisage any compelling need, in principle, for direct government intervention in productive processes and does not postulate changes in the motivation of economic agents. Nor does it entail any need to visualize making sacrifices for faster economic growth, either on the part of the rich or by society as a whole, since it supposes increases to be made, as Keynes did, in both consumption and investment occurring simultaneously, as the frustrated supply resulting from underemployment is absorbed by 'vent-management'. The international implications of Knapp's ideas, their basic analytical foundation as well as their political and administrative implications, will clearly all need much further, careful elaboration.

Meanwhile, what then are the existing Keynesian proposals for the *developed* countries so as to establish international cooperation, both for their own benefit and that of the underdeveloped countries, without, as Keynes put it, 'the need for revolution' (1932b, p. 376)? It is Keynes's own structure built up at Bretton Woods that is now crumbling. It was never given the financial resources, the automatic supply of short-term funds or the genuinely international administration, that Keynes advocated; and these weaknesses provided the main cause of its collapse (Harrod, 1969, p. 268).

Harrod ended his work on *Money* with some cautiously optimistic speculations about the new role of the Group of Ten central bankers in arranging currency swaps (1969, p. 283) and the new international short-term capital market provided by the Euro-dollar system (p. 319). That was in 1968. Two years later he appeared much less happy, either at accepting 'the Federal Reserve system of the United States as the International Monetary Sovran' or about 'the vagaries in this same period of the Euro-dollar market' (1971, pp. 87–8). His 'disquiet about the state of dynamic [growth] economics', which we have already noted, seems to have intensified, and he was emphasizing the value of 'indicative planning, even on a world scale' (1969, p. 319). He was, in fact, putting forward the possibility of 'a world plan . . . only based on rough estimates' but 'which includes the optimum rate of interest and optimum acceptable return on capital [and] involves the optimum capital flow between countries. . . . We also need the basic growth axioms, and that is where we are particularly lacking', and also the overcoming of 'political obstructions . . . to devote sufficient national resources to a world plan and to modify domestic policies . . .' (1971, p. 89).[7]

There have been other proposals for indicative world economic planning which have avoided the obvious political problem referred to by Harrod of accepting decisions from a supra-national agency. The proposal of longest standing is that of Frisch for a planned expansion of trade exchanges corrected for mutual consistency, guaranteed by governments and balanced through a multilateral clearing agency (1948; 1967). It remains the most obvious way of harmonizing the interests of workers in developed countries reaching out to control their

7. It must be recorded that in the same lectures, Harrod expressed 'doubts about any unquestioning duty by Kantian criteria to obey legislation emanating from Brussels'.

own employment opportunities, and of revolutionary movements in underdeveloped countries, looking for the economic means for their development. It could provide a united challenge to the giant trans-national company, which would be expected to resist any such proposals. Less ambitious proposals have included those of Kaldor, Hart and Tinbergen for a commodity currency reserve to replace gold and give to every country a claim on world trade according to its real resources (1964) and of the Food and Agriculture Organization of the United Nations for a *Provisional Indicative World Plan for Agricultural Development* to 1975 and 1985 (1969). Taking out of the hands of the trans-national companies the control of the movements of goods including primary products, and particularly of scarce mineral resources, is an undertaking which schemes even of great theoretical brilliance and of detailed articulation have not yet accomplished.

That would not surprise the Marxists who will be surprised only at the naivety of the proponents of such schemes. The Keynesians will remind them that schemes for managing aggregate demand to maintain full employment in developed national economies were equally ridiculed in the years prior to the mid 1940s. It was, of course, relatively easy to persuade national businessmen to pay taxes to a national welfare state and receive a smaller share of a larger cake. It may be harder to persuade trans-national companies to pay taxes to an international welfare scheme, from which they do not know what their share may be and in which they have little control over the tax authorities – and this would apply, however much they may wish to 'present themselves as benefactors to society', in Robinson's phrase.

By contrast, the basic Marxist view of imperialism originates in the belief that capitalists must find ways of employing labour such that they can realize a surplus and capitalize it, in a process of accumulation in which they are in competition with other capitalists. This involves them in a double conflict at two levels – first, in the relations between capital and labour in production and second, in the exchange of products in the market – and in two respects, in the accumulation of capital and in the employment of labour as a commodity. In the accumulation of capital there is, then, first, a conflict between the aim of higher productivity, to reduce costs of production, and the tendency to a falling rate of profit from the consequent higher capital–labour ratio; and there is, second, a conflict between increased capital-goods production and the profitable sale of increased consumer goods to a labour force displaced by the new capital equipment. In the employment of labour as a commodity there is, first, a conflict between the workers' need to obtain material goods by earning wages at work and the alienation of the workers from the creative activity of work; and second, there is a conflict between the production of commodities for exchange and the needs of human beings for certain use values.

Some of these conflicts are temporarily resolved by crises of overproduction in which capital is destroyed and restructured, labour is unemployed and remobilized. Competition and the search for surplus for capital accumulation drives capitalists to dispossess the self-employed and extend the area of capitalism. But it also leads to the centralization of capital, monopoly restrictions on rivals and the creation of a dual economy both inside and between nations. This holds the world in an artificial division of labour, polarizing, on the one hand, the wealth of the sector where capital is accumulated, where capital goods are manufactured and labour productivity raises real wages and, on the other, the poverty of the sectors where reserves of labour are retained with minimal capital equipment at low levels of productivity to offset the falling rates of profit in the rich sectors. Cyclical crises cannot resolve these conflicts, but only social control over the process of production. This is the general crisis of capitalism which will create the conditions for its overthrow when workers become aware of the contradiction between the vast productive capacity of new technology and the relative impoverishment of their own lives.

The varieties of interpretation of the Marxist view derive from the different emphasis on one or other of the conflicts we have just identified. Various answers will, therefore, be given to the questions raised at the beginning of this chapter.

On the question of the concentration and centralization of capital in the giant trans-national company all Marxists will agree in seeing this process as a continuing one. This was Marx's most successful prediction and has confounded his critics in each generation – from Marshall and Schumpeter to Crosland (see Crosland, 1962; Barratt Brown, 1963). But there is disagreement amongst Marxists about the relationship of the trans-national company and the nation state.

The traditional view most strongly argued by Bukharin (1970; see also Murray, 1971a; Radice *et al.*, 1971), has become incorporated in Marxist orthodoxy as the concept of state monopoly capitalism (Bellamy, 1971), in which the nation state plays not only the role of providing through its executive the 'Committee for managing the common affairs of the whole bourgeoisie' (Marx, 1933a, section 3), but, 'tends to turn the entire "national" economy into a single combined enterprise with an organic connection between all the branches of production' (Bukharin, 1970, p. 70). Some modern Marxists regard the most recent extension of the quantitative role of the state as no 'evidence of a qualitative change' (Baran and Sweezy, 1966, p. 67); others believe that the 'power of the nation state *vis-à-vis* the large firms is *greater* now than ever before (and increasing)' (Warren, 1971, p. 86) with deliberate positive state initiatives replacing a negative, protective role. On this view, the capitalist nation states will be forced 'to become ever more active in their internal economies and their external economic relations' and establish 'an ever closer relationship between the state and the large firms', in order to overcome 'the uncertainty and new problems of economic control' which increasing world-wide economic interdependence creates (Warren, 1971, p. 88).

The opposite view is provided in extreme form by Kindleberger, that 'The nation state is just about through as an economic unit' (1970), in less extreme form by Murray, that 'there was no necessary link between a capital and its state in the area of extension, that capital was rather a political opportunist, and existing states often suffered a decrease in their powers as a result of internationalization [i.e. of capital]';

some smaller states suffered more than others and were thus 'suiting the interests neither of their own besieged capital nor of the foreign investor'; hence 'the demand for some degree of international integration', as in the EEC (Murray, 1971c, p. 187). Murray concludes from this, 'from British experience at least, that it is the corporate rather than the national division of labour that dominates and determines the features of the international economy' (1971a).

In this book, imperialism has been seen, on a Marxist view, essentially in Lee's Luxemburgian phrase, as a process of capitalist 'assimilation' (1971, p. 848). Murray's 'internationalization' of the world division of labour inside the giant corporation implies just the kind of economic development in underdeveloped countries, albeit dependent development, which we saw in looking at neo-colonialism. That this takes place through the direct investment of giant companies, and no longer through indirect loans to overseas governments, more than ever involves each national bourgeoisie in a comprador relationship to metropolitan capital. But this does not exclude antagonism and some economic development. Frank concluded that no sustained development would take place in this way, and revolutionary socialists could look to no possibility of an alliance with a national bourgeoisie against internal feudalism and external imperialism. Lee takes the same view (p. 859). The expectations of Marx, of Lenin, of Hilferding and of Luxemburg also, that new centres of competing capitalist accumulation would develop outside the original metropoles, had been foreclosed. Only further *under*development would follow (Frank, 1972). Yet the United States, Canada and Australia all developed their economies with much direct as well as indirect investment. Even today over 50 per cent of Canadian and Australian industrial capital is foreign owned (Dunning, 1971, p. 20). Industrial development, moreover, has recently been occurring at a rapid rate – albeit from a very low base – in the underdeveloped world.

Whether such development can continue will depend, first, on the internal political economy of each underdeveloped country, in particular the coalition of classes or groups which are involved in neo-colonialism and their influence on the distribution of income and the incentive to invest. In a dual economy, workers and comprador capitalists in the high wage/ high profit sector, associated with the trans-national companies' operations, may identify themselves with feudal or rural capitalist elements in the neo-colonial structure as much as with foreign capital. This does not account for the whole of the industrial working class or exclude the emergence of a local bourgeoisie. Indian Marxists, at least those in the Communist Party of India, insist on the possibility of a 'national democratic front' of workers, working peasants, intellectuals, petty bourgeoisie and non-monopoly bourgeoisie (M. Sen, 1972); but at least, to a visitor in India in 1972, a large section of the non-monopoly bourgeoisie and even of the working class and richer working peasantry did not appear to have any natural conflict with imperialism in the shape of its foreign investment activities. Rather the reverse. Of course, another and larger section of the population does, and it is on the strength of the pressure that the urban and rural poor can exercise, in this case on Mrs Gandhi's government, that the crucial question of income distribution depends.

If incomes were made less unequal in underdeveloped countries by measures of land reform and by the state purchase and sale of essential commodities, the balance of strength inside the 'national democratic front' would shift. Such a redistribution of income would have, on a Keynesian view, the effect of stimulating a higher rate of economic development. Marxists, with support from Kalecki, would expect a high rate of accumulation to imply income inequality, but state taxation could correct the worst polarizing effects of a dual economy. An important factor in United States, Canadian and Australian economic development has always been the commitment to equality (upper bourgeoisie and blacks excepted) especially in newly developing areas (Clark, 1951, p. 538). But these countries had extensive land, and capitalist settlers to develop it.

India suffers from inequality without accumulation. The inequality of incomes, already high in the 1930s, has been increasing. Factory workers' earnings in real terms fell below their wartime peak of 1940 for twenty years, recovering only in 1962, and thereafter falling back again by 10 per cent to 1969; the share of wages, salaries and benefits in the Indian manufacturing industry stayed at 55 per cent after 1955, compared with 65 per cent in 1949; and all estimates of rural poverty show increases in the proportion of the population living below a fixed subsistence level (R. K. Sen, 1972, p. 361). As a result, some 20 per cent of the population, urban and rural, buy half the output of industrial goods, the other 80 per cent the other half. At the same time, industrial capacity is grossly underutilized, a million graduates are unemployed and rich resources of land uncultivated, for lack of adequate state investment to correct the polarization of a dual economy (Alagh and Shah, 1972, p. 379).

Frank gives a similar picture for Latin America, based on data from the United Nations Economic Commission. Steel, paper, cellulose, food, metal and mechanical industries were all operating in 1966 at around 50 per cent of capacity. This is not surprising since the entire output of such industry was destined for some 5 per cent of the local population who received a third of all the income, while at the bottom the poorest half of the population received only a tenth of the income. Future economic development strategy in Brazil is to concentrate income in the upper and middle classes so as to provide a market for developing durable consumer-goods industries; but this will only exaggerate the dualism of the economy. Frank concludes that more repressive and openly fascist movements will spread in the underdeveloped countries, as 'recession deepens into depression' in the metropolitan countries and as inter-imperialist rivalry grows, unless 'the working masses and their Marxist leadership' turn their struggle against the 'immediate enemy', which for him is the native bourgeoisie (1972, pp. 19, 33, 38).

This particular Marxist prediction, then, is of continuing underdevelopment, crisis and breakdown leading to revolutionary struggles. Sutcliffe, in an essay on 'Imperialism and the Industrialization of the Third World', accepts that 'independent capitalist industrialization' has occurred during 'times of acute capitalist crises' in the 1930s and in wartime (as Frank himself noted) and recently also 'in those capitalist countries most obviously satellized by the advanced countries', but believes that 'this is not necessarily a permanent situation'.

Capitalism has not freed itself from crisis, and we cannot be sure that the revived intensive competition within the capitalist system between the United States and the rejuvenated European capitalism and the restrengthened Japanese capitalism will not erupt into war. On these grounds it is not impossible that as a result of changes in the structure of imperialism, we shall see further attempts at independent capitalist industrialization. On the other hand, if the present crisis of capitalism marks its end, then this prospect will cease to have even the limited relevance it still possesses today (Sutcliffe, 1972, p. 192).

We may look at the implications of 'revived competition within the capitalist system', without necessarily assuming an 'eruption into war'. This competition is not only the main external factor likely to influence development in the underdeveloped world, but also the clue to a Marxian answer to most of our other questions about forms of international economic cooperation that take into account the new and dominant position of the trans-national corporation in the international division of labour. It involves also the growth of competition with the communist world, short, that is, of eruption into war.

Recent Marxist writers have offered three alternative scenarios for imperialism in the 1970s which have been categorized by Rowthorn as, respectively, US Superimperialism, Imperial Rivalry and Ultra-Imperialism (1971a, p. 31). The first scenario is that of the American Marxists, Sweezy and Magdoff, who believe that United States capital will continue to dominate the capitalist world because United States companies are 'much bigger, more advanced and faster growing than their foreign rivals'. The main enemy of US capitalism is not its rivals but the world socialist system and the 'revolutionary initiative against capitalism which in Marx's day belonged to the proletariat in the advanced countries, (but which) has passed into the hands of the impoverished masses in the underdeveloped countries' (Baran and Sweezy, 1966, pp. 9, 183).

European Marxists, and especially Mandel, have argued that the challenge of the European and Japanese companies to United States domination involves a real change in the balance of power. Within the EEC superstate, new company laws will permit still further mergers and amalgamations, so that European companies will be born and grow to be as big as those of the United States, especially after Britain's entry into the EEC. Lower wages, plus increasing productivity in both the EEC and Japan, will enable exports from both to break United States domination of world capitalism (Mandel, 1969; 1970a; 1970b).

Rowthorn argues that the rise in unit wage costs in Japan and the EEC has been much greater than in the USA, despite greater increases in productivity, so that a straight argument of more competitive exports is unacceptable. But the EEC and Japan will, nonetheless, present a real challenge to the USA because their giant companies will continue to get larger, and the export surpluses of the EEC and Japan, built up in the past decade, will more and more be converted into investment in subsidiaries in the United States and in areas where large United States companies at present dominate the market. This will be the 'non-American challenge', of those who saw United States investment in Europe as the 'American challenge' (see Hymer and Rowthorn, 1970; Servan-Schreiber, 1968). European and Japanese firms are already catching up with United States firms and expanding their investment in the United States itself. To maintain a position in its own market the giant company has for long now had to expand its sales in its rivals' markets (Barratt Brown, 1958; 1970a, pp. 323–5). Advertisements in the glossy magazines are read the world over. Overseas investment is needed to defend existing markets and capture new ones, and to exploit new sources of raw materials and labour. This is the essence of capitalist competition even in conditions of oligopoly; and behind the giant companies will be arraigned the power they can mobilize in the nation states or super state which claim them as their own.

The third alternative Rowthorn describes as 'ultra imperialism'. He sees this as Kautsky saw it when he first invented the term, as a 'coalition of relatively autonomous imperialist states'[8], establishing through new international institutions a new form of unity between capitalist states. But the situation has changed since Kautsky wrote. The trans-national corporation is now the centre of capitalist power and the new source of capitalist rivalry. So it might be the companies and not the states which would initiate new forms of intercapitalist unity, in order to preserve the stability and growth of the whole capitalist world economy (Barratt Brown, 1972b, p. 225).

This scenario for the future would imply increasing rivalry between giant companies with all the internal contradictions, to which Mandel refers in his use of the Leninist phrase of 'Laws of Unequal Development' (1970b), but with strong pressures for world wide agreements. The model of the cartel seems to be the obvious one. Companies will agree temporarily and according to their current strengths to divide up the world. The spheres of influence, which have persisted so strongly in the past, will provide the starting point – the American hemisphere for the American companies, South East Asia for the Japanese, Europe and Africa for the West Europeans; and, given what we saw of Soviet imperialism in chapter 12, a Soviet sphere of influence in Eastern Europe, the Middle East and India. It is already happening, notably in the claims that are being staked through Treaties of Association by the EEC in Southern Europe and North Africa (Barratt Brown, 1972a, p. 137). That such narrowed spheres of influence will not permanently satisfy the two or three hundred giant corporations, which some have seen as likely to account for half of the world's output by the turn of the century, is obvious (Polk, 1968).

The blockage that a few hundred companies will meet, as cross-investment inside the developed countries increases, can only be overcome by their expanding into the underdeveloped

8. Rowthorn (1971a, p. 31). The reference to Kautsky is to his 1914 *Neue Zeit* articles which Lenin so sharply criticized in *Imperialism – The Highest Stage of Capitalism* (1933), and Rowthorn's own reference is to Varga (1968).

countries and, in the first instance, into *their* underdeveloped countries, to 'assimilate and transform'. In what may be called their 'back gardens' some real economic development by the giant corporations, albeit dependent development, will be encouraged, as fields of development were encouraged by British capital in North America, and Oceania and Argentina in the nineteenth century. Without a framework of international rules for such a process, however, rivalries will become uncontrollable.

Direct investment in manufacturing ties satellite economic development *more* firmly into the world division of labour, operated today by giant trans-national companies, than ever the indirect investment in transport and infrastructure did in the nineteenth century. But direct investment at the same time implies sunk capital in large-scale and ever larger-scale plants which become so many 'individual hostages to fortune'[9] in the underdeveloped countries – steel works, refineries, fertilizer plant, vehicle assembly lines and food processing plant. These are real assets, liable to nationalization, which local staffs are increasingly capable of managing. It will, no doubt, continue to be the policy of trans-national companies to try to retain in the metropoles some of the machine tool and other capital-equipment production, spare parts and technical know-how in research and development. But the Japanese for long showed how easily technology can be copied once a certain level of know-how is reached. Today, indeed, local talent and local subcontracting are increasingly encouraged in the competitive world of the trans-national corporations (Meyer, 1959, p. 89). The brain drain from poor countries to rich requires only quite small changes in expectations of rewarding employment at home to reverse; and the contrast between the potential and its realization in underdeveloped countries creates frustrations that must sooner or later burst into action.

The doubts that some Marxists have about revolutionary

9. The phrase comes from a defence of the multinational company by the coordinator of trade relations of Shell International, Geoffrey Chandler, in an article entitled 'Monsters are not above the law', *The Guardian*, 5 January 1973.

changes within capitalism arise from their expectation that all revolutions must now be socialist ones. At the present low levels of production in the underdeveloped half of the world, Marx would have expected no such thing. We could still see bourgeois and peasant revolutions which fall far short of socialism. The conditions for successful revolutions, as Shanin has summarized them (1971), are a structural crisis of society, and one that raises doubts about the ability of the ruling elite to govern, plus a crystalization of classes around a new elite capable of leading revolutionary struggle. Such conditions are not hard to discern in many underdeveloped countries; and the revolutionary struggles already proceeding in Africa, Asia and Latin America could well loose whole societies from the framework of imperialism, without guaranteeing a transformation from a capitalist to a socialist formation. Nor would the success of such revolutionary struggles imply the end of imperialism as a system of dependent economic relations or the ending of commodity production, as we know from the experience of the Soviet Union, even if capital was brought under state ownership and control in many more nation states.

The contradictions which, on a Marxist view, are above all to be found in capitalism arise from commodity production which capitalism has brought to its climax; they will not easily be resolved, but imperialism as a solution may be losing its relevance. Conscious state management of aggregate demand and supply have gone a long way towards resolving contradictions in a developed private capitalist system. Central state management of all inputs and outputs in the Soviet system has gone further still. The competition between capitalists and the conflict between the different sectors of a dual economy in both the capitalist and Soviet system remains. To the extent that the Soviet system and the Chinese cultural revolution can achieve increasingly abundant production, the chances are raised of the underdeveloped countries drawing upon alternative suppliers and establishing greater independence.

The application to the world economy of proposals like those of Frisch and others will become of importance in the same way that Keynesian measures have in managing the internal economies of developed countries, not just because they incorporate and contain the demands of radical and revolutionary movements but because they show the way to transcending the capitalist system. Whatever the apparent short-term advantages for the richer sector in the dual economy, its wealth is forever under threat from the poorer sector, in respect both of the bargaining power of labour and of the marketing capacity for higher levels of productivity (Barratt Brown, 1972a, pp. 79–121). The great problem of the next decade for the industrial workers of the developed countries and for the liberation movements of the underdeveloped will be to discover the framework of political and economic cooperation that will allow their long-term common interest to prevail over the short-term interests that divide them.

What one can say for certain is that consciousness will steadily grow, that it is not any kind of uncontrollable force of nature but human artefacts that stand between the unemployed capacity of industrial workers in developed countries to produce goods that the peoples of the underdeveloped world want and the underemployed capacity of workers and peasants of the underdeveloped world to produce goods that the developed world wants. We have already seen examples of this growing consciousness in Britain, in the struggle of electrical workers on Merseyside, steel workers in Sheffield and ship builders on Clydeside to find markets in the underdeveloped countries for the products of their factories and yards threatened with closure because they were unprofitable in the going markets (Murray, 1971b).

In essence Marxism is about human consciousness and, in our era, about social and socialist consciousness. For the Marxist the most irreconcilable contradiction within capitalism – that which has driven men to enslave their fellows, to tear out the riches of the earth and of the seas, the precious metals and fossil fuels, the forests and fishes, without thought for the morrow, and leave behind deserts, dereliction, destruction and pollution in great metropolitan waste-lands – is that which exists between, on the one hand, a system of production of commodities for profitable exchange, including the production of labour itself as a commodity, and, on the other, the needs of men and women for things to use and means to create. It is this contradiction which, in Marx's vision, nourishes the seeds in capitalism that will lead to its destruction, through the budding consciousness of human beings that it is capitalism, whether in private or in state hands, that obstructs the 'free development of each [which] is the condition for the free development of all' (Marx and Engels, 1933). As that consciousness flowers, and more and more people take control of their own lives, the era of imperialism will be closed. For Marxists this is not just a matter of faith but of everyday experience wherever the creative activity of work replaces the alienation of commodity production.

References

ALAGH, V. K., and SHAH, J. (1972), 'Utilisation of industrial capacity and agricultural growth', *Econ. Pol. Weekly*, Bombay, February.

ALAVI, H. (1964), 'Imperialism old and new', in R. A. Miliband and J. Saville (eds.), *Socialist Register*, Merlin.

ALAVI, H. (1972), 'The state in post-colonial societies: Pakistan and Bangladesh', *New Left Review*, no. 74, July–August.

ALIBER, R. Z. (1971), 'The multinational enterprise in a multiple currency world', in J. H. Dunning (ed.), *The Multinational Enterprise*, Allen & Unwin.

ALIBER, R. Z. (1970), 'A theory of direct investment', in C. P. Kindleberger (ed.), *The International Corporation*, MIT Press.

ALLEN, G. C. (1965), *Japan's Economic Expansion*, Oxford University Press.

ANDERSSON, J. O. (1971), 'Reflections on unequal exchange', paper submitted to the symposium on *Imperialism – Its Place in the Social Sciences Today*, Elsinore, May.

ANSTEY, V. (1929), *Economic Development of India*, Longman.

ARON, R. (1954), *The Century of Total War*, Weidenfeld & Nicolson.

ARRIGHI, G. (1970), 'International corporations, labour aristocracies and economic development in tropical Africa', in R. I. Rhodes (ed.), *Imperialism and Underdevelopment: A Reader*, Monthly Review Press, New York.

ARRIGHI, G. (1971), 'A critique of A. G. Frank's theory of the development of underdevelopment', paper submitted to the seminar on *Imperialism – Its Place in the Social Sciences Today*, Elsinore, May.

BAILEY, J. D. (1966), *A Hundred Years of Pastoral Banking*, Oxford University Press.

BALOGH, T. (1962), 'The mechanism of neo-imperialism', *Oxf. Univ. Inst. Stat. Bull.*, vol. 24, no. 3, August.

BARAN, P. (1957), *Political Economy of Growth*, Monthly Review Press, New York.

BARAN, P., and SWEEZY, P. M. (1966), *Monopoly Capital*, Monthly Review Press, New York; Penguin, 1970.

BARRATT BROWN, M. (1958), 'The £ and the 1%', *New Reasoner*, Autumn.

BARRATT BROWN, M. (1959), 'The controllers of British industry', *Universities and Left Review*, nos. 5, 6 and 7.

BARRATT BROWN, M. (1960), 'Yugoslavia revisited', *New Left Review*, no. 1, January–February.

BARRATT BROWN, M. (1963), 'Crosland's enemy: A reply', *New Left Review*, no. 25, March–April.

BARRATT BROWN, M. (1968), 'Who controls the economy', in *Can the Workers Run Industry?* Sphere Books.

BARRATT BROWN, M. (1970a), *After Imperialism*, Merlin; first edn 1963, Heinemann.

BARRATT BROWN, M. (1970b), *What Economics is About*, Weidenfeld & Nicolson.

BARRATT BROWN, M. (1972a), *Essays on Imperialism*, Spokesman Books.

BARRATT BROWN, M. (1972b), *From Labourism to Socialism*, Spokesman Books.

BARRATT BROWN, M. (1973), 'Imperialism in our era: spheres of economic influence', *Spokesman*, no. 24, January–February.

BARRY, B. (1965), *Political Argument*, Routledge & Kegan Paul.

BAYKOV, A. (1946), *Soviet Foreign Trade*, Princeton University Press.

BELLAMY, R. (1971), 'State monopoly capitalism', in *Marxism Today*, September.

BERLE, A. A., and MEANS, G. C. (1932), *Modern Corporation and Private Property*, Macmillan Co.

BERNAL, J. D. (1953), *Science and Industry in the Nineteenth Century*, Routledge & Kegan Paul.

BETTELHEIM, C. (1970a), *Calcul économique et formes de propriété*, Paris, summarized by A. Nove in 'Market socialism and its critics', *Soviet Studies*, vol. 24, no. 1, July 1972.

BETTELHEIM, C. (1970b), 'More on the socialism of transition', *Monthly Review*, December.

BETTELHEIM, C. (1972), 'Critical comments', in A. Emmanuel, *Unequal Exchange*, New Left Books.

BEVERIDGE, W. H. (1902), *Unemployment – A Problem of Industry*, Longman.

BEVERIDGE, W. H. (ed.) (1931), *Tariffs – The Case Examined*, Longman.

BOARD OF TRADE (1970), *Journal*, no. 23, September, HMSO.

BODELSEN, C. A. (1960), *Studies in Mid-Victorian Imperialism*, Heinemann.

BODINGTON, S. (1973), *Computers and Socialism*, Spokesman Books.

BOWLEY, A. L. (1937), *Wages and Income since 1860*, Cambridge University Press.

BRAMPTON, C. K. (1938), *History Teaching Atlas*, Wheaton.

BROADBRIDGE, S. (1966), *Industrial Dualism in Japan*, Cass.

BROWN, A. J. (1965), 'Britain in the world economy 1870–1914', *Yorkshire Bull.*, May.

BUCHANAN, D. H. (1934), *The Development of Capitalist Enterprise in India*, Allen & Unwin.

BUKHARIN, N. (1970), *Imperialism and the World Economy*, Merlin; first published 1927.

BUKHARIN, N. (1972), *Imperialism and the Accumulation of Capital*, Allen Lane; first published 1924.

BURNHAM, J. (1941), *Managerial Revolution*, Putnam.

BUTLIN, N. G. (1964), *Australian Capital Formation and Domestic Product, 1860–1938*, Cambridge University Press.

CAIRNCROSS, A. K. (1953), *Home and Foreign Investment, 1870–1913*, Cambridge University Press.

CALDER, R. (1961), *The Inheritors*, Heinemann.

CALDWELL, M. (1971), 'Oil and imperialism in SE Asia', *Spokesman*, June–July.

CARDOSO, F. H. (1972), 'Dependency and development in Latin America', *New Left Review*, no. 74, July–August.

CARR, E. H. (1961), *What is History?*, Macmillan; Penguin, 1964.

CARR, E. H. (1968), 'Revolution from above', *New Left Review*, no. 46, November–December.

CASTLES, S., and LOSACK, G. (1972), 'The function of labour immigration in Western European capitalism', *New Left Review*, no. 73, May–June.

CENTRAL STATISTICAL OFFICE (1965), *The UK Balance of Payments, 1965*, HMSO.

CENTRAL STATISTICAL OFFICE (1970), *The UK Balance of Payments, 1970*, HMSO.

CENTRAL STATISTICAL OFFICE (1972a), *National Income and Expenditure*, HMSO.

CENTRAL STATISTICAL OFFICE (1972b), *Economic Trends*, September, HMSO.

CHANDRA, B. (1973), 'Modern India and imperialism', in *Spheres of Influence and the Third World*, Spokesman Books.

CHATTOPHADHAY, P. (1972), 'On the political economy of the transition', *Monthly Review*, vol. 24, no. 4, September.

CLAPHAM, J. H. (1930), *An Economic History of Modern Britain*, vol. 1 (2nd edn); vol. 2, 1932, vol. 3, 1938, Cambridge University Press.

CLARK, C. (1951), *Conditions of Economic Progress*, Macmillan.

COLE, W. A., and DEAN, P. (1965), 'The growth of national incomes', in the *Cambridge Economic History of Europe*, vol. 6, part 1, Cambridge University Press.

COLEMAN, D. C. (1969), 'Eli Heckscher and the idea of mercantilism', in D. C. Coleman (ed.), *Revisions in Mercantilism*, Methuen.

COPPOCK, D. J. (1956), 'The climacteric of the 1890s – a critical note', *Manchester School of Economic and Social Studies*, vol. 24, no. 1.

CROSLAND C. A. R. (1962), *The Conservative Enemy*, Cape.

DAVIDSON, B. (1950), *Germany, What Now?*, Muller.

DAVIDSON, B. (1955), *African Awakening*, Cape.

DAVIDSON, B. (1969), *The Africans*, Longman.

DAVIDSON, B. (1972), *In the Eye of the Storm*, Longman.

DEANE, P., and COLE, W. A. (1964), *British Economic Growth 1688–1959*, Cambridge University Press.

DEDIJER, V. (1953), *Tito Speaks*, Weidenfeld & Nicolson.

DEFOE, D. (1719), *Robinson Crusoe*; 1937 edn, Oxford University Press.

DEGRAS, J. (ed.) (1960), *The Communist International, 1919–43, Documents*, vol. 2, 1928–38, Oxford University Press.

DEPARTMENT OF TRADE AND INDUSTRY (1970), *A Survey of Mergers, 1958–68*, HMSO.

DEPARTMENT OF TRADE AND INDUSTRY (1972), *Business Monitor*, M4 (also for 1971), HMSO.

DEUTSCHER, I. (1967), 'The unfinished revolution, 1917–1967', *New Left Review*, no. 43.

DEUTSCHER, I. (1970), 'Black dust storms over Russia', in *Russia, China and the West, 1953–1966*, Penguin.

DISRAELI, B. (1834), *Sybil – The Two Nations*; Everyman edn, Dent.

DJILAS, M. (1957), *The New Class*, Thames & Hudson.

DOBB, M. H. (1946), *Studies in the Development of Capitalism*, Routledge & Kegan Paul.

DUBOIS, J. I. (1953), *Generals in Grey Suits*, Bodley Head.

DUNNING, J. H. (1970), 'The multinational enterprise', *Lloyds Bank Review*, July.

DUNNING, J. H. (ed.) (1971), *The Multinational Enterprise*, Allen & Unwin.

DURBIN, E. M. F., and KNAPP, J. A. (1949), *Economics*, Odhams New Educational Library.

DUTT, R. P. (1947), *India Today*, People's Publishing House, Bombay.

EARLEY, J. S. (1956), 'Marginal policies of "excellently managed" companies', *Amer. econ. Rev.*, March.

EMMANUEL, A. (1972a), *Unequal Exchange*, New Left Books.

EMMANUEL, A. (1972b), 'White settler colonialism and the myth of investment imperialism', *New Left Review*, no. 73, May–June.

ENGELS, F. (1888), *Introduction to Marx's Address on the Question of Free Trade*; published with *The Poverty of Philosophy*, Cooperative Publishing Society, Moscow, 1935.

ENGELS, F., and MARX, K. (1933), 'Communist manifesto', in *Karl Marx, Selected Works*, vol. 1, Martin Lawrence; first published 1848.

ENSOR, R. C. K. (1936), *England 1870–1914*, Oxford University Press.

EVELY, R., and LITTLE, I. M. D. (1960), *Concentration in British Industry*, Cambridge University Press.

FAGEN, R. R. (1972), 'Cuban revolutionary politics', *Monthly Review*, vol. 23, no. 11, April.

FEINSTEIN, C. H. (1960), *Home and Overseas Investment 1870–1914*, unpublished thesis, Department of Applied Economics, Cambridge.

FEINSTEIN, C. H. (1961), 'Income and investment in the UK 1856–1914', *Econ. J.*, vol. 21, no. 282, June.

FEINSTEIN, C. H. (1972), *National Income, Expenditure and Output of the UK, 1855–1965*, Cambridge University Press.

FEIS, H. (1930), *Europe the World's Banker 1870–1914*, Yale University Press.

FERNS, H. S. (1953), 'Britain's informal empire in Argentina 1860–1914', *Past and Present*, November.

FERNS, H. S. (1960), *Britain and the Argentine in the Nineteenth Century*, Allen & Unwin.

FIELDHOUSE, D. K. (1967), *Theory of Capitalist Imperialism*, Longman.

FIELDHOUSE, D. K. (1973), *Economics and Empire, 1830–1914*, Weidenfeld & Nicolson.

FINDLAY, R. (1970), *Trade and Specialization*, Penguin.

FISHER, F. J. (1954), 'Commercial trends in sixteenth-century England', in E. M. Carus Wilson (ed.), *Essays in Economic History*, vol. 3, Arnold.

FOOD AND AGRICULTURAL ORGANIZATION (1969), *Provisional Indicative World Plan for Agricultural Development*, C69/4 Rome.

FOOD AND AGRICULTURAL ORGANIZATION (1972), *Ceres*, vol. 5, no. 2.

FORD, A. G. (1958), 'Capital exports and growth for Argentina', *Econ. J.*, vol. 68, no. 271, September.

FORD, A. G. (1965), 'Overseas lending and internal fluctuations, 1870–1914', *Yorkshire Bull.*, May.

FRANK, A. G. (1966), 'The development of underdevelopment', *Monthly Review*, September.

FRANK, A. G. (1969a), *Capitalism and Underdevelopment in Latin America*, revised edn, Monthly Review Press; Penguin, 1971.

FRANK, A. G. (1969b), *Latin America: Underdevelopment or Revolution*, Monthly Review Press, New York.

FRANK, A. G. (1972), 'Imperialism, nationalism and class struggle in Latin America', for a symposium on *Imperialism, Independence and Social Transformation in the Third World*, New Delhi, not yet published.

FRIEDMAN, M. (1969), *Optimum Amounts of Money*, Chicago University Press.

FRIEDMAN, M. (1972), *An Economist's Protest*, Horton, New Jersey.

FRISCH, R. (1948), 'The problem of multicompensatory trade', *Rev. Econ. Stat.*, vol. 30, November.

FRISCH, R. (1967), 'A multilateral trade clearing agency', in *Economics of Planning*, vol. 7, no. 2, Norwegian Institute of International Affairs, Oslo.

FURTADO, C. (1964), *Development and Underdevelopment*, California University Press.

FURTADO, C. (1965), *Diagnosis of the Brazilian Crisis*, California University Press.

GALBRAITH, J. K. (1967), *The New Industrial State*, Hamish Hamilton.

GALLAGHER, J. (1953), 'The imperialism of free trade', *Econ. Hist. Rev.*, vol. 6, no. 1.

GALLAGHER, J., and ROBINSON, R. E. (1953), *Africa and the Victorians*, Macmillan.

GANNAGÉ, E. (1968), 'The distribution of income in underdeveloped countries', in J. Marchal and B. Ducros (eds.), *The Distribution of National Income*, Macmillan.

GATT (1958), *Trends in International Trade*, Geneva.

GATT (1970), *International Trade*, Geneva.

GILLMAN, J. (1958), *The Falling Rate of Profit*, Dobson.

GLYN, A. (1972), 'Capitalist crisis and organic composition', *Conference of Socialist Economists' Bulletin*, Winter.

GLYN, A., and SUTCLIFFE, R. B. (1972), *British Capitalism, Workers and the Profit Squeeze*, Penguin.

GREENBERG, M. (1951), *British Trade and the Opening of China*, Cambridge University Press.

GRIFFIN, K. (1969), *Underdevelopment in Spanish America*, Allen & Unwin.

GUEVARA, C. (1965), *A Common Aspiration: The Overthrow of Imperialism Unites Cuba with Africa and Asia*, Bertrand Russell Peace Foundation, Nottingham.

HALSTEAD, J. L. (1974), 'Huddersfield textile industry', unpublished thesis.

HAMILTON, A. (1791), *Report of Manufactures*, in H. C. Lodge (ed.), *The Works of Alexander Hamilton*, New York, 1885.

HAMILTON, F. J. (1929), 'American treasure and the rise of capitalism', *Economica*, vol. 27.

HARRISON, R. J. (1965), *Before the Socialists*, Routledge & Kegan Paul.

HARROD, R. (1939), 'An essay in dynamic theory', *Econ. J.*, March.

HARROD, R. (1962), A contribution to the Forward Britain Movement Conference, 1962, in *Britain Should Stay Out*, Forward Britain Movement.

HARROD, R. (1963a), A contribution to the Forward Britain Movement Conference, 1963, in *Towards a World Economic Conference*, Forward Britain Movement.

HARROD, R. (1963b), 'Themes in dynamic theory', *Econ. J.*, vol. 73, no. 291, September.

HARROD, R. (1964), 'Are monetary and fiscal policies enough?', *Econ. J.*, vol. 74, no. 296, December.

HARROD, R. (1969), *Money*, Macmillan.

HARROD, R. (1971), *Sociology, Morals and Mystery*, Macmillan.

HART, F. E., and PRAIS, S. J. (1956), 'The analysis of business concentration', *J. roy. stat. Soc.*, vol. 119, part 2.

HAYTER, T. (1971), *Aid as Imperialism*, Penguin.

HECKSCHER, E. (1969), 'Mercantilism', in D. C. Coleman (ed.), *Revisions in Mercantilism*, Methuen.

HENDERSON, W. O. (1962), *The Genesis of the Common Market*, Cass.

HEWINS, W. A. S. (1929), *Apologia of an Imperialist*, Macmillan.

HIBBERT, C. (1961), *The Destruction of Lord Raglan*, Longman.

HICKS, J. (1939), *Value and Capital*, Oxford University Press.

HICKS, J. (1959), *Essays in World Economics*, Oxford University Press.

HICKS, J. (1969), *A Theory of Economic History*, Oxford University Press.

HICKS, U. K. (1938), *The Finance of British Government*, Oxford University Press.

HILFERDING, R. (1923), *Finance Capital*, Vorwärts, Vienna.

HILL, C. (1967), 'Pottage for a freeborn Englishman', in C. H. Feinstein (ed.), *Socialism, Capitalism and Economic Growth*, Cambridge University Press.

HILL, C. (1970), *God's Englishman: Oliver Cromwell and the English Revolution*, Weidenfeld & Nicolson; Penguin, 1972.

HOBSBAWM, E. (1954), 'The crisis of the seventeenth century', *Past and Present*, nos. 5 and 6.

HOBSBAWM, E. (1964), *Labouring Men*, Weidenfeld & Nicolson.

HOBSBAWM, E. (1968), *Industry and Empire*, Penguin.

HOBSON, J. A. (1938), *Imperialism, A Study*, Allen & Unwin, first published 1902.

HOBSON, J. A., and MUMMERY, A. F. (1889), *The Physiology of Industry*, Allen & Unwin.

HODGKIN, T. (1972), 'Africa and third world theories of imperialism', in R. J. Owen and R. B. Sutcliffe (eds.), *Studies in the Theory of Imperialism*, Longman.

HOLZMAN, F. D. (1965), 'More on Soviet bloc trade discrimination', *Soviet Studies*, vol. 17, no. 1, July.

HUBERMAN, L. (1940), *We, The People*, Gollancz.

HUTCHINSON, T. E. (1964), *Positive Economics and Policy Objectives*, Allen & Unwin.

HYMER, S., and ROWTHORN, R. (1970), 'Multinational corporations and international oligopoly: the non-American challenge', in C. P. Kindleberger (ed.), *The International Corporation*, MIT Press.

HYMER, S. (1971), 'Robinson Crusoe and the secret of primitive accumulation', *Monthly Review*, vol. 23, no. 4, September.

IIDA, T. (1965), 'Resource allocation in the dual economy', *Econ. J.*, vol. 80, no. 299, September.

IMLAH, A. H. (1958), *Economic Elements in the Pax Britannica*, Harvard University Press.

INTERNATIONAL MONETARY FUND (1972), *International Financial Statistics*, Washington, July.

JALÉE, P. (1967), *The Pillage of the Third World*, Monthly Review Press, New York.

JENKS, L. H. (1927), *The Migration of British Capital*, Knopf, New York.

JOHNSON, H. G. (1962), *Money, Trade and Economic Growth*, Allen & Unwin.

JOHNSON, H. G. (1965), *The World Economy at the Crossroads*, Allen & Unwin.

JOHNSON, H. G. (1968), *Economic Nationalism in Old and New States*, Allen & Unwin.

JOHNSON, H. G. (1972), 'An economic theory of protectionism, tariff bargaining and the formation of customs unions', in P. Robson (ed.), *International Economic Integration*, Penguin.

KALDOR, N. (1972), 'The irrelevance of equilibrium economics', *Econ. J.*, vol. 82, no. 3, December.

KALDOR, N., HART, P. G., and TINBERGEN, J. (1964), 'The case for an international commodity reserve currency', in *Essays in Economic Policy*, vol. 2, Duckworth.

KALECKI, M. (1943), 'Political aspects of full employment', *polit. Q.*, October–December.

KALECKI, M. (1971), 'Theories of growth in different social systems', *Monthly Review*, vol. 23, no. 5, October.

KAYSERN, C. (1957), 'The social significance of the modern corporation', *Amer. econ. Rev.*, May.

KEMP, T. (1967), *Theories of Imperialism*, Dobson.

KEYNES, J. M. (1920), *The Economic Consequences of the Peace*, Macmillan.

KEYNES, J. M. (1930), *Treatise on Money*, Macmillan.

KEYNES, J. M. (1932a), 'Economic possibilities for our grandchildren', in *Essays in Persuasion*, Macmillan.

KEYNES, J. M. (1932b), 'The end of *laissez faire*', in *Essays in Persuasion*, Macmillan.

KEYNES, J. M. (1932c), 'The Treaty of Peace', in *Essays in Persuasion*, Macmillan.

KEYNES, J. M. (1960), *The General Theory of Employment, Interest and Money*, Macmillan, first published, 1936.

KIDRON, M. (1965), *Foreign Investment in India*, Oxford University Press.

KIDRON, M. (1969), *Western Capitalism Since the War*, Penguin.

KINDLEBERGER, C. P. (1958), *Economic Development*, McGraw-Hill.

KINDLEBERGER, C. P. (ed.) (1970), *The International Corporation*, MIT Press.

KNAPP, J. A. (1949), 'Towards a new theory of capitalism', *Economics – Man and His Material Resources*, Odhams New Educational Library.

KNAPP, J. A. (1956–7), *Some Aspects of Economic Development*, Oxford lectures.

KNAPP, J. A. (1957), 'Capital exports and growth', *Econ. J.*, vol. 67, no. 267, September.

KNAPP, J. A. (1959), 'Capital, exports and growth for Argentina', *Econ. J.*, September.

KNAPP, J. A. (1964–5), 'Marx *versus* Keynes'; contribution to a course of lectures for the Workers' Education Association in Manchester in 1964–5. (Lectures delivered jointly by Knapp and Barratt Brown.)

KNAPP, J. A. (1969), 'Vers une analyse Keynesienne des sous-developpement et des points de croissance', *Le Tiers Monde*, vol. 10, no. 37, January–March.

KNAPP, J. A. (1972), *Divergent Economic Approaches to the Study of the International Economy*, paper delivered to Chatham House Conference, July.

KNAPP, J. A. (1973), 'Economics or political economy', *Lloyds Bank Review*, January.

KNOWLES, L. C. A. (1928), *Economic Development of the Overseas Empire*, vol. 1, Routledge & Kegan Paul.

KRAVIS, I. B. (1970), 'Trade as a handmaiden of growth', *Econ. J.*, vol. 80, no. 320, December.

KREGEL, J. (1972), 'Post Keynesian economic theory and the theory of capitalist crisis', *Conference of Socialist Economists Bulletin*, Winter.

KUZNETS, S. (1958), 'The underdeveloped countries and the pre-industrial phase in the advanced countries', in A. N. Agarwala and S. P. Singh, *The Economics of Underdevelopment*, Oxford University Press.

LACLAU, E. (1971), 'Feudalism and capitalism in Latin America', *New Left Review*, no. 67, May–June.

LANDES, D. (1965), 'Technological change and development in Western Europe 1750–1914', in *Cambridge Economic History of Europe*, vol. 6, part I, Cambridge University Press.

LANGE, O. (1944), *Working Principles of the Soviet Economy*, Research Bureau for Post-war Economies, New York.

LAWSON, J. H. (1950), *The Hidden Heritage*, Citadel, New York.

LEE, G. (1971), 'Rosa Luxemburg and the impact of imperialism', *Econ. J.*, vol. 81, no. 324, December.

LEE, G. (1972), 'An assimilating Imperialism', *J. Contemporary Asia*, vol. 2, no. 1.

LENIN, V. I. (1933), *Imperialism – The Highest Stage of Capitalism*, Little Lenin Library; published in Petrograd 1916 and in a French and German edn 1920.

LENIN, V. I. (1934), *State and Revolution*, Lawrence & Wishart; first published 1917.

LEONTIEFF, W. (1953), 'Domestic production and foreign trade', *Proc. Amer. philos. Soc.*

LEVY, H. (1909), *Monopoly Cartels and Trusts in British Industry*, Macmillan.

LEWIS, A. (1954), 'Economic development with unlimited supplies of labour', *Manchester School*, vol. 22, no. 2, May.

LEWIS, A. (1955), *Theory of Economic Growth*, Allen & Unwin.

LICHTHEIM, C. (1971), *Imperialism*, Allen Lane.

LIPSON, E. (1934), *Economic History of England*, vols. 2 and 3, 2nd edn, Black.

LONDON AND CAMBRIDGE ECONOMIC SERVICE (1967), *The British Economy – Key Statistics, 1900–1966*, The Times Publishing Co.

LUTZ, V. (1962), *Italy: A Study in Economic Development*, Allen & Unwin.

LUXEMBURG, R. (1951), *The Accumulation of Capital*, with introduction by Joan Robinson, Routledge & Kegan Paul; first published Berlin, 1913.

LUXEMBURG, R. (1972), *The Accumulation of Capital – an Anti-Critique*, Allen Lane; first published Berlin, 1915.

MACKAY, D. I. (1971), *Local Labour Markets Under Different Employment Conditions*, Allen & Unwin.

MACPHERSON, W. J. (1955), 'Investment in Indian railways, 1845–75', *Econ. Hist. Rev.*, December.

MACRONE, G. (1969), *Regional Policy in Britain*, Allen & Unwin.

MACROSTY, J. W. (1907), *The Trust Movement in British Industry*, Longman.

MAGDOFF, H. (1970), *The Age of Imperialism*, Monthly Review Press, New York.

MAGDOFF, H. (1972), 'Imperialism without colonies', in R. J. Owen and R. B. Sutcliffe (eds.), *Studies in the Theory of Imperialism*, Longman.

MAIZELS, A. (1963). *Industrial Growth and World Trade*, Cambridge University Press.

MALLET, S. (1970), *Bureaucracy and Technocracy in the Socialist Countries*, Spokesman Pamphlets, Nottingham.

MANDEL, E. (1964), 'After imperialism?', *New Left Review*, no. 25, May–June.

MANDEL, E. (1969), 'Where is America going?', *New Left Review*, no. 5, March–April.

MANDEL, E. (1970a), *Europe Versus America*, New Left Books, first published 1968.

MANDEL, E. (1970b), 'Law of unequal development', *New Left Review*, no. 59, January–February.

MANDEVILLE, B. (1934), *Fable of the Bees*, Lawrence & Wishart; first published 1714.

MAO TSE-TUNG (1954), 'The Chinese revolution and the Chinese communist party', in *Selected Works of Mao Tse-tung*, vol. 3, Lawrence & Wishart.

MARSHALL, A. (1920), *Principles of Economics*, eighth edn, Macmillan.

MARTIN, J. S. (1950), *All Honourable Men*, Little Brown, New York.

MARX, K. (1904), *Contribution to the Critique of Political Economy*, Kerr, Chicago; first published 1859.

MARX, K. (1908), *Capital*, vol. 2, Kerr, Chicago; first published 1885.

MARX, K. (1909), *Capital*, vol. 3, Kerr, Chicago; first published 1894.

MARX, K. (1933), *Civil War in France*, Martin Lawrence; first published 1871.

MARX, K. (1935a), *The Poverty of Philosophy*, Lawrence & Wishart; first published 1848, Cooperative Publishing House, Moscow.

MARX, K. (1935b), 'Critique of the Gotha programme', in *Selected Works*, Martin Lawrence; first published 1875.

MARX, K. (1935c), *Address on the Question of Free Trade*, Lawrence & Wishart; first published 1848, Brussels.

MARX, K. (1946), *Capital*, vol. 1, Allen & Unwin; first published 1867.

MARX, K. (1950), 'The results of British rule in India', in *On Colonialism*, Lawrence & Wishart; first published *New York Daily Tribune*, 11 July 1853.

MARX, K. (1951), 'Theories of surplus value', in G. A. Bonner and E. Burns (eds.), *Selections*, Lawrence & Wishart; first published 1905.

MARX, K. (1959), *Economic and Philosophical Manuscripts of 1844*, Lawrence & Wishart; first published 1844.

MARX, K. (1960), 'The East India Company – its history and results', *On Colonialism*, Lawrence & Wishart; first published in New York *Daily Tribune*, 11 July 1853.

342 References

MARX, K., and ENGELS, F. (1933), 'The communist manifesto', in *Karl Marx Selected Works*, Martin Lawrence; first published 1848.

MASON, E. J. (1958), 'The apologetics of managerialism', in *J. Business*, January.

MATHIAS, P. (1969), *The First Industrial Nation*, Methuen.

MATTICK, P. (1969), *Marx and Keynes, The Limits of the Mixed Economy*, Porter Sargent, Boston.

MEADE, J. E. (1956), *The Theory of Customs Unions*, North-Holland Publishing Co., Amsterdam.

MEADE, J. E. (1964), *Efficiency, Equality and the Ownership of Property*, Allen & Unwin.

MEADOWS, D. H. *et al.* (1972), *The Limits of Growth*, Earth Island.

MEDIO, A. (1972), 'Profits and surplus value: appearance and reality', in F. K. Hunt and J. G. Schwartz (eds.), *A Critique of Economic Theory*, Penguin.

MEEK, R. (1967), *Economics and Ideology*, Chapman & Hall.

MEYER, A. J. (1959), *Middle Eastern Capitalism*, Harvard University Press.

MIKESELL, R. F. (ed.) (1971), *Foreign Investment in the Petroleum and Mineral Industries*, Baltimore Press.

MILL, J. S. (1880), *Principles of Political Economy*, Longman.

MITCHELL, B. R., and DEANE, P. (1962), *Abstract of British Historical Statistics*, Cambridge University Press.

MONTIAS, J. M. (1964), 'Background and origin of the Roumanian dispute with Comecon', *Soviet Studies*, vol. 16, no. 2, October.

MOODY, J. (1904), *The Truth about the Trusts*, New York.

MORRIS, H. C. (1900), *The History of Colonization*, New York.

MUIR, R., and PHILIP, G. (1929), *New School Atlas of Universal History*, Philips.

MUN, T. (1964), *England's Treasure from Foreign Trade*, Blackwell; first published 1664.

MURRAY, R. (1971a), 'The internationalisation of capital and the British economy', *Spokesman*, nos. 10 and 11, March–April.

MURRAY, R. (1971b), *Anatomy of Bankruptcy*, Spokesman Books.

MURRAY, R. (1971c), 'The internationalisation of capital', in J. H. Dunning (ed.), *The Multinational Enterprise*, Allen & Unwin.

MURRAY, R. (1972), 'Underdevelopment, international firms and the international division of labour', in *Towards a New World Economy*, Rotterdam University Press.

MURRAY, R. (1973), 'Productivity, organic composition and the falling rate of profit', *Conference of Socialist Economists' Bulletin*, Summer.

MYER, A. J. (1959), *Middle Eastern Capitalism*, Harvard University Press.

MYINT, H. A. (1958), 'The classical theory of international trade and the underdeveloped countries', *Econ. J.*, vol. 68, no. 270, June.

MYRDAL, G. (1954), *Economic Theory and Underdeveloped Regions*, Duckworth.

MYRDAL, G. (1970), *Challenge of World Poverty*, Routledge & Kegan Paul.

MYRDAL, J., and KESSLE, G. (1971), *China: The Revolution Continued*, Chatto & Windus.

NAIRN, T. (1972), 'The Left against Europe', *New Left Review*, no. 75, September–October.

NEF, J. U. (1954), 'The progress of technology and the growth of large-scale industry in Great Britain, 1540–1640', and 'Price and industrial capitalism in France and England, 1540–1640', in E. M. Carus Wilson (ed.), *Essays in Economic History*, vol. 1, Arnold.

NEWENS, S. (1972), *N. Ceaucescu, The Man and His Ideas*, Spokesman Books.

NKRUMAH, K. (1965), *Neo-Colonialism: The Last Stage of Imperialism*, Nelson.

NORTH, D. C., and THOMAS, R. P. (1970), 'An economic theory of growth in the western world', *Econ. Hist. Rev.*, vol. 23, no. 1.

NOVE, A. (1972), 'Market socialism and its critics', *Soviet Studies*, vol. 24, no. 1, July.

NURKSE, R. (1960), *Problems of Capital Formation in Underdeveloped Countries*, Blackwell.

NURKSE, R. (1961), *Equilibrium and Growth in the World Economy*, Oxford University Press.

O'CONNOR, J. (1970), 'The meaning of economic imperialism', in R. I. Rhodes (ed.), *Imperialism and Underdevelopment: A Reader*, Monthly Review Press, New York.

OECD (1968), *Statistical Bulletin: Foreign Trade by Commodities*, January–December, Paris.

OECD (1970a), *Development Assistance – 1970 Review*, Paris.

OECD (1970b), *National Accounts, 1950–1968*, Paris.

ORME, R. (1768), *History of the Military Transactions of the British Nation in Indostan*.

OWEN, R. J. (1972), 'Egypt and Europe: from French expedition to British occupation', in R. J. Owen and R. B. Sutcliffe (eds.), *Studies in the Theory of Imperialism*, Longman.

OWEN, R. J., and SUTCLIFFE, R. B. (eds.) (1972), *Studies in the Theory of Imperialism*, Longman.

OXFORD (1972), *Economic Atlas of the World*, 4th edn, Oxford University Press.

PALLOIX, C. (1971), *The World Capitalist Economy*, Maspero, Paris.

PALLOIX, C. (1972), 'The question of unequal exchange', *Conference of Socialist Economists, Bulletin*, Spring.

PARES, R. (1962), 'The economic factors in the history of the empire', in E. M. Carus Wilson (ed.), *Essays in Economic History*, vol. 1, Arnold.

PATINKIN, D. (1965), *Money, Interest and Prices*, Harper & Row.

PATNAIK, P. (1972), 'Imperialism and the growth of Indian capitalism', in R. J. Owen and R. B. Sutcliffe (eds.), *Studies in the Theory of Imperialism*, Longman.

PEARSON, L. B., *et al.* (1969), *Partners in Development*, Praeger.

PENROSE, E. (1959), *Theory of the Growth of the Firm*, Blackwell.

PENROSE, E. (1968), *The Large International Firm in Developing Countries, The International Petroleum Industry*, Allen & Unwin.

PENROSE, E. (1971), 'The state and multinational enterprise in less developed countries', in J. M. Dunning (ed.), *The Multinational Enterprise*, Allen & Unwin.

PEP (1959), *Tariffs and Trade in Western Europe*, Political and Economic Planning.

PERLO, V. (1957), *The Empire of High Finance*, International Publishers, New York.

PERLO, V. (1963), *Militarism and Industry*, Lawrence & Wishart.

PHELPS-BROWN, E. H., and HANDFIELD-JONES, S. J. (1952), 'The climacteric of the 1890s', *Oxf. econ. Paps.*, vol. 4, no. 3, October.

PIGOU, A. C. (1920), *Essays in Applied Economics*, Macmillan.

PLATT, D. C. M. (1972), 'Economic imperialism and the businessman, Britain and Latin America before 1914', in R. J. Owen and R. B. Sutcliffe (eds.), *Studies in the Theory of Imperialism*, Longman.

PLUMMER, A. (1934), *International Combines in Modern Industry*, Pitman.

POLLARD, S. (1965), 'Trade unions and the labour market 1870–1914', *Yorkshire Bull.*, May.

POLK, J. (1968), 'The new-world economy', *Columbia Journal of World Business*, January–February.

POPPER, K. (1937), *The Poverty of Historicism*, Routledge & Kegan Paul.

POPPER, K. (1959), *The Logic of Scientific Discovery*, Hutchinson, first published, Vienna 1934.

PORTES, R. D. (1972), 'Strategy and tactics of economic decentralization', *Soviet Studies*, vol. 23, no. 4, April.

PREOBRAZHENSKY, E. (1965), *The New Economics*, Oxford University Press, first published 1926.

PRESCOTT, H. (1845), *History of the Conquest of Mexico*, Routledge & Kegan Paul.

PRESCOTT, H. (1847), *History of the Conquest of Peru*, Routledge & Kegan Paul.

PRYBLA, J. S. (1964), 'Sino–Soviet competition in the communist world', *Soviet Studies*, vol. 15, no. 4, April.

PRYOR, F. L. (1963), *The Communist Foreign Trade System – The Other Common Market*, Allen & Unwin.

QUIJANO, A. (1971), 'Nationalism and capitalism in Peru, a study of neo-imperialism', *Monthly Review*, July–August.

RADICE, H., *et al.* (1971), 'European integration: capital and the state', *Conference of Socialist Economists' Bulletin*, Winter.

RAWIN, S. J. (1965), 'The manager in the Polish enterprise', *Brit. J. indust. Rel.*, vol. 3, no. 1, March.

REDDAWAY, W. B. (1967), *Effects of UK Direct Investment Overseas*, Cambridge University Press.

RHODES, R. I. (ed.) (1970), *Imperialism and Underdevelopment: A Reader*, Monthly Review Press, New York.

RICARDO, D. (1912), *The Principles of Political Economy and Taxation*, third edn, J. M. Dent; first published 1821.

RIPPY, J. E. (1959), *British Investments in Latin America*, Minnesota University Press.

ROBBINS, L. (1935), *Economic Planning and International Order*, Macmillan.

ROBINSON, E. A. G. (1954), 'The changing structure of the British economy', *Econ. J.*, vol. 64, no. 255, September.

ROBINSON, J. (1942), *An Essay on Marxian Economics*, Macmillan.

ROBINSON, J. (1951), Introduction to Rosa Luxemburg, in *Accumulation of Capital*, Routledge & Kegan Paul.

ROBINSON, J. (1962), *Economic Philosophy*, Penguin.

ROBINSON, J. (1966a), *Economics: An Awkward Corner*, Allen & Unwin.

ROBINSON, J. (1966b), *The New Mercantilism*, Cambridge University Press.

ROBINSON, J. (1969), *The Cultural Revolution in China*, Penguin.

ROBINSON, J. (1970a), *Freedom and Necessity*, Allen & Unwin.

ROBINSON, J. (1970b), 'Harrod after 21 years', *Econ. J.*, vol. 80, no. 319, September.

ROBINSON, J. (1971a), *Economic Heresies*, Macmillan.

ROBINSON, J. (1971b), 'The production function and the theory of capital', in G. C. Harcourt and N. F. Laing, *Capital and Growth*, Penguin.

ROBINSON, J. (1971c), 'The relevance of economic theory', *Monthly Review*, vol. 11, no. 8, January.

ROBINSON, R. E. (1972), 'Non-European foundations of European imperialism – a sketch theory of collaboration', in R. J. Owen and R. B. Sutcliffe (eds.), *Studies in the Theory of Imperialism*, Longman.

ROSTOW, W. W. (1948), *British Economy in the Nineteenth Century*, Oxford University Press.

ROWTHORN, R. (1971a), 'Imperialism in the seventies – unity or rivalry?', *New Left Review*, no. 69, September–October.

ROWTHORN, R. (1971b), *International Big Business, 1957–67*, Cambridge University Press.

ROYAL COMMISSION ON THE DEPRESSION OF TRADE AND INDUSTRY (1884), *Final Report*, HMSO.

RUSSELL, C. E. (1914), *Stories of the Great Railroads*, Chicago.

SAKHAROV, A. D. (1968), *Progress, Coexistence and Intellectual Freedom*, Deutsch; Penguin, 1969.

SAUL, S. B. (1960), *Studies in British Overseas Trade, 1870–1914*, Liverpool University Press.

SAVILLE, J. (1954), 'British economy in the nineteenth century', *Past and Present*, no. 6, November.

SCARR, D. (1967), *Fragments of Empire*, Australian National University Press, Canberra.

SCHLOETE, W. (1952), *British Overseas Trade from 1700 to the 1930s*, Blackwell.

SCHUMACHER, E. P. (1967), 'Intermediate technology – a new approach to foreign aid', *Advance*, April, University of Manchester, Institute of Science and Technology.

SCHUMPETER, J. A. (1943), *Capitalism, Socialism and Democracy*, Allen & Unwin; 2nd and 3rd edns, 1947 and 1949.

SCHUMPETER, J. A. (1954), *History of Economic Analysis*, Oxford University Press.

SCHUMPETER, J. A. (1955), *Sociology of Imperialism*, Meridian books; first published 1919.

SCITOVSKY, I. (1936), 'The theory of tariffs', in *Readings in the Theory of International Trade*, Allen & Unwin.

SCOTT, N. B. (1958), 'Sino–Soviet trade', *Soviet Studies*, vol. 10, no. 2.

SEERS, D. (ed.) (1964), *Cuba: The Economic and Social Revolution*, North Carolina University Press.

SEMMELL, B. (1960), *Imperialism and Social Reform*, Allen & Unwin.

SEMMELL, B. (1970), *The Rise of Free Trade Imperialism*, Cambridge University Press.

SEN, M. (1972), 'The National Democratic front – Indian experience', paper delivered to an International Seminar in Delhi, March 1972; in the author's possession.

SEN, R. K. (1972), 'Indian economic growth: constraints and practice', *econ. polit. Weekly*, Bombay, February.

SERVAN-SCHREIBER, J. J. (1968), *The American Challenge*, Hamish Hamilton.

SHANIN, T. (1971), 'Workers and peasants in revolution'. *Spokesman*, no. 10, March.

SHANIN, T. (1972a), *The Awkward Class*, Oxford University Press.

SHANIN, T. (ed.) (1972b), *The Rules of the Game*, Tavistock.

SIGSWORTH, E. J., and BLACKMAN, J. (1965), 'The home boom in the 1890s', *Yorkshire Bull.*, May.

SIK, O. (1967), *Plan and Market Under Socialism*, Academia, Prague.

SIK, O. (1968), 'The Czechoslovak economy today', in K. Coates (ed.), *Czechoslovakia and Socialism*, Spokesman Books.

SIMON, M. (1967), 'The pattern of new British portfolio foreign investment, 1865–1914', in J. H. Adler (ed.), *Capital Movements*, Macmillan.

SINGER, H. W. (1950), 'Distribution of gain between investing and borrowing countries', *Amer. Econ. Rev.*, vol. 40.

SINGER, H. W. (1970), 'Dualism revisited', *J. Devel. Stud.*, vol. 7, no. 1, October.

SINGLETON, F. (1971–2), 'Yugoslavia's market socialism', *Spokesman*, nos. 19–20.

SINGLETON, F. (1972), 'Yugoslavia: from crisis to crisis', *New Society*, 23 November.

SMITH, A. (1812), *Wealth of Nations*, Ward Lock; first published 1776.

SRAFFA, P. (1960), *Production of Commodities by Means of Commodities*, Cambridge University Press.

SRAFFA, P., and DOBB, M. H. (eds.) (1951), *Works of David Ricardo*, Cambridge University Press.

STALEY, E. (1935), *War and the Private Investor*, Chicago University Press.

STALIN, J. (1952), *Economic Problems of Socialism in the USSR*, Foreign Languages Publishing House, Moscow.

STAMP, D. (1960), *Our Developing World*, Oxford University Press.

STEINDL, J. (1952), *Maturity and Stagnation in American Capitalism*, Blackwell.

STRACHEY, J. (1959), *The End of Empire*, Gollancz.

STREETEN, P. (1971), 'Costs and benefits of multinational enterprise in less developed countries', in J. H. Dunning (ed.), *The Multinational Enterprise*, Allen & Unwin.

SUNDELSON, J. (1970), 'US automotive investments abroad', in C. P. Kindleberger (ed.), *The International Corporation*, MIT Press.

SUPAN, A. (1906), *The Territorial Development of European Colonies*, Berlin.

SUTCLIFFE, R. B. (1972), 'Imperialism and the industrialization of the Third World', in R. J. Owen and R. B. Sutcliffe (eds.), *Studies in the Theory of Imperialism*, Longman.

SUTTON, L. D. (1955), *Persian Oil*, Lawrence & Wishart.

SWEEZY, P. (1942), *Theory of Capitalist Development*, Dobson.

SWEEZY, P. (1970), 'On the transition to socialism', *Monthly Review*, vol. 22, no. 7, December.

SWEEZY, P. (1972), 'Towards a programme of studies of the transition to socialism', *Monthly Review*, vol. 23, no. 9, February.

TARBUCK, K. (ed.) (1972), Introduction to Rosa Luxemburg and N. Bukharin, *Imperialism and the Accumulation of Capital*, Allen Lane.

TAUSSIG, F. W. (1925), 'The change in Great Britain's foreign trade terms after 1900', *Econ. J.*, no. 35.

TAYLOR, A. J. P. (1965), *English History, 1914–1945*, Oxford University Press.

THOMAS, B. (1954), *Migration and Economic Growth*, Cambridge University Press.

THOMAS, B. (1967), 'The historical record of international capital movements to 1913', in J. H. Adler (ed.), *Capital Movements*, Macmillan.

TINBERGEN, J. (1962), *Shaping the World Economy*, McGraw-Hill.

TORRENS, R. (1844), *The Budget*, Kelley, New York.

TOYNBEE, A. J. (1931), *A Study of History*, Oxford University Press.

TRAVIS, W. P. (1964), *The Theory of Trade and Protection*, Harvard University Press.

TURNER, H. A., and JACKSON, D. A. S. (1970), 'On the determination of the general wage level – a world analysis; or unlimited labour for ever', *Econ. J.*, vol. 80, no. 320, December.

TURNER, L. (1969), *Politics and the Multinational Company*, Fabian Pamphlet, no. 179.

UNITED NATIONS (1949), *International Capital Movements in the Inter-War Years*, New York.

UNITED NATIONS (1960), *Statistical Yearbook*, New York.

UNITED NATIONS (1964), Conference on Trade and Development, vol. 3, *Commodity Trade*, New York.

UNITED NATIONS (1966), *Statistical Yearbook*, New York.

UNITED NATIONS (1968a), *Economic Survey of Europe, 1967*, Economic Commission for Europe, Geneva.

UNITED NATIONS (1968b), *Economic Survey of Asia and the Far East*, New York.

UNITED NATIONS (1969a), *Statistical Yearbook, 1969*, New York.

UNITED NATIONS (1969b), *Economic Survey of Europe, 1968*, Economic Commission for Europe, Geneva.

UNITED NATIONS (1972a), *Monthly Bulletin of Statistics*, November, New York.

UNITED NATIONS (1972b), *Statistical Yearbook, 1969*, New York.

UNITED NATIONS (1973), *Monthly Bulletin of Statistics*, December.

UNITED STATES DEPARTMENT OF COMMERCE (1952), *Historical Statistics of the United States, 1789–1945*, Washington.

UNITED STATES DEPARTMENT OF COMMERCE (1960), *United States Business Investment in Foreign Countries*, Washington.

UNITED STATES DEPARTMENT OF COMMERCE (1968), Board of Trade Journal, 26 January.

UNITED STATES DEPARTMENT OF COMMERCE (1970), Board of Trade Journal, 23 September.

UNITED STATES DEPARTMENT OF COMMERCE (1971a), *Survey of Current Business*, September, Washington.

UNITED STATES DEPARTMENT OF COMMERCE (1971b), Board of Trade Journal, 7 April.

VARGA, E., and MENDELSOHN, L. (1940), *New Data for Lenin's Imperialism*, International Publishers, New York.

VARGA, Y. (1968), 'The problems of inter-imperialist contradictions and war', in *Politico-Economic Problems of Capitalism*, People's Publishing House, Moscow.

VERNON, R. (1960), 'International investment and international trade in the product cycle', *Q. J. Econ.*, vol. 80, May.

VERNON, R. (1970), 'The future of the multinational enterprise', in C. P. Kindleberger (ed.), *The International Corporation*, MIT Press.

VINER, J. (1955), *Studies in the Theory of International Trade*, Allen & Unwin.

VON ECKARDSTEIN (1919), *Ten Years at the Court of St James, 1895-1905*.

WAKEFIELD, E. G. (1834), *England and America: A Comparison of the Social and Political State of Both Nations*, Kelley, New York.

WAKEFIELD, E. G. (1835), *Notes Upon the Wealth of Nations* in M. F. L. Prichard (ed.), *Collected Works of Edward Gibbon Wakefield*, Collins.

WARREN, B. (1971), 'How international is capital?', *New Left Review*, no. 68, July–August.

WARREN, B. (1973), 'Imperialism and capitalist industrialization', *New Left Review*, no. 81, September–October.

WEHLER, H. U. (1972), 'Industrial growth and early German imperialism', in R. J. Owen and R. B. Sutcliffe (eds.), *Studies in the Theory of Imperialism*, Longman.

WESTLAKE, M. (1973), 'Distributing the profits of migrant labour', *The Times*, 30 May.

WHEELWRIGHT, E. L., and MACFARLANE, B. (1973), *The Chinese Road to Socialism*, Penguin.

WILES, P. T. D., and MARKOWSKI, S. (1971), 'Income distribution under communism and capitalism; some facts about Poland, the UK, the US and the USSR', in *Soviet Studies*, vol. 22, no. 3, January.

WILLIAMS, E. (1964), *Capitalism and Slavery*, Deutsch.

WILSON, C. H. (1954), *The History of Unilever*, vol. 1, Cassell.

WINCH, D. (1965), *Classical Political Economy and Colonies*, Harvard University Press.

WOOD, G. H. (1909), 'Real wages and the standard of comfort since 1850', *J. roy. stat. Soc.*

WOODRUFF, P. (1953), *The Founders*, Cape.

WOODWARD, R. L. (1938), *The Age of Reform, 1815-1870*, Oxford University Press.

WOYTINSKY, W. S., and WOYTINSKY, E. S. (1953), *World Population and Production*, Twentieth Century Fund, New York.

WOYTINSKY, W. S., and WOYTINSKY, E. S. (1955), *World Commerce and Government*, Twentieth Century Fund, New York.

YATES, P. L. (1959), *Forty Years of Foreign Trade*, Allen & Unwin.

ZAUBERMAN, A. (1955), *Economic Imperialism, The Lesson of Eastern Europe*, Bellman Books.

Author Index

Subject Index

More about Penguins and Pelicans

Books on Economics
published by Penguins

Books on Economics
published by Penguins